DESCRIPTIVE PHONETICS

Second Edition

DESCRIPTIVE PHONETICS

Second Edition

DONALD R. CALVERT, Ph.D.

Director
Central Institute for the Deaf
St. Louis, Missouri

Chairman
Department of Speech & Hearing
Washington University

1986
Thieme Inc., New York
Georg Thieme Verlag Stuttgart · New York

Publisher: Thieme Inc.
381 Park Avenue South
New York, New York 10016

Library of Congress Cataloging in Publication Data

Calvert, Donald R.
   Descriptive phonetics.

   Includes bibliographies and index.
   1. English language—Phonetics.   2. Phonetics.
3. Speech.   I. title.   [DNLM: 1. Phonetics.   2. Speech.
WV 501 C167d]
PE1135.C274   1986   414   85-17344
ISBN 0-86577-201-0

Printed in the United States of America

DESCRIPTIVE PHONETICS: SECOND EDITION
Donald R. Calvert

TI ISBN 0-86577-201-0
GTV ISBN 3-13-608002-5

5   4   3   2   1

CONTENTS

To Ruth,
whose generation taught me,
and to Clay,
whose generation I now gladly teach.

PREFACE

Descriptive Phonetics was written to present the features of American-English speech that will be most useful to a broad spectrum of readers. It was developed especially with those in mind who are preparing to be "modifiers" of the speech of others—speech/language pathologists, teachers of speech for children with language and hearing impairment, instructors in English as a second language, and coaches of dramatics and elocution. Such persons need not only to "know about" speech but to develop the rare skill of analysis that is essential for successfully undertaking to change the speech of another person. In this endeavor, they will share the lineage of a long historical continuum of English and American phoneticians and teachers of speech.

The early British phoneticians honed to a fine edge the ability to describe speech as they heard it and to figure out how it was produced. Their most important instruments in this intimate art were their own ears and their essential skills—the facility to analyze and to interpret on the spot. Some admitted to the use of Edison's recording device after its invention in 1877, but only to confirm the observation of their senses. Although collectively immortalized by the irascible Henry Higgins of Shaw's "Pygmalion," they were individualists, working parallel but apart. It was a major achievement of compromise to form the International Phonetic Association near the end of the 19th century and for its members to promulgate an acceptable set of phonetic symbols, the International Phonetic Alphabet, still in use today. Of course, that apparent show of agreement has never deterred phoneticians—notable recently, Trager and Smith—from using other symbols they believed superior for their particular purpose. Neither has there been unanimity in respect to the proper segmentation of speech, the number of phonemes in the language, or the way speech sounds should be described.

Among those early phoneticians were some who considered themselves "teachers of speech." Alexander Melville Bell (1819–1905) of Edinburgh, like his father before him, was one of these who used his talent to change the speech of his students to more acceptable patterns. For such teachers, the scope of analysis required determination of how changes could be made, and their repertory included techniques to effect these changes. But the foundation for their teaching remained a critical ear and the capability of instantaneous analysis.

The prime importance of the individual's cultivated ear, and the talent for what may be called the "power of analysis," are often overlooked in our understandable urge to be scientific. Experimental or instrumental phonetics transfers reliance from the ear to the eye, and from broad analysis to the studied measurement of single parameters. Intuitive individual perception, suspect as a means to derive immutable fact, has sometimes been rejected as a worthy means to achieve a number of applied purposes. This is not to denigrate the contribution of the laboratory approach to phonetics. It has been, and will in the future be, immense. But the abundance of elegant instruments with lights, needles, scopes, dials, screens, or printouts of the speech investigator in his laboratory are no substitute for the clinician or teacher on the spot with a discriminating ear, a nervous system trained for analysis of what he hears, and a selection of strategies for changing speech behavior.

With this in mind, *Descriptive Phonetics* emphasizes the detailed analysis of, and understanding for, how our speech units are formed, in the same sense that "descriptive linguistics" examines a language in terms of its internal structure. Chapters I and II provide the reader with important tools of analysis—a phonetic transcription system and an understanding of the speech mechanism and processes. Exercises at the end of each chapter provide opportunity for developing transcription skill and gaining familiarity with useful vocabulary. Chapters III and IV examine the formation of each of the primary American-English phonemes, with notes on coarticulation effects that are then amplified in Chapter V. Exercises direct the student in analyzing the actions essential for forming various speech units. Further complexity in the task of analysis is added in Chapter VI with speech rhythm and supra-segmental features of speech. Variable pronunciations are presented for analysis in Chapter VII, which deals with standard and nonstandard speech and the dialectical differences thereof. Finally, Chapter VIII describes the products of speech production available for our sensory perception—acoustic, visual, tactile, and kinesthetic.

This book is designed primarily as a text for students beginning the study of phonetics. For those who wish to develop or improve skill in phonetic transcription using symbols of the International Phonetic Alphabet, this text has a companion *Descriptive Phonetics Transcription Workbook* available from the same publisher. More is said about this and its use as a supplement to course lectures in the Foreword To The Instructor that follows. Chapters II and VIII introduce the fields of physiologic and acoustic phonetics, respectively, preparing the student for further study in either area. However, the book may also serve as a resource for the advanced student who wishes to review the detailed descriptions of phonemes in Chapters III and IV, or for the professional clinician and teacher who makes use of the analysis of spellings, and of the list of words, sentences, and contrast pairs that accompany the description of each phoneme in those chapters.

Not all phoneticians will be happy with what I have written. One may feel that there is not enough detail on acoustic phonetics, whereas another may lament the omission of neurology in dealing with physiologic phonetics. Others may object to my categorization of phonemes, perhaps disappointed that /h/ does not follow the traditional classification as a "glottal" fricative, or they may miss the semantic flatulence of calling /l/ a "liquid" of either a "light" or a "dark" character. Still others may observe that the text does not share the currently popular enthusiasm for the concept of distinctive features, or does not carry heavy documentation for all its statements. One can scarcely put to paper his thoughts about phonetics without offending a phonetician somewhere who will become provoked enough to respond with a treatise on the subject. So be it! Descriptive phonetics is not an exact science, and efforts to develop a consistent nomenclature are well overdue.

The pronunciations in this book reflect my personal linguistic heritage. Born and reared within 100 miles of Omaha, Nebraska, I have lived for significant periods in Portland, Oregon, the San Francisco Bay Area, Arlington, Virginia, and St. Louis, Missouri, always with my ears unstopped. I speak my own peculiar dialect of "traveled" General American-English.

I acknowledge with gratitude the advice and suggestions of my colleagues at Central Institute, especially Randall Monsen, S. Richard Silverman, Ira Hirsh, and Carol DeFilippo, and the invaluable editorial assistance of Helen Roberts. The comments of Elizabeth Carr Holmes of Honolulu and of Akiro Honda of Sapporo, Japan, were extremely helpful.

D.R.C.

FOREWORD TO THE INSTRUCTOR

This text follows sequences designed to help college-level students learn from its contents. No previous knowledge of phonetics, and only rudimentary knowledge of anatomy, physiology, and physics, is prerequisite. Its general pedagogic path begins with introduction of material in the chapter text associated with relevant illustrations and examples, followed by exercises at the end of chapters for practice and familiarity, and then reinforcement here and there in the book through application in some practical context or related to something the student is likely to know well already. The chapters follow an order the author has found advantageous in presenting a semester's course of three credits (about 45 lecture hours). Although *Descriptive Phonetics* may help the student as a course of study for self-instruction, its best use is as a supplement to lectures that include presentation of a generous sampling of live speech or recordings for students to transcribe and analyze.

The primary purpose of this book is to present to the student an opportunity to develop listening and analytic skills, to gain knowledge and understanding of speech, to be introduced to some of the special areas of phonetics, and to have access to resource materials that may be helpful for future application. These objectives are outlined below with chapter designations:

SKILLS

1. Phonetic transcription, broad and narrow IPA (I through VII)
2. Use of common symbols to indicate speech rhythm features (VI)
3. Analysis of how speech units are produced (II through VI)

KNOWLEDGE AND UNDERSTANDING

4. Development and purposes of orthographic systems (I)
5. Anatomy and physiologic processes of speech production (II)
6. Categorization of consonants by place and manner of production (II, III)

7. Categorization of vowels by place and height of tongue elevation (II, IV)
8. Influences of phonetic context and coarticulation (III, IV, V)
9. Nature of tongue twisters and difficult articulations (V)
10. Relation of speech rhythm and pronunciation (IV, VI)
11. Relation among standards, dialects, and defects of speech (VII)
12. Historical perspective on speech and phonetics (I, VII)
13. Sensory products of speech—acoustic, visual, tactile, kinesthetic (II, VIII)
14. Relation of acoustic parameters to oral positions (II, III, IV, VIII)
15. Vocabulary associated with phonetics (I through VIII)

INTRODUCTION TO AREAS OF PHONETICS

16. Physiologic phonetics (II, III, IV, V)
17. American-English pronunciation (I, III, IV, V, VII)
18. Dialects (VII)
19. Acoustic phonetics (II, VIII)

RESOURCE MATERIAL FOR REFERENCE

20. Formation of primary American-English phonemes (III, IV)
21. Spellings for primary phonemes (I, III, IV)
22. Word examples of phonemes—initial, medial, and final positions (III, IV)
23. Examples of phonemes in sentence units (III, IV)
24. Sets of words contrasting similar or often confused phonemes (III, IV)
25. The General American symbol system for reading and spelling use (I)

Each of these objectives, which collectively form a basis for examination of the student, is pursued in various parts of the book. For example, skill in phonetic transcription is developed over the course of several chapters. First, the International Phonetic Alphabet (IPA) is put into perspective with other orthographic systems, as the difference between alphabet spelling and the sounds of speech is emphasized in Chapter I. Exercises at the end of the chapter proceed from distinguishing phonemes common to groups of words having varied spellings through transcription tasks of gradually increasing difficulty, to word transcription using broad IPA symbols for all common American-English phonemes. In Chapter II, the newly learned IPA symbols are immediately applied in the text to indicate pronunciation of possibly unfamiliar terms for anatomy of the speech mechanism and speech processes. The task is then reversed at the end of the chapter with exercises requiring the student to sound out the new vocabulary, using the increasingly familiar IPA symbols before spelling the words in Roman alphabet letters. In Chapters III and IV, the student is again required to review knowledge of the IPA in order to understand the production of consonants and vowels. Exercises at the end of Chapter IV require the student to sound out nonsense speech units written in IPA symbols, and then transliterate them into alphabet symbols he believes most appropriate. Chapter V directly instructs the student in transcribing connected speech units with suggestions and illustrations in the text, followed by exercises in using some narrow transcription symbols. By now the student should be learning to transcribe connected speech the way it is actually spoken, including numerous coarticulation effects, rather than simply the more typical word transcription. Chapter VI helps prepare the student to use basic symbols for stress, intonation, and phrasing, again reinforced by exercises at the end of the chapter. Then IPA symbols are used extensively to define non-standard speech and to compare dialects in Chapter VII with exercises now requiring finer phonetic distinctions.

For the instructor especially interested in IPA phonetic transcription, this text has a Thieme-Stratton companion publication, *Descriptive Phonetics Transcription Workbook*, that provides the student with pencil-and-paper exercises. These follow a sequence of **recognition** of the common phoneme in a list of words, **discrimination** requiring a decision about whether a target phoneme does or does not occur in certain words, and IPA **transcription** from words spelled in their usual way. These exercises can be accomplished by the student as homework. Of course, the written text cannot replace the spoken word for developing careful listening and transcription skills. The fourth exercise in this sequence, therefore, is **transcription** of words **from dictation.** The *Workbook* provides numbered spaces for the student's transcription from the instructor's dictation. The words can be presented either recorded (for consistency and review) or live for control of the rate of presentation and for repetition as needed. Word lists for dictation that emphasize target phonemes and review those previously learned are available in the Instructors Section of the *Workbook*. Of course, the instructor may wish to develop his own material graded for difficulty. Dictation of nonsense units is especially valuable to help the student with careful listening to speech sounds without semantic context to depend upon.

A similar sequence is followed to help the student learn to analyze how units of speech are produced. Phonetic transcription is just the beginning of this sequence. Prepared with IPA symbols, and with the vocabulary and understanding of speech production processes from the first two chapters, the student is presented with direct descriptions of the articulatory sequences involved in producing phonemes in Chapters III and IV. From these simple sequences for individual phonemes, Chapter V presents step-by-step, detailed descriptions of connected units of speech, taking into account important effects of coarticulation. The student participates in the process by pursuing exercises at the end of these chapters. Features of speech rhythm are added to the analysis of coarticulated phonemes in Chapter VI. Again, the text may be supplemental to live presentations by the instructor in leading the student to analyze speech units as they are actually spoken.

Important vocabulary is defined within the text, and selected words and phrases are emphasized in bold type with definitions reviewed at the end of each chapter. Important words and concepts related to phonetics are cross referenced in the index. Words likely to be unfamiliar when introduced in one chapter are used again for reinforcement in later chapters whenever possible. Annotated references for suggested reading are presented at the end of each chapter to provide the student with direction for a next step in learning, should his interest or that of the instructor suggest it.

To the skills, knowledge, introductions, and resource materials, which are the main objectives of the book, may be added an **attitude** about speech. This is concerned with the student's sensitivity to variations in speech. A growing child naturally adopts the speech patterns of the people around him, especially his immediate family, and does not question whether the patterns are good or bad, right or wrong, better or poorer than that of others. They are his and his family's, and of course they are good. When he encounters a pattern markedly different from his, such as a major dialect variation, it is to be expected that he may judge that such people "talk funny," and may even judge them inferior because of this. Those around him may voice agreement, reinforcing his belief. Such secure beliefs associated with self-image die hard. For some, this pleasant myth persists throughout a lifetime. On the other hand, if he moves or expands his activities, the growing child may find himself in a group, a school, or even a society in which his speech pattern is considered "funny" and inferior by the majority of his new peers. His response of rebellion or adaptation may be devastating, reflecting confusion and uncertainty. Whatever has been the student's experience with speech variations, he is likely to be ready to develop his own philosophy and attitudes about them and his own speech.

Chapter VII leads the student through some of the thinking about standards, non-standard speech patterns, and the variations of dialects so that he may reach some of his own conclusions. Arbitrary standards and value judgments are de-emphasized, and the dialects of American-English are given historical perspective. The intention is to prepare the student to accept his own dialect as the result of where he happened to be born and grow up, and to accept the dialect of others on the same basis rather than consider either on a scale of value. However, it is unrealistic to leave the student thinking that no value judgments about speech are made, and the subject of nonstandard speech is examined with some care.

A common use students make of a course in phonetics is improvement of their own speech. This is not unlike students who study psychology in order to gain an understanding of or a solution to their own emotional problems. Students' speech patterns are among their most important personal attributes, probably second only to physical appearance, in shaping self-image and influencing those around them. At high school and college age especially, students will wish to improve their speech. In *Descriptive Phonetics*, opportunity to practice pronunciations are abundant in the word and sentence lists of Chapters III and IV, and Chapter VII presents a sequence of exercises for improving enunciation. Future speech/language pathologists and teachers, of course, will be interested in developing speech patterns that will be good models for their clients or students.

In this book, I have attempted to present to the student a prose style that will directly convey ideas and information and yet be fairly lively and interesting. Historical sequences have been included in association with phonetic concepts. References to English literature have included some works of Lewis Carroll, Bernard Shaw, Joel Chandler Harris, E.B. White, H.L. Mencken, and the King James version of the Old Testament. I have avoided the heavy documentation style of theses and research papers in favor of a more smoothly flowing narrative that I hope will lend some pleasure to reading and learning about *Descriptive Phonetics*.

ORTHOGRAPHIC SYSTEMS

Systems of written language symbols are as old as civilization. In fact, they are the mark of a civilized society that senses the need to place in a more permanent form the spoken thoughts and experiences that constitute its culture. Early man used **pictograms** to express his ideas simply and directly. Drawings of a man hunting a deer commemorated a successful deer hunt. The Chinese and Japanese reduced their pictograms to simplified lines representing the form of the object. Over many generations, they developed highly stylized characters or **logograms,** with each symbol representing an entire word (Figure I–1). Egyptian hieroglyphics included pictograms and some **ideograms** with characters expressing a symbolic idea associated with the object. The ostrich feather, for example, was a common symbol for truth. Hieroglyphics also included a few characters that represented either a speech sound or a syllable. A simplified drawing of an owl represented the [m] sound as in *man,* the shape of a loaf of bread the [t] as in *too,* and a lion the [l] as in *lip.* The Phoenicians went further in developing a set of **phonograms,** written symbols unrelated to objects to represent all the various sounds of their speech. Our **alphabet** of written symbols comes by this route; from the Greeks, who named their first two symbols

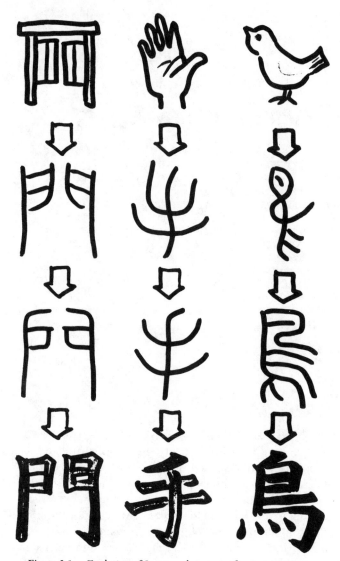

Figure I-1.   Evolution of Japanese logograms from pictograms.

"alpha" and "beta," to the Romans, from whom we have the *Roman Alphabet* that English and several other languages use (Figure I–2).

Orthography refers to the accurate or accepted spelling of words using the symbols of an alphabet. Most orthographic systems relate written language to spoken language, using alphabet letters as phonograms. Ideally, an orthographic system would have one written symbol for each spoken sound, and every time that symbol appeared, it would always be given that

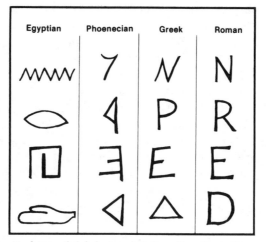

Figure 1–2. Evolution of alphabet symbols from Egyptian to Roman alphabets.

same sound. This would enable us to "sound out" any new word we read so that we could pronounce it correctly. Conversely, if we knew how to pronounce a word, we should also be able to spell it correctly. Such an ideal one-to-one sound/symbol correspondence seldom occurs, unfortunately.

ALPHABET SPELLING AND SPEECH SOUNDS

As spoken language grows and changes, written language follows, but at a slower pace and sometimes at a great distance. English developed from a mixture of the language of Europe. Anglo-Saxon, derived primarily from Germanic dialects, was influenced by the Scandinavian languages of northern Europe, French, the Romance languages of southern Europe, and classic Greek and Latin. A word has been borrowed here and there from Arabic, East Indian, and American Indian languages. American-English is still growing, absorbing new words from languages around the world and adopting words from its own ethnic groups. While this richness of origins enhances our facility in expressing ourselves, it has left spelling and pronunciation in some cases far apart.

By listening carefully to the way speech is pronounced, we become aware that our American-English speech consists of a number of sounds that recur in words and phrases so that we recognize them in connected speech. For example, we hear a highly similar sound at the beginning of the word *cab* and at the end of the word *tack*. We also hear this sound in such words as *ski, occur, ache,* and *liquor,* and we note that although the spelling changes the common sound is essentially the same. Each of these similar sounds is actually produced in a slightly different manner because of the different speech sounds around them. Yet they have enough in common to be considered as examples of a class of sounds we will later see is written as /k/. Such classes of sounds are called **phonemes.** Phonemes are abstractions derived by generalizing from a number of similar sounds that actually occur in speech. Variations among the sounds within a phoneme class are called **allophones.** They differ slightly from each other both in the way we produce them and in the way they sound to our ear. Allophonic variations do not influence the meaning of words. However, when the phoneme changes to another phoneme, the meaning also changes. For example, if the *k* in *key* is produced by a particular speaker farther back in the mouth than usual—as might happen for the *c* in *cool*—it is still an example of the phoneme /k/, and *key* is heard so that the listener envisions a metal object that unlocks doors. But if the sound produced is an example of the phoneme /t/, produced with the front of the tongue instead of the back, the listener will hear *tea* and think of the drink, instead.

One major problem of orthography is that the Roman alphabet does not contain enough symbols to represent all the different speech sound classes, or phonemes, of American-English. We have only 26 alphabet letters to represent 43 basic phonemes. The five letters that we call vowels (*a, e, i, o, u*) must represent 18 different vowel and diphthong phonemes. The 21 consonant letters represent 25 different consonant phonemes. There is, for example, no special letter that represents the medial consonant in the words *leisure* and *pleasure*. A number of other phonemes have to be represented by a combination of two letters such as *sh, th, wh, ch,* and *ng*.

A second related irregularity of American-English is that the letters are not always pronounced the same way each time they appear. Whereas most consonant letters represent a single sound, none of the vowel letters does so exclusively. Note how pronunciation of the letter *o* changes in these words: *ton, top, told, tomb, woman, women*. A third inconsistency of our orthography is that a single speech sound may be represented by a number of different letters or combinations. The sound of /f/, for example, may be spelled *f* (*fir*), *ff* (*differ*), *ph* (*phone*), or *gh* (*rough*). Still a fourth irregularity is that we have a number of letters in spelling that sometimes represent no sound. These silent letters include the *p* in *pneumonia*, the *l* in *half*, the *k* in *knife*, the *t* in *listen*, the *b* in *debt*, and the *gh* in *through*. If these variants were not enough, we have words that are spelled the same but are pronounced differently (*read/read, bow/bow, live/live, uses/uses, tear/tear*), and those that are spelled differently but pronounced the same (*him/hymn, bare/bear, mince/mints,* and *rite/right/write/wright*).

These inconsistencies and irregularities, which most Americans take for granted and learn in stride, cause immense problems for non-English speakers and for children who have a reading disability. Just when a rule of spelling or pronunciation seems to be emerging, a number of important exceptions appear. We could hardly have made the spelling and pronunciation more difficult if we had set out to do so. As the English dramatist George Bernard Shaw said in the preface to his play, *Pygmalion,*

> The English have no respect for their language, and will not teach their children to speak it. They cannot spell it because they have nothing to spell it with but an old foreign alphabet of which only the consonants— and not all of them—have any agreed speech value. Consequently no man can teach himself what it should sound like from reading it. . . . Most European languages are now accessible in black and white to foreigners: English and French are not thus accessible even to Englishmen and Frenchmen.

Despite these obvious problems of our system of orthography, attempts at spelling reform have been largely unsuccessful. Benjamin Franklin and Noah Webster made some early attempts in this country. Notable among more recent efforts was the 40-year experiment by the *Chicago Tribune.* Beginning in 1934, the *Tribune* published lists of words that were to be simplified when spelled in that newspaper. These included such changes as *catalog* for *catalogue, fantom* for *phantom, burocracy* for *bureaucracy,* and *iland* for *island.* New words were added to the list such as *frate* for *freight,* and others that had not been well accepted, such as *sodder* for *solder,* were dropped. Teachers, writers of spelling books, and scholars of language complained persistently, and the new spellings just did not catch on with the public. With an editorial entitled "Thru is through and so is tho," the experiment was abandoned in 1975.

Even though our conventional spelling has a less-than-perfect relation to the sounds of all our words, the relation is often useful. We can and do "sound out" new words when reading. **Phonics** is an application of the alphabet symbol-to-speech sound relation organized into a tool for teaching beginners to read. Cartoonists rely on our knowledge of the symbol/sound relation when they spell the sounds of noises such as *pow* and *zap,* or have a dog bark *arf* or *woof woof.* Similarly, when a foreign language does not use the Roman alphabet and we wish to spell its words for English pronunciation, we judge which of our letters would most closely reflect the sound of the words. This process is called **transliteration.** Languages such as Russian, Chinese, and Japanese, which are in occasional use by people with Roman alphabet languages, are often transliterated by journalists, or by those who make maps and must spell place names. An example is the Russian word for *no,* which is written нет in the Russian Cyrillic alphabet. It has the sound roughly of our word *net,* but with the vowel *e* corresponding to the first two sounds in *yes* so that the word is commonly transliterated "*nyet.*" At times, native speakers seek to correct transliteration that they believe misrepresents their pronunciation. For example, in 1978, the government of the People's Republic of China decreed that all publications printed in that country in English, French, German, Spanish, and other Roman alphabet languages be transliterated into its standard Pinyin phonetic system, developed in 1958. *Peking* is to be written *Beijing* and *Chunking* as *Zhongquing* to approximate better their native pronunciation.

GENERAL AMERICAN SPEECH AND PHONIC SYMBOLS

Many people have tried to analyze our spelling and pronunciation in order to determine its intrinsic system and rules and to make these available to help children and foreigners who wish to learn our language. Alice Worcester, a teacher of deaf children at the Clarke School in Northampton, Massachusetts, published in 1885 a set of symbols taken from the Roman alphabet that she found beneficial in teaching speech and reading. These **Northampton symbols** were revised and organized into systematic charts in 1914 by Caroline Yale, and have been used for years in teaching deaf children.

In order to reflect more closely the pronunciation used throughout most of the United States, and to reduce the complexity of secondary spellings and numerals that children have found difficult, as well as to improve the system for teaching speech, the symbols of the Northampton system were modified to form the **General American speech and phonic system.** *

The principle of the General American Speech and Phonic Symbols system is to use as primary symbols either the alphabet letters that most frequently occur for particular speech sounds or letters that almost invariably represent the sound. To handle the many irregularities, secondary and even tertiary symbols are also used. For example, the letter *k* is the primary symbol for the /k/phoneme, as in *kind*, because it almost always represents that sound when it appears in spelling. But the letter *c* is written for that sound in the spelling of such common words as *car, cat, can, come, could,* and *cup,* and it actually occurs more frequently in common usage than *k* to represent the /k/phoneme. Unfortunately, the letter *c* also frequently has the sound that is associated with *s,* as it does in *city,* or that associated with *sh,* as occurs in *ocean.* The letter *c* was therefore designated a secondary spelling for the /k/ sound, and it is also used as a secondary spelling for the /s/ sound (see Figure I–3).

A special contribution of this system is its handling of vowels. It was noted, for example, that when the letter *a* is followed by a consonant and then the letter *e,* the combination has the sound of *a* as in *make.* Note this sound and spelling in such words as *cake, fame, sane, bale, take,* and *safe.*

---

*Calvert, Donald R., General American Speech and Phonic Symbols, *Amer. Annals of the Deaf,* 127, pp. 405–410, 1982.

GENERAL AMERICAN SYMBOLS	IPA	KEY WORDS	GENERAL AMERICAN SYMBOLS	IPA	KEY WORDS
Stop Consonants			Fricative Consonants		
p	/p/	pie	h	/h/	he
b	/b/	by	wh	/ʍ/	why
t	/t/	tie	f	/f/	fan
d	/d/	day	ph		phone
k	/k/	key	v	/v/	vine
c(a)		cat	th	/θ/	thin
c(o)		cot	th	/ð/	then
c(u)		cut	s	/s/	see
g	/g/	go	c(i)		city
Oral Resonant Consonants			c(e)		cent
			c(y)		cycle
y-	/j/	yes	z	/z/	zoo
l	/l/	lie	sh	/ʃ/	she
r	/r/	red	zh	/ʒ/	vision
w-	/w/	we	Affricate Consonants		
Nasal Resonant Consonants			ch	/tʃ/	chin
			tch		watch
m	/m/	me	j	/dʒ/	jam
n	/n/	no	-dge		edge
ng	/ŋ/	long	qu	[kʍ]	queen
n(k)		think	x	[ks]	box

Figure 1–3. General American Speech and Phonic Symbols: Consonants. Primary and secondary symbols with associated symbols of the International Phonetic Alphabet (IPA) and example words.

Note also how adding the *e* in the following words changes pronunciation of the vowel sound:

mad   made
at   ate
dam   dame
hat   hate

To represent the vowel sound in *mad*, the written symbol -*a*- is used. For the vowel sound in *made*, the symbol *a-e* is used, the dash indicating an intervening or adjoining consonant. Table I–1 shows the regularity with which the written symbol corresponds to the vowel sound it is to represent. The reader encountering a new word that includes one of these vowel letters or combinations of letters could be reasonably confident of the pronunciation.

On the right side are spelling symbols which do not correspond very

TABLE I–1   THE PROPORTION OF TIMES EACH OF 19 ALPHABET SPELLINGS
REPRESENTS THE DESIGNATED VOWEL SOUNDS IN 7,500 COMMON WORDS

SYMBOLS	WORD	VOWEL SOUND	SYMBOLS	WORD	VOWEL SOUND
a-e	make	100%	-a-	cat	83%
				table	13%
u-e	cute	100%			
			-u-	cup	73%
aw	law	100%		unite	24%
i-e	kite	99%	ea	meat	74%
				head	24%
oi	boil	99%			
			-e-	bet	70%
oa	boat	98%		be	30%
ee	beet	96%	ou	out	60%
				rough	35%
-i-	pin	91%			
	child	9%	oo	boot	59%
				cook	41%
ai	bait	90%			
			-o-	top	53%
au	caught	88%		told	40%
			ow	low	52%
				cow	48%
			o-e	home	34%
				come	66%

well. The spelling "ow," for example, can be pronounced like the vowel in
low or the vowel in *cow* with almost equal frequency. The reader would be
uncertain as to which would be the correct pronunciation. Other vowel
spellings in the right column offer probabilities for predicting the correct
pronunciation much better than by chance, although by no means perfectly.

Figures I–3, I–4 and I–5 contain the General American symbols organized by their manner and place of production. Primary spellings are in
bold type with secondary spellings just below, indented and in lighter type.

The numeral system, diacritical [1] and [2], is used consistently and exclusively to indicate the condition of voicing—[1] to designate a voiceless production and [2] to show a voiced production. The numerals appear above the
primary symbols only to differentiate th[1] as in *thin* from th[2] as in *then*. But
they can also be used to suggest the condition of voicing for other phonemes in relevant situations. Since errors of voicing are prevalent among
deaf speakers, this simple code can be very useful to the teacher. For example, the voiceless production of l and r in blends with voiceless consonants can be indicated by writing *print*, *clay*, *free*, and *sleep*. To suggest
the voiceless finish on final voiced fricative consonants, the teacher may write

GENERAL AMERICAN SYMBOLS	IPA	KEY WORDS	GENERAL AMERICAN SYMBOLS	IPA	KEY WORDS
Front Vowels			Back Vowels		
ee	/i/	bee	oo	/u/	boot
ea		meat	ew		grew
-y		busy	-oo-	/ʊ/	foot
-i-	/ɪ/	bit	oo(k)		book
-e-	/ɛ/	bet	aw	/ɔ/	lawn
-a-	/æ/	bat	au		caught
			a(l)		walk
Mixed Vowels			-o-	/ɑ/	top
			ah		rah
ur	/ɝ/	burn	a(r)		car
er	/ɚ/	better			
-u-	/ʌ/	but			
	/ə/	upon			

Figure 1–4. General American Speech and Phonic Symbols: Vowels. Primary, secondary and tertiary symbols with associated symbols of the International Phonetic Alphabet (IPA) and example words.

leave.$^{2-1.}$ When a voiceless fricative is given too much breath force between vowels, correction of the error may be indicated by writing the voicing numeral ^{2} as in *behind*. When a child produces a voiced/voiceless error, such as *die* for *tie*, the teacher can suggest the nature of the error by prompting the child with the written symbols *tie*.

Bracketed General American symbols suggest the influence of one sound upon the pronunciation of another. The letter *n* before *k* is usually pronounced **ng**. The *c* before *e, i,* and *y* becomes **s**, while before *a, o,* and *u* it is usually pronounced **k**. When *oo* is followed by *k* it is almost invariably pronounced **-oo-** rather than **oo**.

GENERAL AMERICAN SYMBOLS	IPA	KEY WORDS	GENERAL AMERICAN SYMBOLS	IPA	KEY WORDS
High Nucleus Diphthongs			Low Nucleus Diphthongs		
u-e	[ju]	cute	oi	/ɔɪ/	coin
a-e	/eɪ/	made	oy		boy
ai		bait	i-e	/aɪ/	bite
oa	/ou/	boat	igh		fight
-o		no	ou	/aʊ/	mouth
			ow		cow

Figure I-5. General American Speech and Phonic Symbols: Dipthongs. Primary and secondary symbols with associated symbols of the International Phonetic Alphabet (IPA) and example words.

The General American speech and phonic symbols are best used as a teaching medium. They serve to give the young child who has speech or language delay written symbols to associate with the speech units upon which he is working, coincidentally providing a written record of his progress for him and his parents to see. It also has served, with the aid of a skillful teacher, to help poor readers establish a link between their own speech production and our orthography, providing a phonic system for sounding-out unfamiliar words. Adaptations of the system have been used similarly to help foreign students pronounce English words.*

VISIBLE SPEECH SYMBOLS

A number of attempts have been made to produce written symbols related to articulatory positions so that the reader would have cues to aid in producing the associated speech sounds. Francis Mercurius Van Helmont† in 1667 promoted the belief that letters of the Hebrew alphabet were based on the configuration of the speech organs in producing certain sounds (Figure I–6).

In the 19th century, Alexander Melville Bell‡ devised a system of written symbols with curves and lines roughly corresponding to a profile view of the organs of speech: the nose, the lower lip, the point of the tongue, the throat, etc. The symbols were essentially directions to do something with the mouth. The /n/, for example, was represented by the symbol illustrated in Figure I–7. The direction of the opening at the top of the crescent in that symbol indicated the tongue tip was upward. Closure of the tongue against the upper gum ridge was shown by closure of the character by lines at the top. Voicing was suggested by the vertical line, and open nasal resonance was shown by the sigmoid line completing the closing at the top. With such symbols, the speech sounds of any language could be represented. For a time, the Bell symbols were used in teaching speech to deaf children, but these were eventually abandoned because of their complexity and unfamiliarity to most teachers and the inevitable need to transform them to the symbols of the Roman alphabet.

THE INITIAL TEACHING ALPHABET

Sir James Pitman introduced his Initial Teaching Alphabet to the United States in the 1960's.§ He attempted to eliminate ambiguity by having only

---

*Laubach, Frank C. et al.: *The New Streamlined English Series.* Syracuse, N.Y., New Readers Press, Revised 1971.
†abHelmond, F. M. B. *Alphabeti vere Naturalis Hebraici Brevissima Delineatio,* 1667.
‡Bell, A. M., *The Mechanism of Speech.* New York, Funk & Wagnalls Co., 1916.
§Pitman, Sir James K.B.E.: Can i.t.a. Help the Deaf Child? *Proceedings: International Conf. on Oral Educ. of the Deaf.* Wash. D.C., A. G. Bell Assn, 1967, Vol. 1, pp. 514–542.

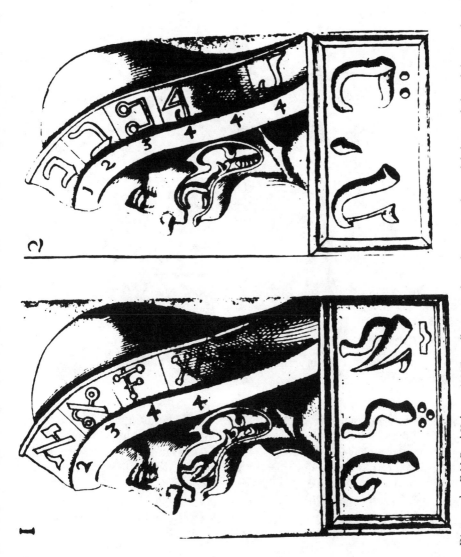

Figure 1–6. Diagrams by F.M.B. abHelmont (1667) to illustrate relation between Hebrew alphabet symbols and the speech mechanism.

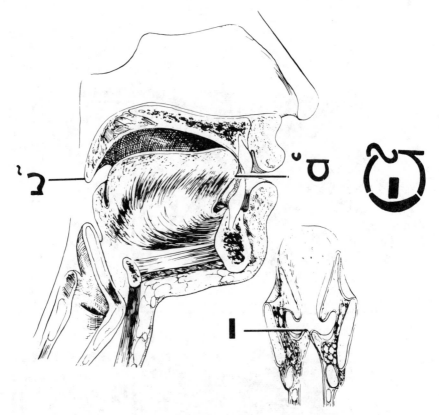

Figure 1-7. Alexander Melville Bell's phonetic symbol for /n/ based on place and manner of production.

one symbol for each spoken sound. The symbols he used were either regular alphabet letters or were made to look like alphabet letters, augmenting the Roman alphabet for a total of 44 symbols (Figure 1–8). The intention was that the young child might learn this system of reading first, then transfer easily to our usual system of orthography for reading and writing. It would be necessary for many children's books to be printed in these symbols. Although there was a flurry of interest in the 1960's, the Initial Teaching Alphabet has not found common use in the United States.

DICTIONARY DIACRITICAL MARKINGS

Pronouncing dictionaries have had to develop systems to indicate how words are commonly pronounced. They use modifying symbols, attached to letters, which are called **diacritical markings.** Pronunciation of the let-

a apple	ɑ father	æ angel	au author	b bed	c cat	ch chair
d doll	ee eel	e egg	f finger	g girl	h hat	ie tie
i ink	j jam	k kitten	l lion	m man	n nest	ŋ king
œ toe	o on	ω book	ω food	ou out	oi oil	p pig
r red	r bird	s soap	sh ship	ʒ treasure	t tree	th three
th mother	ue due	u up	v van	w window	wh wheel	y yellow
z zoo	z is					

this is printed in the inishial teeching alfabet, the purpos ov which is not, as miet bee suppœsd, tω reform our spelliŋ, but tω imprωv the lerniŋ ov reediŋ. it is intended that when the beginner is flωent in this meedium hee shωd bee confiend tω reediŋ in the tradishonal alfabet

if yω hav red as far as this, the nue meedium will hav prωvd tω yω several points, the mœst important ov which is that yω, at eny ræt, hav eesily mæd the chænj from the ordinary rœman alfabet with convenshonal spellings tω the inishial teeching alfabet with systematic spelliŋ.

Figure I–8. The Initial Teaching Alphabet (i.t.a.) of Sir James Pitman. At top, symbols arranged alphabetically with key words. At bottom, example of spelling using the i.t.a. symbols.

TABLE I-2   PRIMARY CONSONANT SYMBOLS OF THE INTERNATIONAL
PHONETIC ALPHABET, THE GENERAL AMERICAN SYSTEM, AND COMMON
DICTIONARY MARKINGS, WITH ASSOCIATED KEY WORDS

INTERNATIONAL PHONETIC ALPHABET SYMBOLS	PRIMARY GENERAL AMERICAN SYMBOLS	COMMON DICTIONARY SYMBOLS	KEY WORDS
h	h-	h	he, ahead
ʍ	wh	hw	when, everywhere
p	p	p	pie, stopped, sip
t	t	t	tie, later, sit
k	k	k	key, become, back
f	f̦	f	fan, coffee, leaf
θ	th	t̪h th	thin, nothing, tooth
s	s	s	see, upset, makes
ʃ	sh	s̪h sh	she, sunshine, fish
tʃ	ch	c̪h ch	chair, teacher, such
w	w-	w	we, awake
b	b	b	boy, rabbit, cab
d	d	d	day, fading, mud
g	g	g	go, begged, log
v	v̦	v	vine, every, give
ð	th	t̶h̶ th t̶h̶ TH	the, bother, smooth
z	z	z	zoo, lazy, size
ʒ	zh	zh	vision, beige
dʒ	j	j	jam, enjoy, edge
m	m	m	my, camera, team
n	n	n	new, any, tin
ŋ	ng	ng n͡g	singer, song
l	l	l	low, color, bowl
r	r	r	red, oral, bar
j	y-	y	yes, canyon
kʍ	qu	kw	queen, liquid
ks	x	ks	taxi, box

ters with attached markings are suggested by key words. These systems
constitute the most available and constant references to pronunciation for
most people. However, they assume some knowledge of the language for
pronunciation of the key words, the symbols vary from dictionary to dictionary, and they are not available in general reading without a dictionary as
ready reference. A teacher may effectively use the diacritical markings to
indicate pronunciation once the system of markings has been learned. Some
common dictionary symbols are presented in Tables I–2 and I–3.

THE INTERNATIONAL PHONETIC ALPHABET

The International Phonetic Association founded a symbol system in 1886,
based upon an alphabet developed earlier by the British phonetician Henry

TABLE I–3 PRIMARY VOWEL SYMBOLS IN THE INTERNATIONAL PHONETIC ALPHABET, THE GENERAL AMERICAN SYSTEM, AND COMMON DICTIONARY MARKINGS, WITH ASSOCIATED KEYWORDS

INTERNATIONAL PHONETIC ALPHABET SYMBOLS	PRIMARY GENERAL AMERICAN SYMBOLS	COMMON DICTIONARY SYMBOLS	KEY WORDS
i	ee	ē	east, beet, me
ɪ	-i-	ĭ	if, bit
ɛ	-e-	ĕ	end, bet
æ	-a-	ă	at, bat
ɑ	-o-	ŏ ä	odd, father, pa
a	-o- -a-		path, Boston, car (Eastern U.S.)
ɒ	-o-	ȯ	hot, top, box (British, New England)
ʌ	-u-	ŭ u	up, cub (stressed)
ə	-u-	ŭ ạ ə	upon, nation, cobra (unstressed)
u	oo	o͞o ȯȯ	ooze, boot, too
ʊ	-oo-	o͝o oo	book, could
ɔ	aw	ô aw	awful, caught, law
ɝ	ur	ûr ur	urn, burn, fur (General U.S.)
ɜ	ur	ûr	urn, burn, fur (Eastern and Southern U.S.)
ɚ	ur	êr er	urbane, obliterate, burner, (unstressed)
eɪ	a-e	ā	able, made, may
e	a-e	ā̤	vibrate (unstressed)
oʊ	oa	ō	own, boat, no
o	oa	ō̤	obey, rotation (unstressed)
aɪ	i-e	ī	ice, mine, my
aʊ	ou	ou	out, loud, now
ɔɪ	oi	oi	oil, coin, boy
ju	u-e	ū	use, cute, few

Sweet. The system was to have a different symbol for each of the sounds of speech and was to be used for all the languages of the world. It was therefore called the **International Phonetic Alphabet** (IPA). It provided a way for phoneticians from different languages to communicate with each other and a common system for scholars of language to use in the literature. With a few modifications, this system continues to be the most widely used for phonetic notation.

The IPA is not intended to be used as a system of spelling for any language but as a system to symbolize visually any speech sound. The symbols *p, b, t, d, k, g, l, m, n, r, f, v, s, z, h,* and *w* come directly from the Roman alphabet (see Table I–2). Other symbols are from Greek or were especially created for the purpose. When one wishes to designate a phoneme, the

IPA symbol is traditionally placed in virgules, or slash marks, as in /k/ for the phoneme that is common to *key, coo, class, bark, account,* and *ski.* To designate a particular sound that was spoken or a group of connected speech sounds, the symbol is placed in squared brackets as in [k] for the sound in the unit [ki] for pronunciation of the word *key.*

There are two levels of transcription. **Broad transcription** uses the primary symbols of the IPA to designate phonemes and the speech sounds as they are usually produced. **Narrow transcription** uses symbols, somewhat like the diacritical markings of dictionaries, to indicate something special about the way the sound has been produced. For example, the symbol [̺] indicates the sound was made on the teeth. Thus, a /t/ phoneme written as [t̪] was made with the tongue tip closing against the upper front teeth rather than the gum ridge. Note how this narrow transcription can be useful in describing how the [d̪] sound in *width* [wɪd̪θ] is produced, or how the Russian [n̪] is made.

Symbols of the International Phonetic Alphabet will be used to designate speech sounds throughout this book. Broad transcription symbols are presented in Tables I–2 and I–3. Exercises are presented at the end of this chapter to help the reader learn to use these symbols. Some useful symbols of narrow transcription are presented in Table I–4.

Consonants.   In addition to the familiar symbols of the Roman alphabet, the IPA uses the Greek capital Theta /θ/ to represent the voiceless sound written *th* as in *thin, thank,* and *thumb,* and it uses the /ð/ to represent the voiced *th* as in *this, that,* and *those.* A printed *w* turned upside down, /ʍ/, is used for the voiceless *wh* as in *why, which, when,* and *where.* A lengthened sigmoid /ʃ/ is written for the voiceless *sh* as in *shoe, bush,* and *ocean.* A symbol like a cursive *z* is produced as /ʒ/ for the middle consonant in *vision* and *measure.* The symbol /ŋ/, written like an *n* with one side length-

TABLE I–4   SOME SYMBOLS OF IPA NARROW TRANSCRIPTION USEFUL IN DESCRIBING VARIATIONS IN AMERICAN-ENGLISH ARTICULATION

SYMBOL	MEANING	EXAMPLES		COMMENTS
z̪	dentalized	[wɪd̪θ]	*width*	Made against upper front teeth
~	nasalized	[mĩn]	*mean*	Made with excess nasality
○	voiceless	[pl̥eɪ]	*play*	Made without usual voicing
˅	voiced	[əhɛ̬d]	*ahead*	Made with some voicing
ˌ	syllabized	[batl̩]	*bottle*	Given duration of a syllable without a vowel present
ː	lengthened	[tɛnːaɪts]	*ten nights*	Sound held longer than usual
⊥	tongue raised	[mɛ̝t]	*met*	Tongue slightly higher than usual
⊤	tongue lowered	[mɛ̞t]	*met*	Tongue slightly lower than usual
ʿ	aspirated	[læpʻ]	*lap*	Stop consonant exploded
ʾ	unaspirated	[pɛkˈt]	*pecked*	Stop consonant not exploded

ened and hooked to suggest the *g* is used for the final sound written *ng* as in *song, wing,* and *bang.* The letter *j* is used for the brief glide sound found initially in *yes* [jɛs].

The two affricate phonemes that combine a stopping of breath and then release with friction at the same point of contact are commonly written as two symbols touching each other to indicate that they are produced with a single impulse. For example, the *ch* sound in *chew, chin,* and *church* is written with the /t/ and /ʃ/ symbols combined as /tʃ/. Note that this sound, produced as a single impulse as in *why chew* [ʍaɪtʃu], is more compact than the simple combination of [t] and [ʃ] in *white shoe* [ʍaɪt ʃu]. Similarly, the initial sound in *John, jam,* and *jaw* is written [ʤ].

Vowels. Vowel symbols combine various kinds of common script with a few invented symbols. The /u/ and /i/ are typical lower case letters, whereas the /ʊ/ and /ɪ/ are capital letters reduced to the size of lower case. The /e/ and /ɛ/ use two kinds of script for writing the letter *e,* and the /a/ and /ɑ/ are different ways to write the letter *a.* The /æ/ is a combination of *a* and *e,* a symbol once used in English orthography. The /ɔ/ is like a reversed *c,* the /ʌ/ an inverted *v,* and the /ə/ is an *e* written upside down and reversed. The /ɜ/ and /ɝ/ is like a number 3 with a hook on the latter one to show [r] quality. The diphthongs, which move from one position to another in a single syllable, are written as combinations of the simple vowel symbols, but they are not attached.

The International Phonetic Alphabet attempts to provide symbols for differences in stress, or the force with which a sound is produced. Very useful is the /ʌ/ for the stressed vowel in *up, cut,* and *bump,* and the /ə/ for essentially the same vowel when it is unstressed as the first sound in *above* [əbʌv]. The /ə/, which is called the "schwa" vowel from the German "schwach" meaning weak, is softer and of shorter duration than the /ʌ/. Many vowels when unstressed become the /ə/. For example, notice what happens to the written *a* in *table* [te'ɪbl̩] when it is unstressed in *vegetable* [vɛʤ-ətəbl̩]. The /ə/ can occur as the unstressed sound for any of the vowel letters in connected speech, for example the *o* in *command* [kəmænd], the *a* in *above* [əbʌv], the *u* in *upon* [əpɑn], the *e* in *release* [rəlis], and the *i* in *attic* [ætək].

IPA representation for stressing and unstressing is more ambiguous for other vowel sounds. The /i/ is often written as /ɪ/ when unstressed, By convention, the final *y,* unstressed in such words as *many, very, happy,* and *baby,* is written as [ɪ]. To the ear, the American-English sound is closer to /i/ but of shorter duration and of less intensity. The convention of transcribing the final *y* as /ɪ/ stems from the British-English pronunciation, which was thought desirable for "good speech," but it seems ill suited for transcribing common American-English speech. Compare the two vowels in *easy* [izɪ], which actually sound more similar than the vowels in *busy* [bɪzɪ]. A completely different symbol for the unstressed /i/ might be helpful. The reader may wish to use for accuracy an accompanying narrow transcription symbol (see Table I–4) for [ɪ̝], which indicates the tongue is raised in producing this sound. This accounts for the tongue position closer to the high position for /i/ but also for the unstressed condition of reduced duration and intensity with the conventional /ɪ/ transcription.

Diphthongs. Diphthongs [dɪfθɔŋz] are combinations of two vowel sounds in a single syllable. One of the vowels, called the **nucleus,** is longer and more intense, whereas the other vowel, called the **glide,** is shorter and weaker. The stronger nucleus is written with its own symbol; the unstressed glide is written with a symbol for the vowel of slightly lower tongue position than its sound to the ear would suggest. For example, the [aɪ] as in *pie* has [a] written for its nucleus and [ɪ] written for its unstressed glide, even though the unstressed glide sounds more like [i]. Similarly, the diphthong [oʊ] as in *go* has its glide written [ʊ] despite its sound heard closer to the [u]. This transcription of the diphthong glide follows in the [aʊ] as in *cow,* the [eɪ] as in *bay,* and the [ɔɪ] in *boy.*

When the diphthongs [oʊ] and [eɪ] occur in unstressed syllables, they are written with the single symbols [o] and [e]. Examples of the unstressed [o] are in the words *obey* and *donation.* Examples of the unstressed [e] are in the words *vacation* and *fatality.* By convention, the other diphthongs /aɪ/, /aʊ/ and /ɔɪ/ are transcribed the same in stressed and unstressed syllables.

THE IDEAL ORTHOGRAPHIC SYSTEM

Several systems of orthography have been described in this chapter, none of which seems to be ideal for all uses. Perhaps no single system could meet all our needs for written language symbols, but the ideal system should meet the following criteria:

1. It should have a consistent one-to-one sound/symbol correspondence. That is, each time a symbol appears, it should always have the same speech sound, and each speech sound should be written by only one symbol.
2. There should be symbols to correspond to all the different speech sounds of our language. Different symbols should be available for all the important sounds, including those that are different in stressed and in unstressed syllables. If possible, additional symbols, rather than modifying markings, should be included in the systems to correspond to all the sounds of all the world's spoken languages.
3. The symbols should be those familiar to the culture. Symbols needed for English should be symbols that English speaking people commonly use. The Roman alphabet letters are most common, but other common

symbols, such as those on a typewriter (#, &, @, %, *) or numerals would have to be added to cover all the English speech sounds.

4. The symbols should be sufficiently simple so that persons of all ages could write them. The symbols would need to be within the capability of writing by almost all the people in the culture. Ideally, too, the symbols should be so simple that one might use them to transcribe connected speech at the rate it is spoken, much as we use shorthand writing systems.

5. The symbols should be distinctive enough to avoid visual confusion. Such similarities as the IPA has in the groupings /ɜ/, /ɝ/, /ɛ/, and /e/, /ə/, /ɚ/, for example, may cause visual confusions to the reader or transcriber.

6. The system should have internal consistency. The method for showing that some vowels are unstressed, for example, should apply to all vowels. When a sound changes its characteristics because of coarticulation, the notation should be consistent for all similar changes. Perhaps symbols for a group of sounds of similar manner or place of articulation could have common characteristics.

7. The symbols should, if possible, tell the reader something about the manner and place of articulation. The Bell Visible Speech symbols were an attempt at this.

Analysis of these several criteria suggest that some may be conflicting. It would be difficult to develop symbols that suggested manner and place of articulation and yet be familiar symbols of the culture, or to account for all the sounds of spoken language and yet have only symbols that could be simply written. The ideal orthographic system may, therefore, be that which is best for a specific purpose, with a number of systems available for various uses.

REVIEW VOCABULARY

Allophones—examples of variations within a phoneme class resulting from different phonetic environments.

Alphabet—the system of written symbols common to a language.

Broad transcription—in IPA, transcribing in phoneme symbols only, without modifying markings to indicate allophonic or other phonetic differences.

Diacritical markings—symbols used to modify alphabet letters or phonetic symbols to indicate differences in pronunciation.

Diphthong—a sequence of two vowel sounds produced in a single syllable with one sound dominant.

Glide—the shorter, less stressed vowel of a diphthong.

Ideograms—written symbols representing symbolic ideas.

Logograms—written symbols representing entire words.

Narrow transcription—in IPA, transcribing in phoneme symbols plus modifying markings to indicate variation in production.

Nucleus—the longer dominant vowel of a diphthong.

Orthography—the commonly accepted spelling using alphabet symbols.

Phoneme—an abstract class of speech sounds containing common elements and influencing the meaning of speech.

Phonics—an application of the relation between alphabet letters or groups of letters and speech sounds as an aid to improving reading.

Phonograms—written symbols representing speech sounds.

Pictograms—drawings that represent only the objects or events depicted.

Roman alphabet—the system of written symbols used in English and several other European languages, transmitted from the Romans.

Transliteration—the process of selecting alphabet letters to represent a group of speech sounds.

EXERCISES

1. Determine the IPA symbol for the consonant phoneme common in each of the following lists of words. Note the differences in spelling.

(a)	(b)	(c)	(d)
stay	speed	malt	then
washed	city	plan	bother
two	science	sleep	bathe
hot	kiss	ballot	the
try	psychology	pillow	other
better	assume	clear	teethe
wasted	desks	elbow	that
twice	splice	blue	leather

(e)	(f)	(g)
laugh	legend	who
phone	judge	high
half	giant	ahead
coffee	edge	hers
off	agile	behold
after	orange	whole
Philip	jazz	anyhow
often	ledge	hen

2. Determine the IPA symbol for the vowel or diphthong phoneme common in each of the following lists of words. Note the differences in spelling.

(a)	(b)	(c)	(d)
seek	about	credit	land
easy	south	enter	amble
streaks	our	feather	and
evil	bound	bend	tan
we	cow	said	rack
being	clown	leopard	fast
teams	power	get	manual
chic	towel	nest	attack

(e)	(f)	(g)
tomb	book	find
soon	put	time
chew	should	by
rule	shook	cried
group	wouldn't	higher
fruit	full	type
lose	woman	height
boost	foot	ride

Transcribe in IPA symbols only the consonants as you would say them (or from another's dictation) in the following words:

3. /p, b, t, d, k, g, l, m, n, r, f, v, s, z, h, w/

goat	cave	soap	maybe
hog	mount	sleep	gained
walk	race	balloon	bottom
who	waffle	vacate	roof
doze	half	five	license

4. /ʍ, θ, ʃ, ð, ʒ, ŋ, j, tʃ, dʒ/

why	show	wished	whether
the	edge	think	shoe
sing	vision	where	wealth
church	change	usual	those
thin	yellow	when	which
pleasure	singing	enjoy	badge

Transcribe in IPA symbols all consonants and vowels as you would say them (or from another's dictation) in the following words:

5. /u, ʊ, ɔ/

book	caught	all	moon
law	boots	tools	balls
put	shook	thought	could
choose	June	good	tomb

6. /i, ɪ, ɛ/

beet	mean	when	zen
dim	quenched	these	sing
quick	sheet	yet	geese
then	jig	whip	pin

7. /æ, ɑ, ʌ/

at	chants	arm	bunk
mom	much	thus	an
tuck	bomb	Tom	palm
lack	judge	thank	back

8. /ə, ɝ, ɚ/ plus previously practiced vowels

butter	third	furnace	burner
bird	girl	zebra	Adam
above	upon	fern	evil
banner	turning	better	liquor

9. All pure vowels. Review Table I–3.

ahead	whose	under	yawn
foot	each	youth	went

learning	imagine	doctor	should
turn	bath	son	whim
fought	cause	watch	spurn

Transcribe in IPA symbols all consonants, vowels, and diphthongs as you would say them (or from another's dictation) in the following words:

10. /eɪ, oʊ, aɪ, aʊ, ɔɪ/

eight	own	time	foil
load	cold	boys	around
stain	mile	date	choice
light	now	rain	spoil
tried	toasts	drown	clown

11. All consonants, vowels, and diphthongs. Review Tables I–2 and I–3.

looks	them	hawk	about
quickly	watched	temper	leisure
branch	tomatoes	whimper	filing
weaves	thirst	gusher	yesterday
omen	wonder	tuba	just

12. All consonants, vowels, and diphthongs. Review Tables I–2 and I–3.

yeast	chalk	Utah	girl
occasion	hinder	method	voices
allow	whose	father	badge
why	put	wish	once
changes	wrong	queen	supper

SUGGESTED READING

Albright, Robert W.: The International Phonetic Alphabet: Its Backgrounds and Development, *International Journal of American Linguistics*. Volume 24, #1, Part III, January, 1958.

This scholarly work traces the International Phonetic Alphabet from phoneticians of 16th Century England to development of the first IPA in 1888, and through its various modifications. It is based on Albright's doctoral dissertation at Stanford University and also appears as a 78-page monograph, Publication #7, of the Indiana University Research Center in Anthropology, Folklore and Linguistics. It includes descriptions of a number of early orthographic systems.

Calvert, Donald R. and Silverman, S. Richard, *Speech and Deafness*. Washington, D.C., A. G. Bell Ass'n. for the Deaf, revised 1983.

Chapter I, "Speech and its production," includes description of use of the General American Speech and Phonic Symbols in teaching speech and reading. These symbols are used throughout the text.

International Phonetic Association: *The Principles of the International Phonetic Association*. London, 1979.

A reprint of the 1949 pamphlet that describes the IPA and shows specimens of its use with several languages.

Chapter II

THE SPEECH PRODUCTION MECHANISM AND PROCESSES

Among the creatures of Earth, only man has achieved speech. All species of animals communicate, many by vocal noises, but none has approached the complexity and sophistication of our spoken language. Yet the body parts we use to produce speech do not appear to be greatly different from those of other animals with teeth, tongues, and palates. And we, as they, regularly use these oral structures for more basic bodily functions, especially breathing and eating. However, we know that a healthy human baby has the innate potential to speak, a potential that apparently is specific to our species. This suggests a unique nervous system capable of abstracting, associating, memorizing, recognizing, recalling, and formulating—a nervous system that has evolved to make use of our given body parts for the production of speech.

THE SPEECH MECHANISM

The term "speech mechanism" should not appear to imply a simple mechanical system of pulleys and levers, or even an electronic system of transistors and capacitors. Our anatomy and physiology are too complex for that. But "speech mechanism" is a useful term to refer collectively to the body parts used in producing speech. This chapter aims to present those anatomic and physiologic concepts that will contribute most to the study of descriptive phonetics, rather than an exhaustive exposition of the subject. Where possible, we will use the common Anglicized terms along with Latinized names, prefixes, and suffixes that commonly describe place of articulation and manner of speech production. The typical General-American pronunciation will be indicated with symbols of the International Phonetic Alphabet, aided by accent marks to show the stressed syllable. We begin with the most obvious part of the speech mechanism, the lips.

Lips (Prefix *labio*- [leíbɪo], suffix -*labial* [leɪbɪəl])

The lips are a complex of muscles and other tissues. Running vertically in the center of the upper lip, just below the nose, is a grooved indentation called the **philtrum** [fɪltrəm]. At the lip border, the skin changes to form the characteristic reddish **vermilion** [vɝmíljən], which is an adaptation of the mucous membrane that lines the mouth. Inside both the upper and lower lips at the midline is a thin flexible membrane called the labial **frenum** [frinəm] that connects the lip to the alveolar [ælvíolɚ] processes between the central incisors. These can be felt with the tongue tip. The lips have a great capacity for varied movements, and much of their range of movements is utilized in producing our speech sounds.

The versatility of the lips results from a complex system of muscles. Of central importance is the **orbicularis oris** [ɔrbɪkjuláris óris] muscle with its fibers in a circular pattern around the periphery of the mouth. It can contract to round the lips with a wide to small opening, even closing the rounded lips and protruding them. The orbicularis oris is actually a layer of muscle fibers coming from other muscles that are inserted into the lips, rather than having an origin and insertion of its own. These other facial muscles contribute greatly to lip movement and versatility. From the upper jaw or **maxilla** [mæksílə] come muscles that raise and lower the upper lip and draw up and back the corners of the mouth. From the lower jaw or mandible [mǽndɪbəl] come muscles that raise and lower the lower lip, protrude it, and draw down and back the corners of the mouth. From the cheeks or **bucca** [bʌ́kə] comes the wide, flat **buccinator** [bʌ́ksɪneɪtɚ] muscle, mingling its fibers in the orbicularis oris and controlling the corners of the mouth. From the neck come muscles that can pull down the corners of the mouth. These varied muscles also affect the facial expressions (frown, grin, smile, sneer, pout) we use in association with speech and to communicate non-speech information.

Although the primary bodily function of the lips is to help receive and contain food and fluids in the oral cavity, they perform a number of actions in speech production. The lips can be closed passively by elevating the lower jaw, or mandible, until the teeth close together. However, the closures of speech articulation require variability in firmness and rapid motions of short duration, and they are usually made with the teeth apart. This action requires active muscular closure by the upper and lower lips moving simultaneously to the center of the mouth. In most speakers, the lower lip is the more mobile in rapid connected speech, and in some speakers, the upper lip may move very little. The lips close by muscular action to stop the breath stream, as in articulating /p/, /b/, and /m̃/, the **bilabial** [baɪleíbɪəl] consonant sounds. Closure for the /p/ requires the greatest bilabial firmness to contain the air pressure built up in the oral cavity. Less firmness is required for /b/, and still less for /m/, which has nasal emission of air flow. By bringing the lower lip close to the upper front teeth, the breath stream can be constricted to create friction for the /f/ and /v/, the **labio-dental** consonant sounds. This articulation requires that the lower lip be moved upward without simultaneous lowering of the upper lip, while the teeth remain open. Many speakers pull the lower lip slightly inward toward the upper teeth, also. Then too, the lower lip must be held briefly close to the upper front teeth, just far enough away to permit air to escape between them, but close enough to constrict air flow for audible friction. This position of closeness is called **approximation** [əprɑ́ksəmeɪʃən]. Rounding the lips with varying degrees of opening contributes to the production of the bilabial consonants /w/ and /ʍ/, the vowels /u/, /ʊ/, and /ɔ/, and the diphthongs [dɪfθɔ́ŋz] /ou/, /ɔɪ/, and /aʊ/. Some lip rounding is also present in fricative [fríkətɪv] consonants /ʃ/ and /ʒ/, and in affricates [ǽfrɪkəts] /tʃ/ and /ʤ/.

Teeth (Prefix *dento-*, suffix *-dental*)

The teeth play a passive but important role in speech production. Their primary function is to cut and grind in chewing food. For the growing child, dentition undergoes significant changes (Figure II-1) that influence speech. The **deciduous** [dɪsídjuəs] teeth, sometimes called the primary or "baby" teeth, erupt during a period of from six months to two years of age to include

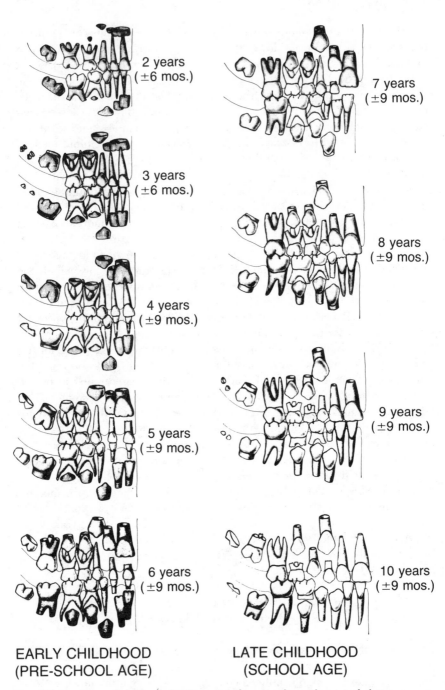

2 years
(±6 mos.)

3 years
(±6 mos.)

4 years
(±9 mos.)

5 years
(±9 mos.)

6 years
(±9 mos.)

7 years
(±9 mos.)

8 years
(±9 mos.)

9 years
(±9 mos.)

10 years
(±9 mos.)

EARLY CHILDHOOD
(PRE-SCHOOL AGE)

LATE CHILDHOOD
(SCHOOL AGE)

Figure 11-1. Stages of children's dentition. Deciduous teeth are shown in dark tint, permanent teeth in white. From the chart, "Development of the Human Dentition," I. Schour & M. Massler, American Dental Association, 211 East Chicago Avenue. Chicago, Illinois 60611.

20 teeth—10 in the maxilla and 10 in the mandible. They are arranged in symmetrical sets of five teeth on each side, beginning from the midline: **central incisor** [ɪnsáɪzɚ], **lateral incisor, canine** [keínaɪn] (or eye tooth), **first molar** [moulɚ], and **second molar.** Starting at about age six, the deciduous teeth are gradually replaced by 32 **permanent** teeth—16 in the maxilla and 16 in the mandible—arranged in symmetrical sets of eight teeth on each side. Beginning from the midline, these are as follows: **central incisor, lateral incisor, canine, first bicuspid** [baɪkʌspɪd] (having two sharp points, or cusps, and sometimes called a "premolar"), **second bicuspid, first molar, second molar,** and variably in the teens or early twenties, the **third molar** or "wisdom" tooth. No further development occurs into adulthood, but with decay or damage, teeth may be altered by extraction or repair, or the set may have to be partially or completely replaced with dentures.

When the teeth are closed, the maxillary and mandibular molars and the bicuspids rest intermeshed with each other, normally with the inner **cusps** or points of the maxillary teeth against the midline of their mandibular counterparts. The maxillary canines and incisors overlap the outer surface of their mandibular opposites. This fitting together or "bite" when closed is called the dental **occlusion** [oklúʒən], and an abnormality of the bite is referred to as a **malocclusion** [mǽloklúʒən].

The sides of the tongue pressed against the molars help direct the breath stream toward the front of the mouth as in /ʃ/ and /ʒ/. The lower lip approximates the maxillary incisors to constrict the breath stream for the labio-dental consonants /f/ and /v/. The tongue tip similarly approximates the maxillary incisors for production of the lingua-dental /θ/ and /ð/. The slightly opened maxillary and mandibular incisors provide friction surfaces for the /s/, /z/, /ʃ/, and /ʒ/. When the incisors are absent, as they are for a time between deciduous and permanent dentition at about age seven (see Figure II-1), sounds that require friction against the teeth cannot be produced well. Similarly, when decayed teeth must be replaced, or when there is a malocclusion, production of these consonants is adversely affected.

Alveolar Ridge (Prefix *alveolo-* [ælvíolo], suffix *-alveolar* [ælvíolɚ]

In both the maxilla and the mandible, the teeth are contained in alveolar processes or sockets, commonly called the "gum ridges." The alveolar processes behind the maxillary incisors and canine teeth form a rather pronounced ridge that figures prominently in consonant articulation. The tongue presses against this alveolar ridge to stop the breath stream for the /t/, /d/, and /n/, and just behind the ridge for /tʃ/ and /dʒ/. Pressing the narrow point of the tongue against the center of the ridge permits the breath stream to escape around both sides of the tongue for the /l/ sound. The tongue tip

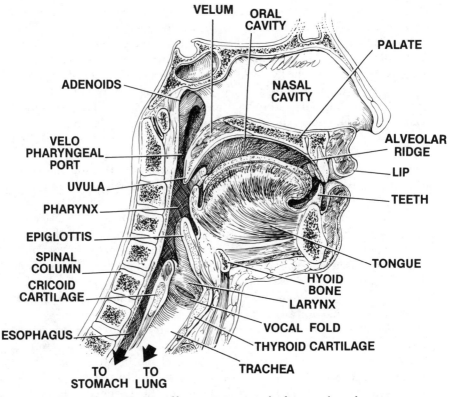

Figure II–2.   Diagram of basic structures involved in speech production.

approximates the alveolar ridge in the most common formation of the /s/ and /z/. The front of the tongue, at a greater distance from the ridge, forms constriction of the breath stream to produce the /ʃ/ and /ʒ/ sounds.

Palate (Prefix *palato-* [pǽlətou], suffix *-palatal* [pǽlətəl] and *palatine* [pǽlətin])

Farther inside the mouth, just beyond the alveolar ridge of the maxilla, is the **palate**, commonly called the "bony" or "hard" palate. It forms part of the roof of the mouth, but it is both a roof and a floor, as it separates the nasal cavity from the oral cavity. Its primary bodily functions are to help contain food in the oral cavity and to provide a hard upper surface for the action of swallowing. From the alveolar processes of the maxillary teeth, the palate arches upward. The height and narrowness of the arch, sometimes called the palatal "vault," varies greatly with facial structure. Evidence of the palate's embryologic manner of development from the two sides is apparent by feeling the midline suture running from between the central incisors the length of the palate to disappear at the juncture of the hard and soft palates. As the superior (upper) surface of the oral cavity, the palate contributes to vowel resonance by determining the shape of the cavity. It helps to direct the breath stream toward the front of the mouth for consonant articulation. The back of the tongue presses against the back of the palate or the velum in the production of /k/, /g/, and /ŋ/. The tip of the tongue is lifted toward the palate, just behind the alveolar ridge, to help form the /r/ sound.

Velum (Prefix *velo-* [vílou], suffix *-velar* [vilɚ])

Farther back on the roof of the mouth, posterior to and adjoining the palate, is the **velum** [viləm], commonly called the "soft palate." It consists of muscle and connective tissue covered by a continuation of the mucous membrane of the palate. Its primary purpose is to help keep food and fluids from entering the nasal cavity. The velum is very flexible and mobile, opening to permit air to flow through the nasal cavity to and from the throat. To achieve this control, the velum participates in opening and closing the **velopharyngeal** [vilofɛrínʤəl] **port,** the aperture that connects the nasal cavity and the oral cavity. It is sometimes referred to as the "nasopharyngeal" port (Figure II-2). At the midline of the posterior border of the velum is the **uvula** [júvjulə], from the Latin meaning "little grape," an appendage that apparently serves little function in man.

The mobility of the velum derives from having muscles coming from above, below, and behind it. The paired **levator** [livéɪtɚ] muscles enter the velum at the midline and contract to raise it toward the posterior wall of the throat. The **tensor** [tɛnsɚ] muscles contract to make the velum taut, especially during swallowing, and they influence the opening and closing of the orifice of the **Eustachian** [justéɪkɪən] **tube,** which lies near the origin of these muscles in the throat (see Figure II-3). The **glossopalatine** [glásopǽlətin] muscles pass from the undersurface of the tongue to the palate along each side of the oral cavity, making noticeable bundles called the **anterior pillars of the fauces** [fɔsiz]. When the glossopalatines contract, they draw down the sides of the velum and at the same time, draw up and back the sides of the tongue. The **pharyngopalatine** [fɛríŋgopǽlətin] muscles rise from the larynx and pass along each side of the oral cavity, forming another pair of prominent bundles called the **posterior pillars of the fauces,** and then they insert into the midline of the velum. They act to depress the velum while elevating the throat and larynx [lérɪŋks].

By helping to close the velopharyngeal port, the velum helps direct the breath stream to the oral cavity for articulation and for primarily oral reso-

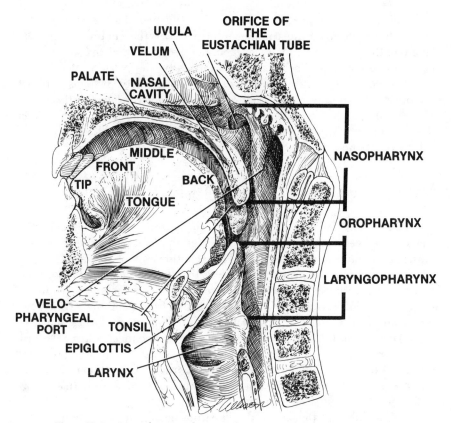

Figure II-3.   Sagittal section diagram of structures of the pharyngeal area.

nance as in vowel sounds. When the velum is relaxed and the port is opened, the breath stream can enter the nasal cavity for predominantly nasal resonance as in /m/, /n/, and /ŋ/.

Tongue (Prefixes *lingua-* [lɪŋgwə] and *glossa-* [glɑsə], suffixes *-lingual* [lɪŋgwəl] and *-glossal* [glɑsəl])

The Latin root *lingua*, the same for "tongue" and for "language," reflects the historic importance ascribed to the tongue as the vehicle for spoken language. We commonly speak of "foreign tongues" or of the "mother tongue" when we mean the spoken language. Without a doubt, the tongue is of very great importance in producing speech. Its exceptional mobility permits it to shape the oral cavity almost infinitely. Its primary bodily purpose is to direct food to the back of the oral cavity during swallowing. This highly mobile muscular organ arising from the floor of the oral cavity derives its remarkable versatility from dual control by **intrinsic** [ɪntrɪ́nsɪk] muscles that change its shape and **extrinsic** [ɛkstrɪ́nsɪk] muscles that are largely responsible for its movement within the oral cavity.

The intrinsic muscles are named for their direction within the tongue: the **vertical,** which widens and flattens the tongue tip; the **inferior longitudinal** (from base to apex), which widens and shortens the tongue, depresses the tip, and makes the upper surface convex; the **superior longitudinal,** which widens, thickens, and shortens the tongue, raises its tip and edge, and makes the upper surface grooved or concave; and the **transverse** (from midline to both sides), which elongates, narrows, and thickens the tongue, and can lift its sides. The extrinsic muscles connect the tongue to the temporal bone of the skull, the mandible, the **hyoid** [haɪ́ɔɪd] bone, and the velum. They include the following: the **styloglossus** [staɪ́loglɑ́səs], running forward and downward from the styloid process of the temporal bone to enter the sides of the tongue, which elevates the rear of the tongue and retracts it when protruded; the **genioglossus** [ʤɪ́nɪoglɑ́səs], running upward from the mandible as a great fan-shaped muscle, forming a large part of the tongue's bulk and providing for the majority of its activity, which depresses, retracts, and protrudes the tongue; and the **hyoglossus** [haɪ́oglɑ́səs], extending upward from the hyoid bone into the posterior half of the sides of the tongue, which helps retract the tongue and depresses its sides. These extrinsic muscles interweave with the intrinsic muscle fibers to form a very complex pattern.

The anatomic landmarks of the tongue include its **root** or posterior portion connecting with the hyoid bone and epiglottis, the **apex** [eɪ́pɛks] at the anterior end, its **dorsum** [dorsəm] or superior surface, and the septum [sɛptəm] or midline structure of connective tissue. The surface under the front of the tongue is connected with the mandible centrally by the lingual **frenum** [frinəm]. For describing speech, it is convenient to label positions on the dorsum that figure prominently in articulatory activity. These positions are the **back,** the **middle,** the **front** (sometimes called the "blade"), the **tip,** and the **point,** which is derived when the tongue is narrowed and pointed (Figure II–4).

The tongue can narrow and point, as it does for the /l/, or it can present a broad front as in producing /ʃ/ and /ʒ/, where there is no tip or point evident. It can close off the oral cavity and quickly release compressed breath as it does for /t/, with the tongue tip against the alveolar ridge, and for /k/, with the back of the tongue against the velum or palate. With somewhat reduced closure pressure, the same action is involved in producing /d/ and /g/. The tongue can close the oral cavity at the alveolar ridge for /n/ and at the velum for /ŋ/, with nasal emission of voice. It can form a central groove to direct the breath stream as it does for /s/, or the tip can be elevated and drawn back (retroflexed) toward the back of the oral cavity as in /r/. The front and back of the tongue can be raised and lowered by subtle degrees in order to alter the

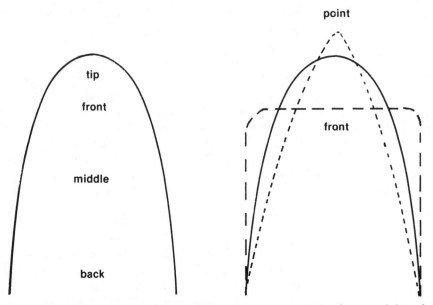

Figure II–4.   Top or superview diagram of the tongue in its normal relaxed position (left), and in positions of a narrow point (as in /l/) and a broad front (as in /ʃ/).

oral cavity for vowel resonance. All the vowel sounds are influenced by tongue action, and the only consonants in English that do not have direct tongue involvement are the following: /m/, /p/, /b/, /v/, and /f/.

Mandible (Prefixes *mandibulo-* and *genio-*, suffixes *-mandibular* and *-genial*)

The mandible, or lower jaw, plays both a passive and an active role in articulation. It serves as a foundation for the large genioglossus muscle of the tongue and it houses the mandibular teeth. It can be elevated to close and lowered to open the jaw for vowel articulation. This movement is accomplished by four muscles, the primary muscles of mastication (Figure II–5). These are as follows: the **temporal** muscle, originating over a large fan-shaped area of the temporal bone of the skull and converging downward and forward to form a tendon inserted into the mandible, which elevates and retracts the mandible to close the jaw; the **masseter** [mǽsətɚ], which also closes the jaw and runs downward from the **zygomatic** [zaɪgomǽtɪk] arch or "cheek bone" to insert into the lateral surface and angle of the mandible; the **internal pterygoid** [tɛ́rəgɔɪd] muscle, which arises from the pterygoid (wing-like) plate at the base of the skull and runs downward and backward to

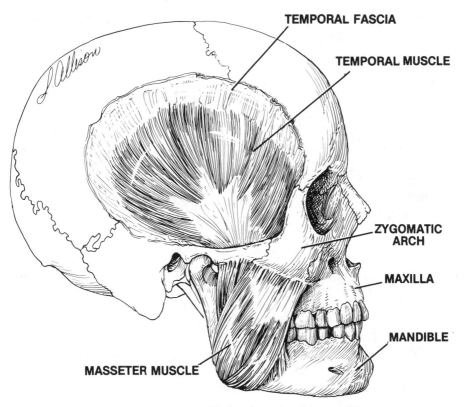

Figure II-5. Diagram of skull and muscles of the mandible.

insert onto the medial surface of the posterior vertical portion and angle of the mandible, assisting in closing the jaw and protruding the mandible; and the **external pterygoid** muscle, which also arises from the base of the skull but runs horizontally to insert into the top of the posterior portion of the mandible, permitting it to assist gravity in depressing the mandible as well as giving it lateral movement needed in chewing.

Oral Cavity (Prefix *oro-*, suffix *-oral*)

This cavity extends from the oral aperture or mouth in front to the posterior wall of the pharynx or throat, from the palate and velum above to the base of the tongue, and laterally between the teeth or the cheeks if the jaws are open. Its primary purpose is to contain food for chewing and swallowing. For speech, it changes size and shape for vowels and resonant consonants through action of the mandible, tongue, velum, and lips. It also channels the breath stream out of the mouth for other than nasal sounds to be articulated by the tongue, lips, and mandible.

For vowel production, one end of the oral resonating cavity is opened at the mouth while the velopharyngeal port is closed for primarily oral resonance. Then the combined action of the tongue and mandible alters the size and shape of the cavity to determine its resonant characteristics, and the lips relax, round, or protrude to influence resonance of the cavity further. For the nasal consonants /m/, /n/, and /ŋ/, the oral cavity is closed off at the lips, alveolar ridge, or velum, respectively, whereas the back of the oral cavity is opened to the nasal cavity through the open velopharyngeal port. In producing /n/ and /ŋ/, the lips are apart to form an open front oral cavity, which contributes to the resonant characteristics of these sounds. If the lips were to be closed, even though the tongue might be in position for /n/ or /ŋ/, the sound would be perceived as sounding closer to /m/.

The oral cavity provides various surfaces between which the breath stream can be constricted and turbulence can be created. The /h/ is the least constricted of the fricative consonants and, accordingly, requires the greatest breath effort to produce turbulence. Positioning for resonation of surrounding vowels forces the breath stream across the velum and palate above and the tongue below to make /h/ a **lingua-palatal** or **lingua-velar** fricative, depending on the adjoining vowels. When the lips are rounded with a small aperture to constrict breath, the /ʍ/ is produced as a **bilabial** fricative. The tongue, lips, teeth, palate, and alveolar ridge participate in constricting breath for other fricative consonants.

Nasal Cavity (Prefix naso-, suffix -nasal)

The nasal cavity extends from the nostrils or **nares** [nɛ́riz] in the front to the posterior wall of the pharynx, and from the base of the skull above to the palate and velum below. It is primarily designed to receive inhaled air and to filter it, warm it, and direct it toward the **trachea** [treɪkɪə] or "windpipe." An ample blood supply in the mucous membrane lining of the nasal cavity warms the inhaled air before it travels into the lungs. This soft moist lining contributes to the distinctive resonance characteristics of the cavity.

The nasal cavity participates in speech resonance with either closure or opening of the velopharyngeal port. It is always open at the nostrils unless blocked by mucous or infection. With the velopharyngeal port closed, the nasal cavity resonates voice vibration in conjunction with the oral cavity for the overall quality of voice that is distinctive for a particular speaker. While vocalizing /ɑ/, the speaker can noticeably influence vocal resonance characteristics by pinching the nostrils closed, making the nasal cavity closed at both ends. With the velopharyngeal port open, the nasal cavity has open resonance characteristic of /m/, /n/, and /ŋ/.

Pharynx (Prefix *pharyngo-*, suffix *-pharyngeal*)

The **pharynx** [férɪŋks], throat, or pharyngeal cavity extends from the posterior portion of the nasal cavity downward through the back of the oral cavity to the larynx [lérɪŋks]* (see Figure II–3). The anatomic functions of the pharynx are (1) to receive food from swallowing and move it toward the esophagus and stomach and (2) to channel air from respiration between the nose and the mouth and the trachea and lungs. The pharynx is a vertical tube with three parts: the **nasopharynx** [neízoférɪŋks], a continuation of the nasal cavity; the **oropharynx** [óroférɪŋks], a continuation of the oral cavity, and the **laryngopharynx** [lɛríŋgoférɪŋks], the area just above the larynx. The tube is lined with mucous membrane over a number of muscles. The nasopharynx houses the funnel-shaped orifice of the **Eustachian** tube, which permits ventilation of the middle ear.

The nasopharynx can be closed off from the oropharynx where they join at the **velopharyngeal port.** Closure is achieved by a complex muscular action involving the levator muscle of the velum (described earlier) that raises the velum and uvula toward the posterior pharyngeal wall. The **velopharyngeal sphincter** [sfɪŋktɚ], which runs from the midline of the velum around the sides of the pharynx to insert into the midline of the back of the pharynx, protrudes and elevates the pharyngeal wall and also aids in pulling the velum posteriorly. The **superior constrictor** muscle contracts the pharynx in the nasopharyngeal region, aiding further with a raising and circular closing action of the velopharyngeal port.

For speech production, the pharynx acts as a resonating chamber for voice. Its primary alteration is the velopharyngeal closure that not only directs voice into the oral cavity but reduces the length of the pharyngeal tube. The pharynx can also be altered in its circumference throughout its length, first by the action of three pharyngeal constrictor muscles that can contract the pharynx—primarily as an aid to moving food toward the esophagus—and then by two pharyngeal levator muscles that elevate and widen the pharynx. The changes can alter the resonating characteristics of the pharynx and thus the sound of the voice.

Larynx (Prefix *laryngo-*, suffix *-laryngeal*)

The **larynx** [lérɪŋks] is a structure of cartilage and muscles situated atop the trachea. Its primary bodily purpose is to protect the lungs by preventing food particles and fluids from entering the trachea through the **glottis** [glɑtəs], its port or opening to the pharynx (see Figure II–3). Directly above the glottis and posterior to the root of the tongue is the leaf-shaped and

---

*The pronunciation [fǽrɪŋks] and [lǽrɪŋks] is also common.

flexible **epiglottis** [ɛ́pɪglɑ́təs], a cartilaginous structure that is moved downward and backward with the tongue during swallowing to cover the glottis, thus channeling food and fluids to the esophagus [isɑ́fəgəs] and stomach (see Figure II-7). Food materials that accidently enter the larynx are expelled by coughing. A secondary bodily purpose of the larynx is to close the trachea at the glottis so that air in the lungs keeps the **thoracic** [θorǽsɪk] or chest cavity rigid as a help in such action as elimination, childbirth, and heavy lifting.

The larynx may be viewed as an extension and specialized adaptation of the cartilaginous rings that form most of the circumference of the trachea (Figures II-6 and II-7). The bottom ring of the larynx is the **cricoid** [kraɪkɔɪd] cartilage, which completely encircles the trachea as a foundation for the larynx. Its name, cricoid, comes from its resemblance to a signet ring. From its narrowest part in the front, the cricoid widens upward as it extends

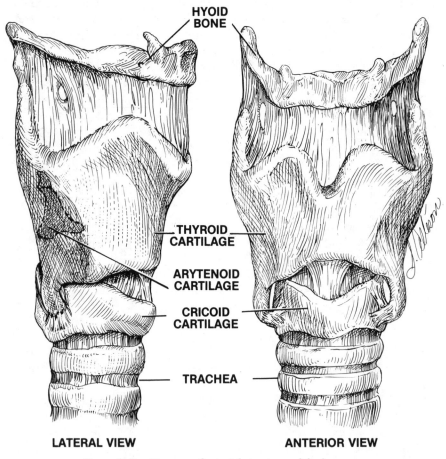

HYOID
BONE

THYROID
CARTILAGE

ARYTENOID
CARTILAGE

CRICOID
CARTILAGE

TRACHEA

LATERAL VIEW   ANTERIOR VIEW

Figure II-6.   Diagrams of external structures of the larynx.

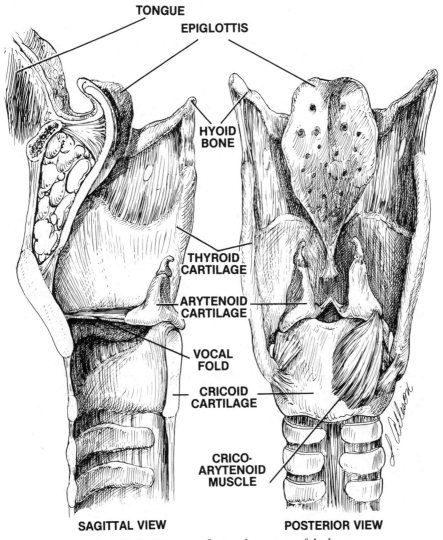

Figure II-7. Diagrams of internal structures of the larynx.

backward into its tall, broad signet portion. Upon this posterior shelf of the cricoid rests the paired **arytenoid** [ɛrətínɔɪd] cartilages. The forward angle of these highly mobile, pyramidal-shaped cartilages aids in attachment of the **vocal folds,** commonly but inaccurately called the "vocal cords." The vocal folds attach anteriorly inside the angle of the largest structure of the larynx, the **thyroid** [θaɪrɔɪd] cartilage, named for its shape resembling a shield. The thyroid cartilage is prominent in the neck, especially in post-adolescent males, as the "Adam's apple." It overlaps the sides of the cricoid cartilage but does not complete the circumference of the larynx in the back (see Figure II–7). The two sides of the thyroid meet in a sharp angle in the front with a V-shaped notch at the top and extend backward on both sides, widening both downward and upward at its posterior borders into inferior and superior **cornua [kornúə]** or horns (see Figure II–6). The inferior horns of the thyroid cartilage form joints in contact with the lateral surfaces of the cricoid cartilage, which lies below and inside the thyroid. The superior horns are connected by ligaments to the posterior extensions of the horseshoe-shaped **hyoid [haíɔɪd]** bone, which lies horizontally just above them. The front of the hyoid's "U" may be felt in the neck, just above the notch at the frontal angle of the thyroid cartilage.

The **hyoid** bone plays a prominent role as attachment and foundation for muscles and ligaments involved in swallowing and phonation. Uniquely, it is not articulated with other bones of the body but gets its support from ligaments and muscles coming from the mandible and skull. It sits in an intermediate position at the back of the base of the tongue and directly at the top of the larynx. Their common attachment to this bone brings about a muscular interaction between the tongue and larynx. For example, when raising the tongue high, as in producing a tense /i/, one may feel the thyroid cartilage rise simultaneously.

The **vocal folds** are like horizontal curtains protruding from the lateral walls of the larynx, joined at the anterior end of their common attachment to the angle of the thyroid cartilage and open (at rest) at the posterior end, where each fold attaches to one of the arytenoid cartilages (see Figure II–11). Each fold is lined with mucous membrane, which encloses a vocal ligament medially and vocal muscles at the sides. Just above each vocal fold, and lying beneath a pair or protrusions called "ventricular" folds or "false" vocal folds, are mucous glands that lubricate the vocal folds during their rapid action.

The important structures that participate in laryngeal function are summarized as follows:

1. The **cricoid** cartilage at the base of the larynx and atop the trachea
2. The paired **arytenoid** cartilages sitting on the high back of the cricoid cartilage ring
3. The **thyroid** cartilage with its two sides wrapping around the cricoid cartilage and open in the back
4. The **hyoid** bone, which lies horizontally just above the thyroid cartilage and at the back of the base of the tongue
5. The two **vocal folds,** which attach separately to an arytenoid cartilage in the back of the larynx and come together in the front to attach inside the angle of the thyroid cartilage.

These structures interact to produce phonation in a complex relationship under the control of extrinsic muscles, those having attachment to structures outside the larynx, and of intrinsic muscles, with both attachments within the larynx.

The **extrinsic muscles** of the larynx have attachments to the mandible in front and above, to the skull above, and to the thorax below. Together they act as a sling that can move the larynx up, down, forward, or backward, or combinations of these. Most of these extrinsic muscles affect the position of the hyoid bone with its resulting movement directly influencing the movement of the laryngeal structures. The **hyoglossus** muscle, mentioned earlier in relation to the tongue, extends downward from the posterior half of the sides of the tongue, attaching to the rear horns of the hyoid bone. The **geniohyoid** muscle arises from the internal surface of the mandible to attach to the front of the hyoid bone, working with the hyoglossus to draw the hyoid bone forward. The **mylohyoid** [maɪlohaɪɔɪd] muscle, which forms the floor of the mouth, also comes from the mandible to raise the hyoid. The **digastric** [daɪgæstrɪk] muscle, which arises both from the mandible and the temporal bone, and the **stylohyoid** [staɪlohaɪɔɪd] from the temporal bone help elevate and draw the hyoid backward. Three other extrinsic muscles that fill out the neck along side the larynx have origins below the hyoid and act to depress the larynx. These include the **sternohyoid** [stɜˈnohaɪɔɪd], which attaches to the clavicle and the sternum, and the **omohyoid** [oʊmohaɪɔɪd], which is attached to the superior edge of the scapula. The **sternothyroid** muscle arises from the sternum and uppermost ribs, attaching directly to the thyroid cartilage to depress it. A continuation of this muscle, the **thyrohyoid**, travels from the thyroid cartilage upward to the hyoid bone and can depress the hyoid bone or elevate the larynx.

Although the extrinsic muscles influence phonation to some extent, it is a group of intrinsic laryngeal muscles that contributes primarily to producing the sound (see Figures II–8, II–10, and II–11). The **cricothyroid** muscle originates at the narrow front of the cricoid cartilage, with one portion rising vertically to insert into the lower surface of the front of the thyroid and the other portion rising at an angle backward to attach on the outside of the lower portion of the thyroid at its lower horn (see Figure II–8). This muscle pulls the cricoid and thyroid cartilages closer together, resulting in a lengthening and tensing of the vocal folds. The **lateral cricoarytenoid** muscle arises from the narrow anterior area of the cricoid cartilage and is inserted onto the base of each arytenoid cartilage, along with the **posterior cricoarytenoid,** which arises below from the broad posterior surface of the cricoid (see Figure II–10). These muscles act as antagonists in adducting (closing) and abducting (opening) the vocal folds and the glottis (Figure II–9). The lateral cricoarytenoids contract to rock the arytenoid cartilages medially, approximating and slightly tensing the vocal folds. The posterior cricoarytenoids contract to rock the arytenoids laterally, separating and relaxing the folds (Figure II–10). A set of **interarytenoid** muscles, one transverse and one oblique, join the posterior surfaces of the arytenoids to contract and adduct them for approximation of the vocal folds (see Figure II–10). The **thyroarytenoid** muscles form a large part of the vocal folds and the

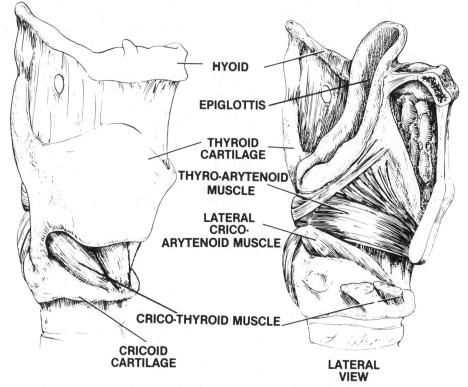

Figure II-8. Lateral view diagrams of structures and intrinsic muscles of the larynx.

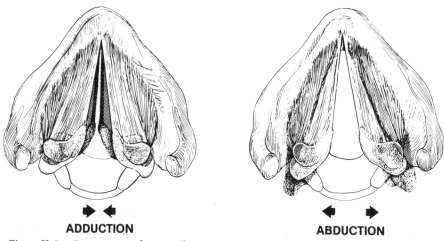

Figure II-9. Superior view diagram of actions involved in abduction (opening) and adduction (closing) of the glottis.

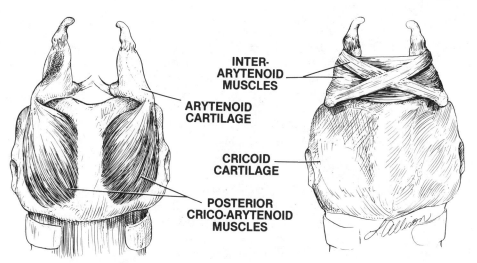

Figure II–10. Posterior view diagrams of cricoid and arytenoid cartilages, and intrinsic muscles of the larynx.

lateral walls bounding them (Figure II–11). They arise from the angle of the thyroid cartilage, inserting into the arytenoid cartilages on either side. When the **thyromuscularis** [θaíromʌ́skjuléɾɪs] portions of these muscles contract, they move the arytenoid cartilages forward, shortening and relaxing the vocal folds. The **vocalis** [vokǽlɪs] portions of the thyroarytenoid muscles are attached similarly but have fibers that also insert along the entire length of the vocal ligament. With contraction of its parts, this muscle can tense portions of the vocal fold differentially, resulting in subtle pitch differences.

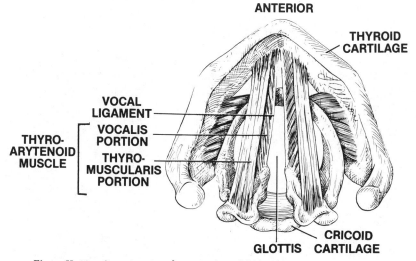

Figure II–11. Superior view diagram of vocal folds and arytenoid cartilages.

Sub-Laryngeal Structures

Beneath the larynx are the organs of respiration that provide breath flow, the basic material of speech. Immediately below the cricoid cartilage of the larynx is the **trachea**, consisting of a tube of 16 to 20 irregular cartilage rings descending downward just in front of the esophagus until the trachea divides into smaller tubes. These paired tubes, the **bronchi** [bráŋkɪ], enter the lungs and further subdivide into small **bronchioles** [bráŋkɪolz], which house numerous air sacs containing the minute **alveoli** [ælvíolɪ]. In the alveoli, oxygen is exchanged for carbon dioxide in the blood of the tiny capillaries of the cell walls. The major muscle influencing the lungs is the large, broad **diaphragm** [daíəfræm]. It arises around the circumference of the lower thoracic cavity to form two semi-circular domes upon which rest the base of the lungs. When they contract, the domes flatten and pull downward, with the soft lung tissue expanding and following. The reduced air pressure inside the expanded lungs forces air from the greater atmospheric pressure outside the body to flow through the respiratory tract and into the lungs. The diaphragm is assisted in this **inhalation** or "inspiration" phase of respiration by expansion and upward movement of the rib cage with contraction of other muscles of the thorax and neck. These include the **external intercostals** [ɪntɚkástəlz] between the ribs, the triangular shaped **scalenes** [skelínz], and the **pectoral** [péktɚəl] muscles, which help elevate the ribs. The **exhalation** or "expiration" of air is achieved by a combination of the (1) effect of gravity, (2) elastic reaction of cartilage and lung tissue, (3) relaxation of the muscles of inhalation, (4) contraction of the **internal intercostal** muscles, and (5) contraction of a group of muscles of the abdominal region that anchor the ribs and compress the abdominal viscera to reduce thoracic volume.

SPEECH PROCESSES

Speech is the end product of four processes or actions occurring simultaneously and cooperatively. These are respiration, phonation, resonation, and articulation, which together are responsible for the variety of sounds we use to transmit spoken language.

Respiration

Respiration is accomplished by a complex interaction of the aforementioned structures and muscles. The exhalation phase provides the flow of breath for speech. Air, which is elastic and occupies space, is forced from the large cavity of the lungs through the bronchi and into the narrow tube of the trachea. Since air pressure increases inversely with tube diameter, the exhaled breath is under considerable pressure as it reaches the trachea below the glottis, and it will expand upward through the vocal tract to equalize pressure on the outside. This positive pressure is essential to produce speech. If allowed to escape through the open glottis during normal respiration, breath may flow into the pharynx and outside through the unobstructed nasal or oral cavity without necessarily being audible to listeners. By taking a "deep breath" and letting it escape rapidly, however, exhalation pressure increases and turbulence with audible friction is created in the open respiratory tract as the breath is forced across surfaces of the tract.

Inhalation while talking occurs at some of the pauses between speech phrases with fairly rapid and brief expansion of the lungs. Outside air usually flows in through the oral cavity during speech, whereas in regular breathing it typically is received by the nasal cavity where it may be filtered, warmed, and moistened. Some speakers habitually, or in excitement, make inhalation audible, resulting from friction in the vocal tract when air pressure is too great. Speakers may practice silent inhalation during speech by balancing the volume and rate of inhaled air with vocal tract openness.

In normal breathing, the relative duration of inhalation and exhalation is about the same. But when speaking, the duration of exhalation in a single respiratory cycle is usually about 10 times as long as that of inhalation and may be as much as 50 times as long for practiced speakers. Since no more breath is used in speaking than in regular breathing exhalation, the extended duration of exhalation during speech reflects a remarkable control and economy in using the breath stream in order to sustain connected speech. This efficiency, realized by the synergistic [sɪnə·dʒístɪk] functioning of the respiratory muscles, larynx, and articulatory mechanism, apparently is learned. Think of the difference in control, for example, between the baby crying violently and always "running out of breath," and the trained singer or speaker who can easily sustain voice for long periods.

The sounds of friction, created when air flow passes against the various surfaces of the vocal tract, can transmit very limited speech information. For example, in whispering, the vocal folds are closed but a chink between the arytenoid cartilages allows the escape of subglottal air under great pressure into the vocal tract. Considerable friction and turbulence is set up at the glottis as the primary sound source to be amplified and shaped by the resonating cavities above, forming the resonant consonants and vowels. The articulators of the oral cavity narrow or stop the breath flow for other consonants such as /f/, /s/, and /t/. Speech can thus be transmitted, but the range of distance is extremely limited, since such friction sounds are of low acoustic intensity, audible only to the listeners close at hand.

Phonation

In order to transmit speech over a distance, **phonation** [foneí ʃən] or voicing is required. Phonation is accomplished by rapid rhythmic closing and opening of the glottis with the vocal folds. The muscles described earlier help close the glottis by adducting the arytenoid cartilages and steadily approximating the vocal folds, but lightly enough so that they can be parted by accumulated subglottal air pressure. Once they are parted, the subglottal pressure is released and the folds again approximate through a combination of muscular tension and aerodynamic effect. For phonation to occur, subglottal pressure must be greater than supraglottal [súprəglátl̩] pressure and greater than glottal resistance. During phonation, the vocal folds follow this rhythmic cycle:

1. Closing of the glottis
2. Increasing of air pressure beneath the glottis
3. Bursting apart of the folds from air pressure with release of a puff of compressed breath
4. Closing of the folds again under constant muscle tension, with temporarily decreased air pressure at the glottis "sucking" the folds back together.

Air pressure beneath the glottis increases as air continues to flow from the lungs and trachea, and the pattern is repeated. Viewed by high-speed motion picture photography, it is apparent that the phonation cycle is not a simple opening and closing, like two sliding doors abutting over their length on a horizontal plane. Rather, there is usually a greater opening centrally, and the adduction and abduction occur with undulating, aerodynamically influenced waves of the vocal folds in both vertical and horizontal dimensions. The subglottal portions of the vocal folds, increasing in thickness as they approach the glottis, also show upward wave-like movements during phonation.

The periodic puffs of breath that occur during phonation form a string of pulses of **compression** and **rarefaction** [rɛrəfækʃən] of air molecules that constitute **sound waves.** When sufficiently amplified by the resonant cavities of the vocal tract above, the sound of phonation is easily audible to listeners. The rate or frequency at which the glottis is forced open so that puffs of compressed breath result determines the **fundamental frequency,** or F_0, of the resulting voice sound. If, for example, the glottis completes 125 of the closing-opening phonation cycles in a second, the fundamental frequency, or F_0, of the resulting sound will be 125 cycles-per-second, written in physical terms as 125 Hertz (Hz). As the rate of opening-closing cycles increases or decreases, the F_0 increases and decreases accordingly, and listeners judge that the pitch of the voice rises or falls.

Changes in fundamental frequency come about through interaction of the lungs and the larynx. The size and mass of the vocal folds determine the range of frequencies possible for a speaker. Adult males with larger, heavier larynges [lɛríndʒiz] typically have a lower average F_0 (about 100 to 125 Hz) than do adult females (about 180 to 220 Hz), and the developing larynx of a pre-adolescent child may have an even higher fundamental. Changes in F_0 of a given speaker occur through a combination of alterations in (1) tension of the vocal folds and (2) subglottal air pressure. The folds are lengthened and thus tensed by the muscles influencing the airflow of exhalation. When F_0 is to rise, as for a question requiring a yes-or-no answer or to give stress to a syllable, the principal mechanism is tensing of the folds with some increase in subglottal pressure. When F_0 drops, as it might at the end of a declarative sentence, a reduction of subglottal pressure appears to be the primary mechanism. In rapid connected speech, changes in vocal fold tension and in subglottal pressure are involved in combination.

An increase in **intensity** of voice, heard by listeners as increased loudness, occurs when the amplitude of horizontal vocal fold movement is increased and muscle tension controlled so that the glottis is opened wider and closed more suddenly, permitting a volume of very compressed breath to be released. This comes about by a complex interaction of (1) increased subglottal pressure, (2) control of the vocal folds for rapid and firm closure and for longer closure periods so that no breath flow is wasted, and (3) expansion of the vocal tract for reduced supraglottal pressure. One or more of these mechanisms is involved when voice intensity is increased during speech. For a decrease in intensity, the opposite of these conditions is applicable. Of course, overall intensity of speech may be increased or decreased by alteration of the resonating cavities of the vocal tract as well. Surprisingly, instrumental studies have shown that loud speech (less than shouting) may require no more breath than quiet speech, and that stressed vowels consume no more air than unstressed vowels. This suggests an efficiency and economy of air flow at the glottis when loud speech is produced. It is apparently possible to reduce the intensity of a sound by only partially closing the glottis in such a manner as to permit some of the non-vibrating air to escape.

In their rhythmic opening and closing of the glottis to produce the fundamental frequency of voice, the vocal folds actually open more slowly than they close and create a complex sound with secondary vibrations of air molecules resulting from wave-like motions. The resulting sound thus includes **overtones** that are higher in frequency than the fundamental. The overtones of voice are whole number multiples of the fundamental frequency called **harmonics** [hɑrmɑnɪks]. Harmonics are numbered so that the fundamental is considered the first harmonic. The second harmonic has twice the frequency of the fundamental, the third three times, the fourth four times, etc. If the fundamental frequency were 125 Hz, for example, the second and successive harmonics would be 250 Hz, 375 Hz, 500 Hz, 625 Hz, and so on. The lower the fundamental frequency, the greater the number of harmonics possible within the range of hearing. Since the harmonics result from vibrations of parts of the vocal folds, each successive harmonic is less intense than the previous one, until the highest ones cannot be heard at all. Considering the combinations of fundamental frequency and harmonics occurring in unison, the sound produced by the larynx is a complex one resulting from a complex sound wave.

Resonation

The complex sound produced by the larynx itself is not loud, but it can be amplified for easy audibility by the cavities above the larynx through the process of **resonation.** A similar kind of amplification occurs when we speak through a megaphone, shout into a cave, sing in a shower enclosure, or pass a vibrating tuning fork over a glass partly filled with water. Many kinds of objects, including a cavity filled with air, will tend to vibrate when struck or when another vibrating body is placed near them. The frequency of their vibration depends upon various factors such as the size of the object or cavity and the shape of the cavity and its openings. As we fill a glass with water while occasionally tapping it with a spoon, the pinging sound will rise in frequency as we pour more water in, reducing the volume of air in the glass. If we sing or play a musical note of the same frequency near the glass, the glass and the air in it will "ring" with sympathetic vibration, resulting in an increased loudness of the sound. The frequency at which an object or cavity of air can be set to ringing loudest is called its **natural frequency.** We say it is "tuned" to that frequency. A resonating cavity will respond not only to a simple sound such as tapping with a spoon or playing a musical note but also to a complex sound like that which results from phonation—the fundamental frequency of voice plus its overtones. The resonator will respond to and amplify the overtones to which it is tuned or "in tune." The closer the cavity's natural frequency is to the original sound, the greater the resonation. But if the original sound and the resonating cavity are greatly out of tune, there can be little resonation and may even be a reduction of the sound. Thus, resonating cavities selectively amplify parts of the complex vocal sound.

The vocal tract above the glottis acts as a resonator for the sound produced by phonation. While the tract was previously described as three cavities (oral cavity, nasal cavity, and pharynx), it may be treated as a single resonating cavity, with coupling of its component cavities, that is capable of a great variety of adjustment to alter the sounds it will resonate. Figure II–12 shows a schematic diagram of the vocal tract viewed as a resonating system with mechanisms for some of these alterations.

The distinctive sound of an individual's voice, referred to as its **quality** or "timbre" [tɪmbɚ], is produced primarily by a combination of the person's habitual range of fundamental frequency blended with the overtones that are amplified or subdued through resonation. The manner in which a person's vocal folds habitually perform may also contribute to quality—for example, a sound of "breathiness" is heard resulting from frequent incomplete closure of the glottis during adduction of the vocal folds. Influences of resonation on voice quality include:

1. The overall size of the vocal tract
2. The relative size of the three major cavities

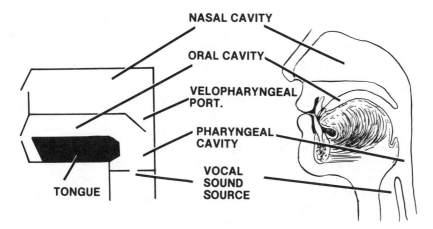

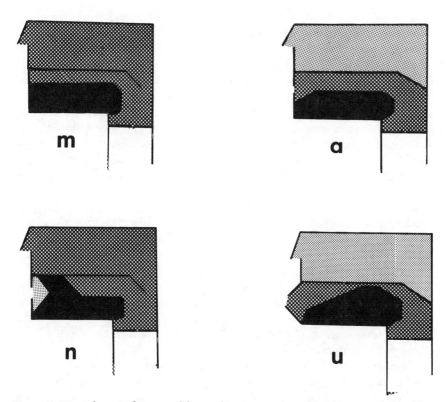

Figure II-12. Schematic diagrams of the vocal tract as a system of variable resonating cavities for speech sounds.

3. Habitual muscle tensing that may raise the larynx and change the size and shape of the pharynx
4. The size of the tongue in relation to the oral cavity
5. The moistness and softness of the cavity walls, which reduce resonation and "damp" some components of voice
6. The relative openness of the jaw and lips during speaking
7. The relative openness of the velopharyngeal port during production of vowels and oral resonant consonants.

Accumulations of mucous during upper respiratory infections or abnormal growth of adenoid tissue influence nasal resonance. General bodily factors such as the weight of bones and other tissue and size of the chest cavity may also contribute to overall voice quality.

Articulation

Resonance not only contributes to speech by amplifying the voice and determining its quality, but it participates importantly in articulation. **Articulation** may be defined as shaping the breath stream that flows from the glottis, voiced or unvoiced, to form the sounds of speech. The vowels and resonant consonants are articulated primarily by adjustments in resonance (see Figure II–12). The nasal resonant consonants /m/, /n/, and /ŋ/ derive their distinctive character from openness of the velopharyngeal port, while the oral cavity is closed off at the lips for /m/, at the alveolar ridge for /n/, and at the velum for /ŋ/. The resonance for /l/ and /r/ is produced by partially blocking the oral cavity and reducing its air volume by intruding the tongue into it. The /w/ and /j/ are produced with resonance similar to /u/ and /i/, respectively, but with shorter duration. Differences among American-English vowels are produced entirely by adjustment in the oral cavity to influence resonance. For vowels and resonant consonants other than /m/, /n/, and /ŋ/, the velopharyngeal port is closed off but air in the nasal cavity is set into resonant vibration by the palate, which vibrates with the oral cavity. Except for the small openings at the nostrils, the nasal cavity operates for vowels as a nearly closed resonating cavity. If one closes off the nostrils during vowel production, though, the change in sound can be noticeable. The primary determiners of oral resonance for producing different vowels are (1) the height of the tongue, (2) the place at which the tongue is elevated, and (3) the shape and openness of the lips (see Figure II–12).

For consonants other than the resonant consonants, the tongue, jaw, and lips act as shapers of the breath stream. They may constrict the flow of the stream, acting like a valve system, to cause audible friction against the velum, palate, alveolar ridge, or teeth, as in /h/, /f/, and /s/, or they may constrict it by themselves as the lips do for /ʍ/. The other primary action of articulation is to stop the flow of breath suddenly, sometimes releasing it with an audible explosion for /p/, /t/, and /k/. A detailed description of articulation is presented in Chapters III, IV, and V.

REVIEW VOCABULARY

Abducting—moving apart as in the vocal folds abducting to open the glottis. (See Figure II-9.)

Adducting—drawing together as in the vocal folds adducting to close the glottis. (See Figure II-9.)

Alveolo-, -alveolar—referring to the prominent alveolar ridge just behind the maxillary incisors and canine teeth. Example: lingua-alveolar, involving the tongue and alveolar ridge.

Approximation—position of closeness of speech organs that permits a constricted flow of air.

Articulation—shaping the breath stream to form the sounds of speech.

Bronchi—cartilaginous ringed tubes leading downward from the trachea to each lobe of the lungs.

Cusps—sharp points of the teeth.

Deciduous—in reference to teeth, the first and temporary set.

Dento-, -dental—referring to the teeth. Example: labio-dental, involving the lips and teeth.

Epiglottis—a cartilaginous structure at the base of the tongue and directly above the glottis.

Eustachian tubes—tubes connecting the nasopharynx with the middle ear cavity, permitting ventilation of the middle ear.

Extrinsic muscles—having an attachment to structures outside of an organ such as the tongue or larynx.

Frenum—a thin, flexible connecting membrane. Examples: labial frenums, lingual frenum.

Fundamental frequency—in reference to voice, rate at which glottis opens and closes during phonation. Written F_0. Heard by listener as pitch of the voice.

Genio-, -genial—referring to the mandible, especially the chin, Example: genioglossus muscle, involving the mandible and tongue.

Glosso-, -glossal—referring to the tongue. Example: the glossopalatine muscle, connecting the tongue and palate.

Glottis—opening that connects the trachea and laryngopharynx. Space between the vocal folds.

Harmonics—overtones that are whole number multiples of the fundamental frequency.

Intensity—in reference to voice, volume of the voice increasing with amplitude of glottal opening. Heard by the listener as loudness of the voice.

Intrinsic muscles—having both attachments within an organ such as the tongue or larynx.

Labio-, -labial—referring to the lips. Example: bilabial, involving both lips.

Laryngo-, -laryngeal—referring to the larynx. Example: laryngopharynx, the portion of the pharynx just above the larynx.

Lingua-, -lingual—referring to the tongue. Example: lingua-alveolar, involving the tongue and alveolar ridge.

Malocclusion—an abnormal or atypical fit of the maxillary and mandibular teeth in relation to each other.

mandible—the lower jaw.

Mandibulo-, -mandibular—referring to the mandible or lower jaw. Example: mandibular incisors, front teeth of the lower jaw.

Maxilla—the upper jaw.

Naso-, -nasal—referring to the nasal cavity. Example: nasopharynx, the portion of the pharynx at the back of the nasal cavity.

Occlusion—intermeshing and overlapping of the maxillary and mandibular teeth.

Oro-, -oral—referring to the oral cavity. Example: oropharynx, the portion of the pharynx at the back of the oral cavity.

Overtones—tones of a complex sound that are of a higher frequency than the fundamental.

Palato-, -palatal, -palatine—referring to the bony or hard palate that separates the oral and nasal cavities. Example: lingua-palatal, involving the tongue and palate.

Pharyngo-, -pharyngeal—referring to the pharynx or throat. Example: pharyngopalatine, involving the pharynx and palate.

Philtrum—indentation in skin between nose and center of upper lip.

Phonation—the process of creating voice at the larynx.

Quality—in reference to voice, the distinctive sound resulting from a combination of habitual range of F_0 blended with overtones amplified or subdued through resonation.

Resonation—the process of modifying a sound by passing it through a cavity of air or by placing a vibrating object against another object capable of vibrating.

Sound waves—a series of pulses of compression and rarefaction of air molecules within the range of hearing.

Sympathetic vibration—the resonant vibration of an object or a cavity of air with its natural frequency the same as that of the sound source.

Trachea—the windpipe or cartilage rings leading downward from the larynx to the bronchi and the lungs.

Velo-, -velar—referring to the velum or soft palate. Example: lingua-velar, involving the tongue and velum.

Velopharyngeal port—the aperture that connects the nasopharynx and oropharynx, sometimes called the nasopharyngeal port.

Vermilion—the reddish skin of the outside surface of the lips.

EXERCISES

Transcribe in Roman alphabet orthography the words that correspond to the following phonetic units:

1. Parts of the speech mechanism

tʌŋ	frinəm	haɪɔɪd
viləm	θaɪrɔɪd	mændɪbəl
fɛrɪŋks	treɪkɪə	keɪnaɪn
pælət	juvjulə	daɪəfræm

2. General phonetic terminology

neɪzəl	dɛntl̩	ædʌkʃən
spitʃ	ɪntrɪnsɪk	kʌɑlətɪ
voukəl	fənɛtɪks	ɛkstrɪnsɪk
okluʒən	ʍɪspɚ	foneɪʃən

3. Parts of the speech mechanism

kraɪkɔɪd	pɛktɚəl	vokælɪs
mæksɪlə	ɛpɪɡlɑtəs	sfɪŋktɚ
ɪnsaɪzɚ	baɪkʌspəd	kɑrtɪlədʒ
kævətɪ	justeɪkɪən	ælviolɚ

4. General phonetic terminology

hɑrmɑnɪks	kəmprɛʃən
tɚbjulənts	fʌndəmɛntl̩
ɪntɛnsətɪ	rɛspɚeɪʃən
vaɪbreɪʃən	frikʍənsɪ

SUGGESTED READING

Zemlin, Willard R.: *Speech & Hearing Science: Anatomy and Physiology.* Englewood Cliffs, N.J., Prentice-Hall, Inc. 1981, second edition

An exceptionally fine text on anatomy and physiology directed to knowledge a serious student of phonetics will need. Includes valuable sections on the ear and the nervous system.

Fink, Raymond B., and Demarest, Robert J.: *Laryngeal Biomechanics.* Cambridge, Mass., Harvard University Press, 1978

This volume includes descriptions and illustrations to help understand the actions of the larynx. It was created by the combined talents of a physician (Fink) and a medical illustrator (Demarest). It uses excellent drawings, X-ray photographs, and schematic diagrams to illustrate the complex relations and actions associated with phonation.

Palmer, John M.: *Anatomy for Speech and Hearing,* 3rd ed. New York, Harper & Row, 1984

This paperback manual features large drawings that simplify anatomic relations. Tables present clear descriptions of structures, muscles, and nerves, and their functions related to respiration, phonation, and articulation.

Chapter III

CONSONANT PRODUCTION

- ANALYSIS OF CONSONANTS
  - STOP CONSONANTS
  - FRICATIVES
  - AFFRICATES
  - ORAL RESONANTS
  - NASAL RESONANTS
- REVIEW VOCABULARY
- EXERCISES
- SUGGESTED READING

Speech sounds have traditionally been divided into **consonants** and **vowels,** with **diphthongs** [dɪfθɔŋz] considered a special kind of vowel. However, the distinction between consonants and vowels is not as sharp as popular usage might suggest. The division is hard to justify on a purely phonetic basis, since many consonants are nearly indistinguishable from vowels, either in the way they are produced or in their resulting acoustic properties. The /w/ and /j/ are very similar to the /u/ and /i/, respectively. There seems little difference between the [r] at the end of *far* [fɑr], which is usually considered a consonant, and the same sound at the end of *fir* [fɝ], where it is treated as part of a vowel sound. However, some differences are apparent. As a group, American-English vowels are all voiced and oral resonant sounds, whereas consonants are more variable. Some consonants, like /p/ and /f/, are voiceless. Some are made with a combination of voicing and friction noise, like /v/ and /ð/. Others, particularly the /m/, /n, and /ŋ/, are voiced with open nasal resonance. Several, like the /r/, /l/, and /w/ are voiced resonants similar to vowels.

One reasonable definition of a vowel is "a speech sound which may constitute a syllable or the nucleus of a syllable," whereas a consonant is considered "a speech sound which is used marginally with a vowel or diphthong to constitute a syllable."* A few consonants can take the place of

*Wise, Claude M. *Applied Phonetics.* Englewood Cliffs, N.J., Prentice Hall, 1957.

vowels, like the [n̩] in the final unaccented syllable of *button* [bʌtn̩]. However, in a single syllable word like *ton* [tʌn] or in a stressed syllable as in *tonnage* [tʌnɪdʒ], the consonant cannot serve the syllable function of a vowel. It is also interesting to observe that some vowels and diphthongs can stand alone as isolated words, although none of the consonants can do so. Note, for example, /aɪ/ as *I* and /eɪ/ or /ə/ as *a*. Even though we cannot formulate a final and entirely consistent distinction with a single dividing characteristic, the dichotomy of consonant and vowel will serve us here to divide the sounds of speech for description in this and the next chapter.

Consonant phonemes have traditionally been described by their place of articulation, their condition of voicing, and by their manner of production. **Place of articulation** refers to those parts of the speech mechanism involved most prominently in production of the sound. Consonants may be classified by their place of articulation using the structures outlined in Chapter II. For example, the /t/ may be described as a "lingua-alveolar" sound (the tongue touches the alveolar ridge), the /f/ as a "labio-dental" sound (the lip approximates the teeth), and the /θ/ as a "lingua-dental" sound (the tongue touches the teeth). Consonants involving phonation, such as /b/, /m/, /v/, and /l/, are called **voiced** sounds. Those without phonation, such as /p/, /t/, /f/, and /h/, are called **voiceless** sounds. Sometimes these are referred to as "unvoiced" or "breath" sounds. **Manner of production** refers to the way the speech mechanism modifies the voiced or voiceless air stream. Although the actual variety of modifications is wide, consonants may be conveniently grouped by five primary classes: **stops, fricatives, affricates, oral resonants**, and **nasal resonants**.

Consonants are conventionally categorized in brief descriptive terms by their distinctive features of place of articulation, voicing, and manner of

MANNER OF PRODUCTION	PLACE OF ARTICULATION					
	Lingua-Dental	Lingua-Alveolar	Lingua-Palatal	Lingua-Velar	**Bilabial**	Labio-Dental
Stops		t d		k g	p b	
Fricatives	θ ð	s z	ʃ ʒ	h ʍ		f v
Affricates		tʃ ⟶ tʃ dʒ ⟶ dʒ				
Oral Resonants		l	r j	w		
Nasal Resonants		n		ŋ	m	

Figure III–1. Consonant sounds of American-English ordered by their place of articulation and manner of production. Voiced sounds are in bold type.

production. For example, the /t/ is called a "lingua-alveolar, voiceless stop" sound; the /v/ a "labio-dental, voiced fricative," and the /l/ a "lingua-alveolar, oral resonant." Figure III-1 orders consonant sounds by these descriptive terms.

ANALYSIS OF CONSONANTS

The consonant phonemes of American-English speech are described individually in this chapter. Their written symbols, as used in the International Phonetic Alphabet (IPA), in dictionaries, and in the General American symbol system are listed, along with key words to assist in pronunciation. A typical place of articulation and manner of production is outlined, using both the conventional descriptive terms and a step-by-step analysis of their production. Then the most common American-English spellings associated with the phoneme are presented, along with some irregular spellings. This is followed by words, sentences, and contrast discrimination exercises for each consonant phoneme. Notes are added about some phonemes.

A word of caution to the reader. These descriptions of the phonemes of our language may suggest there is a single or standard way of producing each sound. This is not the case! The descriptions are generalizations of how most people produce speech sounds. Each of us makes accommodations for our unique anatomy and for our skill in moving the speech mechanism rapidly about. We did not learn speech by carefully watching and copying how someone else moved his tongue and lips, or made closure of the velopharyngeal port. We learned speech by listening, and, by trial-and-error, moving our speech mechanism this way and that until the sound we produced was similar to that which we heard from others. Since there is more than one possible way to produce the same sound, it is to be expected that there will be individual differences in the particular way people habitually produce speech.

Individual analysis begins with the stop consonants, then moves to the fricatives, the affricates, and the resonants. Exercises are included at the end of the chapter.

Stop Consonants

The stop consonant phonemes of General American-English speech are /p/, /t/, /k/, /b/, /d/, and /g/. These consonants are sometimes called "plosives" or "aspirates." The essential action in their production is an interruption of the air stream, whether voiced or voiceless, by a closure within the oral cavity. The interrupting action has two possible phases: first, the necessary **stop** phase with its rapid closure, and second, the more variable **aspira-**

tion or "plosive" phase, when impounded air is released. Some allophones of these stop phonemes are made without aspiration or are made with varying degrees of diminished aspiration. For example, whereas the [p] in *pot* is both stopped and aspirated, the [p] in *spot* is stopped but not aspirated. The differences can be verified by placing the back of the hand just in front of the lips while producing the two words alternately.

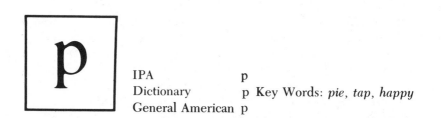

IPA   p
Dictionary   p Key Words: *pie, tap, happy*
General American p

/p/ PRODUCTION—Bilabial Voiceless Stop

The /p/ is made with the velopharyngeal port closed and without voice. There are two phases possible: first, the necessary **stop** phase, with its rapid closure, and second, the **aspiration** or plosive phase, with variable release.

Stop: the lips close and the breath is held and compressed in the oral cavity. Closure is more tense and of greater duration than for /b/.

Aspiration: the breath compressed in the oral cavity is released suddenly as an audible explosion of air between the lips.

In connected speech, the /p/ may or may not be released with aspiration. It is usually released with audible aspiration in these situations:

1. As the initial consonant in a syllable as in *pie, report, bypass.*
2. As the final consonant following /m/, which is **homorganic**, that is, made at the same place of articulation, as in *lamp, blimp, bump.*
3. As the final consonant following /s/ as in *lisp, hasp, cusp.*
4. In the medial position, but somewhat softer, as in *apple, apron, carpet, upon.*

The /p/ is usually released without audible aspiration in these situations:

1. As the final consonant following vowels and most voiced consonants as in *up, harp, hop, stop.*
2. Following /s/ in the same syllable as in *spy, spear, sport, despair* (compare the soft release of the [p] in *spy* with the exploded release in *pie.* The /p/ is released with explosion when it initiates a syllable (compare the soft release in *the sport* with the exploded release in *this port*).

The /p/ is released into the position of the following voiceless consonant in such combinations as *kept, hips, stop sign, sheep shears, hop farm.*

/p/ SPELLING—*p* is Primary Spelling

-*pp*- in medial positions in words such as *apple, happy, pepper, oppose* is given a single [p] sound. When two [p] sounds abut at the end of one word and the beginning of another, as in *stop pushing*, the closure period is held longer for [stɑp:uʃɪŋ].

-*m( )th* results in an intruded [p] sound, not included in spelling, between an [m] and a following breath sound as in *warmth* [wormpθ], *comfort* [kʌmpfɚt], dreamt [drɛmpt], and *something* [sʌmpθɪŋ]. Note that /m/ and /p/ are homorganic.

/p/ WORDS

Initial		Medial		Final		Clusters
pack	pool	upon	paper	up	shop	spy
pie	pun	apple	rapid	cap	cape	spring
peas	peak	approve	repair	chop	deep	split
pill	pot	apply	happy	jump	sharp	carps
pry	place	stopping	keeper	lamp	help	kept
pride	plunge	stupid	oppose	camp	clasp	grasps

/p/ SENTENCES

1. Polly takes pride in preparing apple pie.
2. Please provide a pleasant place to play.
3. The pine wood you chopped is kept upon the pile.
4. The spines on that sponge are spaced apart.
5. Pack the spare parts in the portable package.
6. Purple pleases particular people.

/p/ CONTRASTS

/p/—/b/		/p/—/t/		/p/—/k/	
pack	back	pie	tie	pear	care
pill	bill	pan	tan	pan	can
peas	bees	pin	tin	peep	keep
peak	beak	pop	top	Pope	cope
tap	tab	lip	lit	pain	cane
rope	robe	pop	pot	part	cart
cap	cab	rap	rat	lap	lack
rapid	rabid	sipping	sitting	seeping	seeking

Note: the /p/ is developed early by children and is seldom misarticulated.

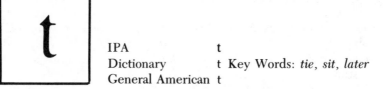

IPA   t
Dictionary   t Key Words: *tie, sit, later*
General American t

/t/ PRODUCTION—Lingua-alveolar Voiceless Stop

The /t/ is made with the velopharyngeal port closed and without voice. There are two phases possible: first, the necessary **stop** phase, with its rapid closure, and second, the **aspiration** or plosive phase, with variable release.

Stop: the tip of the tongue closes against the alveolar ridge with the sides of the tongue against the molars, and the breath is held and compressed in the oral cavity. Closure is more tense and of greater duration than for /d/.

Aspiration: the breath compressed in the oral cavity behind the tongue is released suddenly as an audible explosion between the alveolar ridge and tip of the tongue through slightly open teeth and lips.

In connected speech, the /t/ may or may not be released with aspiration. It is usually released with audible aspiration in these situations:
1. As the initial consonant is a stressed syllable as in *tie, retire, until, attest.*
2. As the final consonant following consonants that are **homorganic**, having the same or nearly the same place of articulation, as in *want, salt, cart.*
3. Following voiceless consonants in the final position as in *kept, act, fished, watched, laughed,* or when a medial consonant as in *after, luster, sitting.*
4. The /t/ is released into the position of the following voiceless consonant in such combinations as *pats, that sign, that part, what for, white car, what thing,* and *that ship.*

The /t/ is usually released without audible aspiration in these situations:
1. As the final consonant following vowels as in *at, but, hot, let, sit.*
2. Following /s/ in the same syllable in *stop, stove, steam, restore* (compare the soft release of the [t] in *stop* with the exploded release in *top*). However, the /t/ is released with aspiration when it initiates a syllable (compare the soft release (in *the store* with the exploded release in *this tore*).

The /t/ between vowels, especially in an unstressed syllable, is sometimes produced as a brief, voiced "flap" of the tongue, rather than a voiceless stop, as in *better, butter, pity, waiting, beautiful.*

/t/ SPELLING—*t* is Primary Spelling

-tt- in medial positions in words such as *lettuce, pretty, better, motto, kitten* is given a single [t] sound. When two [t] sounds abut at the end of one

word and beginning of another, as in *hot time*, the closure period if held longer for [hɑt:aɪm].

-ed following breath consonants as in *fished, watched, laughed, taped, backed, fixed, laced*, except following [t] as in *skated, waited*.

Th- as in *Thomas, Thames, Theresa, Thompson, thyme* may be said as /t/.

-n( )s results in an intruded [t] sound, not included in spelling, between [n] and [s] as in *chance, fence, tense, dance, cancel, stencil*.

Rare Spellings: *yacht, indict, debt, doubt, receipt, eighth, ptomaine, two*. The *t* is silent in *listen, soften, often, castle, thistle, bristle, whistle*.

/t/ WORDS

Initial		Medial		Final		Clusters
too	try	after	potato	at	act	eighth
take	train	into	until	cut	waked	stream
tube	tree	pretty	city	gate	touched	lets
toe	trust	letter	motto	west	dropped	acts
time	twin	sister	shouting	lent	washed	guests
team	twelve	chapter	rotate	salt	next	gifts

/t/ SENTENCES

1. *T*om walk*ed t*wo miles *to* ge*t* tha*t* ha*t*.
2. *T*ed can'*t t*ouch the *t*ip of his *t*ongue.
3. The *t*rain will car*t* the *t*ools *to t*own.
4. *T*win *t*rolleys *t*ravel *t*welve *t*imes.
5. As we watch*ed*, he fish*ed* and caugh*t t*wen*t*y *t*rou*t*.
6. Yes*t*erday *T*heresa bough*t* a beau*t*iful valen*t*ine.

/t/ CONTRASTS

/t/—/d/		/t/—/θ/		/ /—/t/	
tie	die	tin	thin	lass	last
ton	done	tick	thick	necks	next
try	dry	tree	three	pass	past
metal	medal	tinker	thinker	Bess	best
writing	riding	taught	thought	mass	mast
unto	undo	bat	bath	slip	slipped
mat	mad	boat	both	guess	guests
coat	code	fateful	faithful	wash	washed

Note: Europeans may make the /t/ with insufficient aspiration in the initial and the final positions, and they may make closure with the tip of the tongue on the inside surface of the upper front teeth rather than on the alveolar ridge. The /t/ is one of the most frequently occurring consonants in American-English speech.

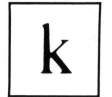

IPA   k
Dictionary   k Key Words: *key, back, become*
General American k (c, ck)

/k/ PRODUCTION—Lingua-velar Voiceless Stop

The /k/ is made with the velopharyngeal port closed and without voice. There are two phases possible: first, the necessary **stop** phase, with its rapid closure, and second, the **aspiration** or plosive phase, with a variable release.

Stop: the back of the tongue closes against the front of the velum or back portion of the palate, and the breath is held and compressed in the back of the oral cavity and in the oropharynx.

Aspiration: the breath compressed in the oral cavity and oropharynx is released suddenly as an audible explosion of air between the tongue and roof of the mouth.

In connected speech, the /k/ may be released with variable aspiration. The /k/ is released with a strong aspiration in these situations:

1. As the initial consonant in a syllable as in *key, come, kite*.
2. As the final consonant following the homorganic sound [ŋ] as in *sink, tank, trunk, drink*.

The /k/ is released with a light aspiration in these situations:

1. As the final sound of most words as in *back, take, thick*, the final /k/ closure producing less acoustic information than either final /p/ or /t/.
2. In the medial position as in *stocking, across, pocket*.

The /k/ is released without audible aspiration in these situations:

1. As the final consonant of a syllable, followed by a voiced consonant that begins the next syllable, as in *backdoor, blackball, like new, bookmark*.
2. Following /s/ in the same syllable in *scold, ski, scare* (compare the soft release of the [k] in *scare* with the strongly aspirated release in *care*). However, the /k/ is released with aspiration when /k/ initiates a syllable (compare the soft release in *the ski* with the aspirated release in *this key*).

The /k/ is released into the position of the following voiceless consonant in such combinations as *backed, black tie, bake pies, backfire, backside, milk shake*.

/k/ SPELLING—*k* is Primary Spelling

-*ck* always has the /k/ sound as in *back, clock, buck, brick, neck.*

c (a, o, u) has the /k/ sound as in *cake, because; core, decorate; cut, biscuit.* The *c* before *l* as in *clerk* and before *r* as in *craft* also has the /k/ sound.

-*c* as in *tic, chic, talc* has the /k/ sound.

-*cc*- as in *occur, accord, staccato* takes the /k/ sound, following the *c* before *a, o,* and *u* pronunciation just described, and is given as a single /k/ sound. When two /k/ sounds abut at the end of one word and beginning of another as in *black cat,* they are given as a single [k] sound but the closure period is held longer for [blæk:æt].

ch in some words has the /k/ sound as in *ache, echo, chorus, chemist, technique, chasm, conch.*

-*que* as in *technique, Basque, pique, baroque* has the /k/ sound.

qu in some words has the /k/ sound as in *liquor, conquer, quay, queue.*

kh- is a rare spelling for /k/ as in *Khan, khaki.*

-*ng( )th* results in an intruded [k] sound, not included in spelling, between [ŋ] and a final [θ] as in *length* [lɛŋkθ] and *strength* [stɹɛŋkθ].

/k/ WORDS

Initial		Medial		Final		Clusters
key	clay	monkey	picture	book	oak	milks
cat	close	basket	stocking	rock	stick	scream
count	cloud	across	jacket	wake	tick	asks
coal	cry	became	pocket	cake	duck	looked
caught	crown	bucket	likeable	park	ink	desks
kite	cream	pumpkin	accident	thank	work	thinks

/k/ SENTENCES

1. Kate could carry the kitten carefully.
2. Carl's book was in his jacket pocket.
3. By accident, the kite caught on the oak.
4. For breakfast at eight o'clock we had cocoa and biscuits.
5. Ask about the desks and the ink on those books.
6. Carol looked like a monkey running across the park.

/k/ CONTRASTS

/k/—/g/		/k/—/t/		/k/—/p/	
cap	gap	kite	tight	care	pear
rack	rag	key	tea	can	pan

tack	tag	back	bat	scare	spare
come	gum	cry	try	lack	lap
could	good	scream	stream	ache	ape
curl	girl	stark	start	cart	part
meeker	meager	scare	stare	cry	pry
bicker	bigger	caught	taught	keep	peek

Note: the /k/ is developed early by children and is seldom misarticulated by those with normal hearing. It is one of the most frequently occurring consonants in American-English speech.

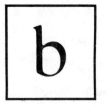

IPA   b
Dictionary   b Key Words: *be, cab, rabbit*
General American b

/b/ PRODUCTION—Bilabial Voiced Stop

The /b/ is made with the velopharyngeal port closed and with voice. There are two phases possible: first, the necessary stop or **closure** phase, and second, the **release** phase, which is variable.

Closure: the lips close as voicing begins or continues, and the air is held briefly in the oral cavity. Closure is usually less tense and of shorter duration than for /p/.

Release: the lips are opened as voicing continues. Voicing begins with the lips closed and the /b/ is released into the following voiced sound when it is the initial sound of an utterance, as in *boy*, or immediately following a breath consonant, as in *this boy*. Between two voiced sounds as in *about*, the /b/ is a brief closure and release with continued voicing. Immediately before a voiceless consonant, as in *lab coat*, the /b/ is closed but not released with voicing. As the final sound of an utterance, as in *lab*, the /b/ is either held without release or is released lightly.

/b/ SPELLING—*b* is Primary Spelling

-*bb*- in medial positions in words such as *rabbit, cabbage, rubber, pebble, ribbon* is given a single /b/ sound. When two /b/ sounds abut at the end of one word and beginning of another as in *tub brush*, the closure period is held longer for [tʌbːrʌʃ].

-*pb*- occurs rarely as [b] in *cupboard, clapboard.*

/b/ WORDS

Initial		Medial		Final		Clusters
be	blue	baby	maybe	tub	orb	absorbed
by	blow	robin	nobody	crab	curb	table
bad	block	number	about	globe	herb	bulbs
bed	bread	rabbit	October	cube	bulb	arbor
boy	brave	pebble	bluebird	sob	cob	number
book	broom	ribbon	remember	bib	crab	tumbler

/b/ SENTENCES

1. The rubber ball absorbed the bounce.
2. Both October and November have bright blue weather.
3. Bring Ben the big brown book by the table.
4. Robins, bluebirds, and blackbirds are above the boat.
5. Maybe somebody will buy Bob's big globe.
6. Rabbits have been breaking into the cabbage.

/b/ CONTRASTS

/b/—/p/		/b/—/v/		/b/—/m/	
back	pack	berry	very	be	me
bill	pill	best	vest	bay	may
bees	peas	boat	vote	by	my
beak	peak	gibbon	given	bear	mare
tab	tap	saber	saver	bath	math
robe	rope	bow	vow	lab	lamb
cab	cap	cabs	calves	Bob	bomb
rabid	rapid	Serb	serve	crab	cram

Note: the /b/ is mastered early by children and is seldom misarticulated. Spanish speakers may not make the sound with firm lip closure, substituting the bilabial fricative /β/, which sounds like /v/, to American-English listeners. Germans and Russians may produce the final /b/ as /p/.

IPA   d
Dictionary   d Key Words: *day, mud, fading*
General American d

/d/ PRODUCTION—Lingua-alveolar Voiced Stop

The /d/ is made with the velopharyngeal port closed and with voice. There are two phases possible: first, the necessary **closure** or stop phase, and second, the **release** phase, which is variable.

Closure: the tip of the tongue closes against the alveolar ridge with the sides of the tongue against the molars, the breath is held briefly in the oral cavity. Closure is usually less tense and of shorter duration than for /t/.

Release: closure of the tip of the tongue on the alveolar ridge is released as voicing continues.

Voicing begins with the closed position, and the /d/ is released into the following voiced sound when it is the initial sound of an utterance as in *day*, or immediately following a breath consonant as in *this day*. Between two voiced sounds as in *eddy*, the /d/ is a brief lingua-alveolar closure and release with continued voicing. Immediately before a voiceless consonant, as in *red car*, the /d/ is closed but not released with voicing. As the final sound of an utterance, as in *bad*, the /d/ is either held without release or is released lightly. As the final consonant following consonants that have the same or nearly the same lingua-alveolar place of articulation (*held, hand, hard*), the /d/ is audibly released.

/d/ SPELLING—*d* is Primary Spelling

-dd- in medial positions in words such as *ladder, ridden, sadder, middle*, and final as in *odd* and *add* is given a single /d/ sound. When two /d/ sounds abut at the end of one word and beginning of another as in *bad day*, the closure period is held longer for [bæd:eɪ].

-ed has the sound of /d/ following vowels, as in *bowed, stayed*, and voiced consonants, as in *saved, bathed, buzzed, judged, opened, steamed, rubbed, begged*, other than after the /d/.

-ld occurs with a silent *l* in *could, should, would*.

-ed has the sound of [əd] following a /d/ as in *waded* [weɪdəd], *molded, deeded*, and after /t/ as in *waited* [weɪtəd], *batted, rated*.

/d/ WORDS

Initial		Medial		Final		Clusters
do	draw	ladder	jaded	did	used	cards
day	dream	lady	handed	dead	loved	bonded

dog	dry	wonder	condition	hand	clothed	molds
dish	drop	somebody	abdicate	bold	stoned	laden
duck	dwarf	children	meadow	bird	changed	hoarding
down	dwell	hardy	nobody	head	dreamed	address

/d/ SENTENCES

1. The la*d*y *d*i*d d*ry the *d*og's *d*ish.
2. The In*d*ian chil*d*ren playe*d* un*d*er cliff *d*wellings.
3. *D*ad*d*y change*d* the *d*amp *d*iaper.
4. Rein*d*eer are her*d*e*d d*own to the san*d*y mea*d*ow.
5. Somebo*d*y han*d*le*d* the cage*d* bir*d*.
6. *D*wight won*d*ere*d* if anybo*d*y coul*d* fin*d* a hun*d*re*d d*ollars.

/d/ CONTRASTS

/d/—/t/		/d/—/ð/		/d/—/n/	
die	tie	den	then	dough	no
done	ton	doze	those	dear	near
dry	try	day	they	done	none
medal	metal	dough	though	down	noun
riding	writing	dare	there	dead	den
undo	unto	fodder	father	bad	ban
mad	mat	ladder	lather	bid	bin
code	coat	reed	wreathe	mad	man

Note: the /d/ is mastered fairly early by children but is often misarticulated. It is one of the most frequently occurring consonants in American-English speech.

IPA	g
Dictionary	g Key Words: *go, log, begged*
General American	g

/g/ PRODUCTION—Lingua-velar Voiced Stop

The /g/ is made with the velopharyngeal port closed and with voice. There are two phases possible: first, the necessary **closure** or stop phase, and second, the **release** phase, which is variable.

Closure: the back of the tongue closes against the front of the velum or back portion of the palate as voicing begins or continues, and air is held briefly in the back of the oral cavity and in the oropharynx. Closure is less tense and of shorter duration than for /k/.

Release: closure of the back of the tongue and the velum—palate is released as voicing continues.

As the initial sound of an utterance (*girl*) or immediately following a breath consonant (*this girl*), voicing begins with the lingua-velar closure, and the /g/ is released into the following voiced sound. Between two voiced sounds (*again*), /g/ is a brief closure and release with continued voicing. Immediately before a voiceless consonant (*big coat*), the /g/ is closed but not released with voicing. As the final sound of an utterance (*big*), the /g/ is closed and released lightly.

/g/ SPELLING—*g* is Primary Spelling

-gg- in medial positions in words such as *buggy, stagger, trigger, wriggle*, and in the final position as in *egg* is given a single /g/ sound. An exception is the word *suggest* [sʌgdʒɛst]. When two /g/ sounds abut at the end of one word and beginning of another as in *big girl*, the closure period is held longer for [bɪg:ɝl].

g(*a, o, u*) has the /g/ sound as in *game, began; gone, forgot; gun, begun.* The *g* before *l* as in *glass* and before *r* as in *grow* also has the /g/ sound.

-gue has the /g/ sound as in *vague, rogue, vogue, intrigue, brogue.*

gu- has the /g/ sound as in *guest, guilty, guess, guile, guard, guarantee.*

gh- has the /g/ sound with silent *h* as in *ghost, gherkin, ghoul, ghastly.*

(e)x- in such words as *exam, exact, exist, exhibit, example* has the sound of [gz].

-ng has the [ŋ] sound as in *sing, singer, ring, wrong, lung, ringing, hanger* except for *finger* [fɪŋgɚ], *linger* [lɪŋgɚ], *longer* [lɔŋgɚ] and *hunger* [hʌŋgɚ].

/g/ WORDS

Initial		Medial		Final		Clusters
go	glad	again	buggy	egg	vague	single
gate	glove	begin	bigger	dog	rogue	angled
gun	glow	ago	stagger	tug	intrigue	tangled
good	grow	forgave	trigger	bag	bag	finger
gone	green	angry	wriggle	dig	big	suggest
guess	ghost	hungry	logger	leg	beg	giggle

/g/ SENTENCES

1. The big gray goose is gone.
2. August has begun and the green bugs are bigger.

3. Greg forgot the grapes on the garden gate.
4. The big girls giggled again.
5. He got his gloves together on the log.
6. We guessed that the single flag was gone.

/g/ CONTRASTS

/g/—/k/		/g/—/d/		/g/—/ŋ/	
gap	cap	go	dough	rug	rung
rag	rack	gate	date	sag	sang
tag	tack	lag	lad	log	long
gab	cab	rig	rid	big	bing
gum	come	goes	doze	hug	hung
good	could	got	dot	bag	bang
girl	curl	gun	done	rig	ring
meager	meeker	bigger	bidder	wig	wing

Note: the /g/ is mastered by children at about age four and is seldom misarticulated.

Fricatives

The fricative [frɪkətɪv] consonants of American-English are /h/, /ʍ/, /f/, /θ/, /s/, /ʃ/, /v/, /ð/, /z/, and /ʒ/. These sounds, sometimes called "spirates," require turbulence heard as audible friction. Some turbulence occurs as air flows through the glottis and pharynx. However, the primary sources of audible friction for consonants are the structures of the oral cavity: the lips, teeth, tongue, alveolar ridge, palate, and velum. Audible friction may occur either with the voiceless breath stream as in /h/, /ʍ/, /f/, /θ/, /s/, and /ʃ/, or combined with voicing as in /v/, /ð/, /z/, and /ʒ/. Several other speech sounds include some degree of friction in their production but are not dependent upon audible friction for their perception.

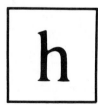

IPA	h
Dictionary	h Key Words: *he, ahead*
General American	h-

/h/ PRODUCTION—Lingua-velar, Lingua-palatal Voiceless Fricative

With the velopharyngeal port closed, breath is directed through the oral cavity, which assumes the configuration of the adjacent vowel, with sufficient force to produce audible friction. The /h/ has no special formation of its own but changes with the vowels that surround it. In the initial position as in *he*, /h/ is produced as a voiceless fricative. In the intervocalic position, as in *ahead*, /h/ is usually produced as a voiced fricative [ɦ]. The /h/ is always followed by a vowel in English and is sometimes considered a glide because of its short duration. The relative lack of constriction in most vowel positions requires that breath be emitted with greater force than for other fricatives in order to make /h/ audible.

/h/ SPELLING—*h* is Primary Spelling

wh- in words *who, whose, whom, whole, whoop* has the [h] sound.

-gh- has the sound of /h/ in Celtic names such as *Callaghan, Caragher, Monoghan*, and is silent in the final position as in *Hugh*.

-h is not pronounced as a final consonant in exclamations *oh* and *ah*.

h- is silent in the words *honor, honest, honesty, honorary, hour, herb, heir*.

/h/ WORDS (The /h/ does not occur in the final position)

Initial		*Medial*	
he	high	ahead	unhook
his	how	behind	mahogany
hat	her	perhaps	anyhow
hoe	hen	rehearse	behold
hail	home	mohair	lighthouse
who	hook	behave	inhuman

/h/ SENTENCES

1. Per*h*aps *h*e *h*as a *h*ome a*h*ead.
2. Un*h*itch *H*arold's *h*eavy *h*orse.
3. *Wh*o *h*as a *h*ouse on the *h*ighway?
4. *H*elen *h*oes *h*er *h*olly*h*ocks.
5. *H*e *h*ides be*h*ind the light*h*ouse.
6. *H*ow can *h*e *h*elp the *wh*ole of *h*umanity?

/h/ CONTRASTS

/∅/—/h/		/h/—/ʍ/		/h/—/θ/	
eat	heat	hen	when	hatch	thatch
it	hit	high	why	high	thigh
ate	hate	heat	wheat	hum	thumb

air	hair	hay	whey	heard	third
you	hew	height	white	hick	thick
Ed	head	hitch	which	hump	thump
add	had	heather	whether	Hank	thank
ooze	whose	heel	wheel	heft	theft

Note: /h/ never occurs as a final sound in English. The cockney dialect pattern of intrusion and omission of /h/, associated with the East End of London, is not apparent in American-English. However, the omission of /h/ before [ju] is found among some speakers in such words as *humid, huge, human,* and *humor.* /h/ is mastered early by children and is seldom misarticulated.

In some phonetic literature, the /h/ is described as a "glottal" fricative, assuming that the source of audible friction is at the glottis. In other than whispered speech, the site of friction is primarily the velum and palate above and the tongue surface below. One can observe the difference between glottal friction and oral friction by alternately whispering [hi̥] and then producing [h] as it would be before a regular oral production of [hi]. In some speakers, part of the turbulence contributing to audible friction for /h/ may be produced at the glottis.

IPA   ʍ
Dictionary   hw, wh   Key Words: *when, everywhere*
General American   wh

/ʍ/ PRODUCTION—Lingua-velar, Bilabial Voiceless Fricative

With the velopharyngeal post closed, the lips are rounded with a small aperture as for the vowel /u/ and may be slightly protruded, and the back of the tongue is raised toward the velum. Breath is directed through the oral cavity and through the constricted opening of the lips with sufficient force to produce audible friction. The /ʍ/ is sometimes considered a glide because of its brief duration. In the intervocalic position, as in *nowhere,* the /ʍ/ usually becomes a voiced fricative [ʍ̬].

/ʍ/ SPELLING—*wh-* is Primary Spelling

-*w*- following *s* as in *swim, swat, sway;* following *t* as in *twin, twirl, twenty,* and following *th* as in *thwart* has the /ʍ/ sound.

(s)u- produces a [ʍ] glide for *u* between [s] and another vowel as in *suede* [sʍeɪd], *persuade* [pɚsʍeɪd], *assuage* [əsʍeɪ3].

/ʍ/ WORDS (The /ʍ/ does not occur in the final position)

Initial		Medial		Clusters	
where	while	anywhere	meanwhile	twelve	sweet
what	which	somewhere	erstwhile	twenty	swing
why	wheat	everywhere	afterwhile	twin	swag
when	wheel	elsewhere	worthwhile	twig	sway
whisper	whine	nowhere	somewhat	twinkle	sweat
whip	whale	overwhelm	horsewhip	thwart	schwa

/ʍ/ SENTENCES

1. Somewhere the white whale swims.
2. Why do the twenty twin wheels whine?
3. What does wheat sell for, meanwhile?
4. The bobwhite's whistle continued awhile.
5. Where is the whip when we need it?
6. Wheeler goes nowhere while White goes everywhere.

/ʍ/ CONTRASTS

/ʍ/—/w/		/ʍ/—/v/		/ʍ/—/h/	
where	wear	whine	vine	where	hair
whet	wet	why	vie	when	hen
what	watt	while	vile	what	hot
whine	wine	whale	veil	white	height
which	witch	wheel	veal	whale	hail
whey	way	whet	vet	wheat	heat
while	wile	where	very	wheel	heel
whether	weather	whence	vents	whim	him

Note: some American-English speakers habitually omit or reduce the friction and add voicing to the /ʍ/ so that it is closer to /w̥/ or /w/, as in [wɛn] for [ʍɛn], or [waɪt] for [ʍaɪt]. In combinations such as *swim* and *twin*, some speakers may make the sound closer to [w̥] for [sw̥ɪm] and [tw̥ɪn]. Continental Europeans frequently have difficulty learning this sound, often substituting the /v/ as in [vɛn] for [ʍɛn], or [vaɪt] for [ʍaɪt]. The /ʍ/ is one of the last sounds mastered by children and is among the most frequently misarticulated consonants.

$$\boxed{\text{f}}$$

IPA	f
Dictionary	f Key Words: *fan, leaf, coffee*
General American	f (ph)

/f/ PRODUCTION—Labio-dental Voiceless Fricative

With the velopharyngeal port closed, the lower lip approximates the upper front teeth, and breath is continuously emitted between the teeth and lower lip as audible friction. The /f/ is usually of greater duration and produced with more force than /v/.

/f/ SPELLING—*f* is Primary Spelling

-*ff*- as in *off, coffee, waffle, office, staff, cuff* is given as a single [f]. When two /f/ sounds combine at the end of one word and beginning of another as in *half free*, the duration of the resulting single fricative is extended for [hæf:ri].

-*gh* as in *rough, laugh, enough, cough, trough* has the /f/ sound.

ph- as in *phone, philosophy, phonetics, aphasia, diphthong* has the /f/ sound.

-*lf* occurs rarely as /f/ with silent *l* as in *calf* and *half*.

/f/ WORDS

Initial		Medial		Final		Clusters
fun	fly	after	refer	if	beef	soft
feet	float	before	effort	off	cough	sifts
fast	flower	elephant	fifteen	wife	tough	reflect
field	free	coffee	office	puff	staff	laughs
four	frost	softly	different	laugh	loaf	surfed
five	friend	coughing	prophet	calf	safe	turfs

/f/ SENTENCES

1. Frank found a knife in the field.
2. The staff had coffee and waffles before flying to the office.
3. Francis studies phonetics and philosophy on Friday.
4. The flowers from the field float on the surf.
5. Four or five flags flew freely.
6. Fifteen different elephants followed his friend.

/f/ CONTRASTS

/f/—/v/		/f/—/θ/		/f/—/p/	
fine	vine	fought	thought	fast	past
safe	save	Fred	thread	fool	pool
belief	believe	fin	thin	fry	pry
surface	service	fret	threat	flee	plea
fat	vat	free	three	pheasant	peasant
file	vile	laugh	lath	laughed	lapped
feel	veal	first	thirst	leaf	leap
proof	prove	reef	wreath	from	prom

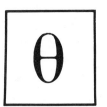

IPA   θ
Dictionary   th, th Key Words: *thin, tooth, nothing*
General American th

/θ/ PRODUCTION—Lingua-dental Voiceless Fricative

With the velopharyngeal port closed and the sides of the tongue against the molars, the tip of the tongue, spread wide and thin, approximates the edge or inner surface of the upper front teeth, and breath is continuously emitted between the front teeth and tongue to create audible friction. The /θ/ is of greater duration and produced with more force than /ð/.

/θ/ SPELLING—*th* is Only Spelling

-*th* as in *bath, teeth, birth, health, width, month,* and in compound words as in *bathtub, birthday, earthquake, faithful, healthy.*

th(r) as in *three, through, throw, thread, threat.*

th- as in *thin, think, thumb, thought,* and in compound words as in *something, anything, nothing.*

-*th-* as in *author, arithmetic, athlete, ether.*

/θ/ WORDS

Initial		*Medial*		*Final*	
thin	three	arithmetic	anything	teeth	north
thaw	through	pathetic	birthday	oath	fourth
thank	threat	cathedral	faithful	growth	month

theater	theme	ether	earthquake	cloth	length
theft	third	ethics	something	booth	width
thud	thief	pathos	nothing	path	wealth

/θ/ SENTENCES

1. *Th*ree *th*in men came *th*rough our *th*eater.
2. Every*th*ing nor*th* or sou*th* will *th*aw *Th*ursday.
3. We *th*ink some *th*ief stole a *th*ousand *th*ings.
4. A fai*th*ful au*th*or *th*inks *th*rough his *th*eme.
5. Great mon*th*ly grow*th* of his mou*th* is a *th*reat to heal*th*y tee*th*.
6. No*th*ing is so pa*th*etic as a *th*irsty a*th*letic you*th*.

/θ/ CONTRASTS

/θ/—/ð/		/θ/—/t/		/θ/—/s/	
thin	this	thin	tin	thin	sin
theme	these	thick	tick	thank	sank
throw	though	three	tree	thaw	saw
ether	either	thinker	tinker	theme	seem
booth	booths	thought	taught	path	pass
teeth	teethe	bath	bat	growth	gross
wreath	wreathe	both	boat	lath	lass
thigh	thy	faithful	fateful	faith	face

Note: the /θ/ is acoustically one of the weakest speech sounds. It is one of the last sounds mastered by children and is among the most frequently misarticulated consonants. The /θ/ is very difficult for most foreign born speakers to learn, present only in English, Gaelic, Greek, and Spanish among European languages. The /t/ or /s/ are frequent substitutions by foreign speakers.

S

IPA   s
Dictionary   ﹅s Key Words: *see, makes, upset*
General American s (c before i, e, y)

/s/ PRODUCTION

There are two prevalent formations for American-English /s/. The lingua-alveolar position is more common than is the lingua-dental formation.

Alveolar /s/—Lingua-alveolar Voiceless Fricative (tongue tip up position)

With the velopharyngeal port closed and the sides of the tongue against the upper molars, the tip of the tongue, narrowly grooved, approximates the alveolar ridge just behind the upper incisors, and breath is continuously directed through the narrow aperture between the alveolar ridge and the grooved tip of the tongue against the closely approximated front teeth with audible friction.

Dental /s/—Lingua-dental Voiceless Fricative (tongue tip down position)

With the velopharyngeal port closed and the sides of the tongue against the upper molars, the tip of the tongue approximates the lower incisors near the gum ridge, and the front of the tongue, slightly grooved, is raised toward the alveolar ridge and forms a narrow aperture through which breath is continuously directed against the closely approximated front teeth with audible friction.

/s/ SPELLING—*s* is Primary Spelling (Extremely variable, sometimes pronounced /z/ as in *business*, /ʒ/ as in *leisure*, and /ʃ/ as in *sugar*)

-*ss* as in *assess, kiss, lass, message, cross, assume* has a single /s/ sound.

-*s* as a plural form, past tense or possessive is /s/ after voiceless consonants (other than *s*) as in *apes, cats, lasts, laughs, cat's, Jack's*.

c-(*i, e, y*) has the /s/ sound as in *city, excite, pencil; fence, cent, accent; cycle, cytology, mercy*.

ps- with a silent *p* is /s/ in *psychology, pseudo-,* and *psalm*.

sc-(*i, e, y*) has the /s/ sound as in *science, scissors; scent, scene, scythe*.

-*st*- with a silent *t* is /s/ in *hasten, listen, fasten, Christmas*.

Less frequently, the /s/ occurs for -*z* as in *waltz* and *quartz*, and as *sch*- in *schism*.

-*x*- forms a derived affricate [ks] in such words as *tax, six, box, taxi, hexagon,* and *rex*.

/s/ WORDS

Initial		Medial		Final		Clusters
see	skin	basket	lesson	us	bats	wasps
swim	spring	Christmas	missile	boss	tops	gasps
slow	splash	fasten	possible	miss	beaks	mists
small	straw	history	basin	this	laughs	beasts
speak	scream	recent	gasoline	horse	else	asks
stay	square	license	asleep	peace	once	risks

/s/ SENTENCES

1. Six boats sped outside the limits.
2. Some nests would soon be destroyed.
3. The message crossed the sea swiftly.
4. Sarah signed for a gasoline license.
5. Psychology may be a science associated with excitement.
6. Jack's cats scooted against the fence.

/s/ CONTRASTS

/s/—/z/		/s/—/θ/		/s/—/ʃ/	
sue	zoo	sin	thin	seat	sheet
seal	zeal	sank	thank	sock	shock
racer	razor	saw	thaw	seep	sheep
lacer	laser	seem	theme	cast	cashed
fleece	flees	pass	path	fasten	fashion
price	prize	gross	growth	gas	gash
bus	buzz	lass	lath	mass	mash
loose	lose	face	faith	Swiss	swish

Note: the /s/ is among the most frequently misarticulated consonants, produced variously toward /θ/ (lisping) or toward /ʃ/. It is degraded by abnormal dentition and often with dentures, and is one of the first sounds affected by hearing loss. The /s/ is one of the most frequently occurring consonants in American-English speech.

IPA	ʃ
Dictionary	sh, sh Key Words: *she, fish, sunshine*
General American	sh

/ʃ/ PRODUCTION—Lingua-palatal Voiceless Fricative

With the velopharyngeal port closed and without voice, the sides of the tongue are against the upper molars, the broad front surface of the tongue is raised toward the palate just back of the alveolar ridge, forming a central aperture slightly broader and farther back than for /s/, to direct the breath stream continuously through and against the slightly open front teeth as audible friction. The lips are usually slightly rounded and protruded, approximating the position for /ʊ/.

/ʃ/ SPELLING—*sh* is Primary Spelling

s as in *sure, sugar, sumac, insurance.*
-c- as in *ocean, specie, facial, special, racial, social.*
-ss- as in *assure, fissure, issue, mission, Russian.*
ch as in *machine, chic, crochet, mustache, creche.*
-t(ion) as in *nation, action, relation, phonation.*

Less frequently as *sch-* in *schist, schwa, schnapps; -sc-* as in *fascist, fascia,* and *conscience; -chs-* as in *fuchsia,* and *-x-* as in *anxious.*

In the following adjectival suffixes: *-c(ious)* as in *precious, delicious; -t(ious)* as in *facetious, fractious; -c(eous)* as in *sebaceous; -s(eous)* as in *nauseous,* and *-sc(ious)* as in *conscious.*

/ʃ/ WORDS

Initial		Medial		Final	
sheep	shop	fashion	wishes	mash	radish
shall	shake	bushel	fished	harsh	English
should	shed	ashamed	rushing	wish	splash
shoe	shower	ocean	pusher	push	foolish
shut	shrink	assure	insure	fresh	establish
ship	shrub	nation	machine	crush	relish

/ʃ/ SENTENCES

1. She washed the shirt in the shower.
2. The nations gave assurance to shed racial persecution.
3. Her facial expressions should show emotion.
4. The English shining brush kept his shoes shipshape.
5. Bashful Shirley shrank from social relations.
6. Washing machines are precious in Russian shops.

/ʃ/ CONTRASTS

/ʃ/—/ʒ/		/ʃ/—/s/		/ʃ/—/tʃ/	
glacier	glazier	sheet	seat	sheep	cheap
Aleutian	allusion	shock	sock	ship	chip
assure	azure	sheep	seep	chic	cheek
pressure	pleasure	cashed	cast	marsh	march
vacation	occasion	fashion	fasten	wash	watch
fuchsia	fusion	gash	gas	wish	witch

vicious	vision	mash	mass	dishes	ditches
dilution	delusion	swish	Swiss	washed	watched

Note: the /ʃ/ is degraded by abnormal dentition and often with dentures. Spanish speakers are likely to substitute /tʃ/. Some Europeans may make the /ʃ/ too far back on the palate, or may round and protrude the lips to a greater degree than for the American-English /ʃ/.

IPA v
Dictionary v Key Words: *vine, have, ever*
General American v

/v/ PRODUCTION—Labio-dental Voiced Fricative

With the velopharyngeal port closed, the lower lip approximates the upper front teeth, and voice is continuously emitted between the teeth and lip with enough force to create audible friction combined with voicing. The /v/ is shorter in duration and usually produced with less force than /f/. In termination of an utterance, the /v/ has a voiceless finish.

/v/ SPELLING—*v* is Only Spelling (With the exception of *-f* in *of* and variable voicing of *-ph* in *Stephen*)

Rare spelling of *-vv-* occurs in the slang words *flivver* and *savvy*. The *-lv* occurs with the *l* silent in *salve, halves, calves*. Intervocalic *-w-* is /v/ for most Hawaiian words (see Chapter VII).

/v/ WORDS

Initial		*Medial*		*Final*	
vine	vowel	ever	servant	have	believe
very	vault	over	fervor	gave	weave
view	vice	river	velvet	live	twelve
vote	vain	divide	envisage	glove	delve
vow	value	heavy	invite	groove	serve
visit	voice	knives	advantage	move	carve

/v/ SENTENCES

1. The river divides the village we visited.
2. Have you voted in the seventy-seventh district?

3. A *variety of* eleven vegetables gives a very heavy flavor.
4. He carved the veal and served the gravy.
5. Divide eleven by five and twelve by seven.
6. The brave servant dove over the waves.

/v/ CONTRASTS

/v/—/f/

		/v/—/ð/	
van	fan	van	than
vine	fine	vat	that
save	safe	veil	they'll
prove	proof	lave	lathe
vile	file	cave	scathe
live	life	ever	weather
veal	feel	glover	brother
service	surface	fever	either

/v/—/b/

		/v/—/w/	
very	berry	vane	wane
vest	best	very	wary
vote	boat	vest	west
given	gibbon	vent	went
saver	saber	vee	we
vow	bow	vail	wail
calves	cabs	vet	wet
serve	Serb	vaults	waltz

Note: the /v/ is mastered late by children, much later than /f/, and is misarticulated with moderate frequency. Spanish speakers may substitute /b/ for initial /v/ and produce the voiced bilabial fricative /β/ in medial positions.

IPA	ð	
Dictionary	t̶h̶, th, t̶h̶	Key Words: *the, bathe, bother*
General American	th²	

/ð/ PRODUCTION—Lingua-dental Voiced Fricative

With the velopharyngeal port closed and the sides of the tongue against the molars, the tip of the tongue approximates the edge or inner surface of the upper front teeth, and voice is continuously emitted between the teeth and tongue with enough force to create audible friction combined with voicing. The /ð/ is usually shorter in duration and produced with less force than /θ/. In termination of an utterance, the /ð/ has a breath finish.

/ð/ SPELLING—*th* is Only Spelling (Frequently has the sound of /θ/)

th- occurs as /ð/ in a few words that are used frequently as in *the, this, that, they, them, then, there, these, those, their.*
-*th* rarely occurs as /ð/ as it does in *smooth* and *with.*
-*th(e)* as in *bathe, teethe, soothe, loathe, scythe, breathe.*
-*th(er)* as in *bother, either, mother, father, feather, another.*
-*th(ing)* as in *breathing, bathing, clothing, mouthing, soothing.*
-*th(s)* has the /ð/ sound when a final /θ/ is pluralized by *s* as in *moth– moths, mouth–mouths, booth–booths.*

/ð/ WORDS

Initial		*Medial*		*Final*	
the	these	bother	other	soothe	smooth
this	though	weather	lather	bathe	with
that	those	rather	feather	tithe	breathe
they	there	either	bathing	clothe	loathe
them	thus	father	soothing	lathe	wreathe
than	then	mother	although	teethe	seethe

/ð/ SENTENCES

1. *Th*ese fea*th*ers bo*th*er *th*em.
2. *Th*ey buy *th*is lea*th*er in *th*ose boo*th*s.
3. Fa*th*er and mo*th*er are *th*ere.
4. *Th*ey ba*th*e wi*th* soo*th*ing la*th*er.
5. O*th*er ba*th*ers swim wi*th* smoo*th* brea*th*ing.
6. *Th*e mo*th*s fly ei*th*er *th*is way or *th*at.

/ð/ CONTRASTS

/ð/—/θ/		/ð/—/d/		/ð/—/v/	
this	thin	then	den	than	van
these	theme	those	doze	that	vat
though	throw	they	day	they'll	veil
either	ether	though	dough	either	fever
booths	booth	wreathe	reed	lathe	lave
teethe	teeth	father	fodder	scathe	cave

wreathe	wreath	lather	ladder	brother	glover
thy	thigh	there	dare	weather	ever

Note: the /ð/ is one of the last sounds mastered by children and is among the most frequently misarticulated consonants. /ð/ occurs very frequently in speech and *the* is among the most common words spoken. The /ð/ is very difficult for most foreign born speakers to learn, present only in English, Spanish, and Danish among European languages.

IPA   z
Dictionary   z Key Words: *zoo, size, lazy*
General American z

/z/ PRODUCTION

There are two prevalent formations for American-English /z/. The lingua-alveolar position is more common than the lingua-dental formation. In termination of an utterance, the /z/ has a breath finish.

Alveolar /z/—Lingua-alveolar Voiced Fricative (tongue tip up position)

With the velopharyngeal port closed and the sides of the tongue against the upper molars, the tip of the tongue, narrowly grooved, approximates the alveolar ridge just behind the upper incisors, and combined voice and breath are continuously directed through the narrow aperture between the alveolar ridge and the grooved tip of the tongue against the closely approximated front teeth with audible friction. Duration and breath pressure is usually less than for /s/.

Dental /z/—Lingua-dental Voiced Fricative (tongue tip down position)

With the velopharyngeal port closed and the sides of the tongue against the upper molars, the tip of the tongue approximates the lower incisors near the gum ridge; the front of the tongue, slightly grooved, is raised toward the alveolar ridge and forms a narrow aperture through which combined voice and breath are continuously directed against the closely approximated front teeth with audible friction. Duration and breath pressure are usually less than for /s/.

/z/ SPELLING—z Is Most Consistent Spelling (s occurs more frequently for /z/)

z as in *zoo, zebra, hazel, lazy, glaze, breeze.*

-zz- as in *dazzle, muzzle, buzz, jazz* has a single /z/ sound.

s as in *close, rise, chasm, is, was, his, bruise*; and in plural forms, past tense, or possessives after voiced consonants, vowels, /s/, /ʃ/, or /tʃ/ as in *dogs, runs, man's, boy's, kisses, washes,* and *matches.*

Less frequently, the /z/ occurs as -ss- in *scissors,* -sth- in *asthma,* and as initial *x* in such words as *xylophone, Xavier,* and *Xanadau.*

-x- forms a secondary affricate [gz] in such words as *exit, exist,* and *examine.*

/z/ WORDS

Initial		Medial		Final		
zoo	zebra	easy	visit	buzz	is	webs
zipper	zinc	dozen	nozzle	jazz	was	adds
zeal	zenith	music	dazzle	breeze	these	eggs
zephyr	zany	hazard	puzzle	use	those	dolls
zone	zen	rosin	dozed	eyes	songs	homes
zero	zodiac	weasel	busy	nose	gives	pans

/z/ SENTENCES

1. These eyes are the eyes of a weasel.
2. Zen and the zodiac are at their zenith these days.
3. A dozen zoo zebras graze lazily.
4. Music dazzled those busy boys.
5. His zipper was used easily.
6. The poison posed a hazard to these trees.

/z/ CONTRASTS

/z/—/s/		/z/—/ð/		/z/—/ʒ/	
zoo	sue	bays	bathe	bays	beige
zeal	seal	breeze	breathe	lows	loge
razor	racer	close	clothe	rues	rouge
laser	lacer	tease	teethe	Caesar	seizure
flees	fleece	lays	lathe	tease	prestige
prize	price	seas	seethe	reason	lesion
buzz	bus	rise	writhe	hazard	azure
lose	loose	ties	tithe	desert	measure

Note: the /z/ is one of the last consonants mastered by children and is among the most frequently misarticulated consonants, produced variously toward /ð/ (lisping) or toward /ʒ/. Some Europeans, particularly Spanish and Swedish speakers, may substitute /s/ regularly. The /z/ is degraded by abnormal dentition and often with dentures.

IPA   ʒ
Dictionary   zh, zh Key Words: *vision, beige*
General American zh

/ʒ/ PRODUCTION—Lingua-palatal Voiced Fricative

With the velopharyngeal port closed and the sides of the tongue against the upper molars, the broad front surface of the tongue is raised toward the palate just back of the alveolar ridge, forming a central aperture slightly broader and farther back than for /z/, to direct voice continuously through and against the slightly open front teeth with enough force to create audible friction combined with voicing.

/ʒ/ SPELLING

There is no alphabet symbol consistently and especially associated with /ʒ/. The most frequent symbol is *s*.

-s- as in *vision, occasion, usual, casual, measure, lesion, usury, aphasia, Asia.*

-g(e) as in *beige, loge, garage, regime, rouge, menage, assuage, prestige.*

-z- as in *azure, brazier, seizure.*

/ʒ/ WORDS—Does not occur initially in English

Medial		Final	
vision	aphasia	beige	corsage
usual	usury	loge	menage
occasion	treasure	garage	prestige
casual	division	rouge	montage
measure	seizure	assuage	persiflage
lesion	regime	camouflage	collage

/ʒ/ SENTENCES

1. His leisure brought unusual pleasure.
2. The envisioned Persian treasure was a delusion.
3. Occasionally decisions lead to confusion.
4. The garage was camouflaged in beige.
5. The collision and explosion caused a lesion affecting his vision.
6. The treasurer measured usury rates.

/ʒ/ CONTRASTS

/ʒ/—/ʃ/		/ʒ/—/dʒ/	
glazier	glacier	pleasure	pledger
allusion	Aleutian	lesion	legion
azure	assure	prestige	vestige
pleasure	pressure	vision	pidgeon
occasion	vacation	Asia	aged
fusion	fuchsia	assuage	cage
vision	vicious	rouge	huge
delusion	dilution	collision	religion

Note: the /ʒ/ is one of the last developed and mastered consonants, and one of the least frequently occurring sounds in English.

Affricates

The affricate [ǽfrɪkət] sounds are sometimes called "stop-fricatives" because they combine a stop immediately followed by a fricative on the same impulse. During the stop phase, the fricative position is anticipated by tongue and lip movement so that the air stream is aspirated directly and immediately into the position of the fricative. The affricate phonemes of American-English are /tʃ/ and /dʒ/. Connecting the stop and the fricative symbols into a single written symbol emphasizes that the affricate is a phoneme and is made on a single impulse. The stop and fricative portions of each of these phonemes are **homorganic**, that is, they are produced at the same place of articulation. These two affricates can also initiate an utterance in American-English as, for example, in *chin* and *just*. An affricate, to be considered a phoneme in our speech, must be homorganic and able to initiate an utterance. A number of other affricates occur in speech, which are derived from **coarticulation**—that is, from producing two sounds in sequence so that they influence how each other is produced. Such derived affricates are considered a cluster of consonants rather than a phoneme. For example, the commonly derived affricate of [ts] as in *bits*, although the stop and fricative portions a.e homorganic, is not a combination that can begin an utterance in American-English (as it does in *tsetse* [tsɛ́tsi] of Bantu origin). Other examples of derived affricates are the [kʍ] as in *queen* and the [ks] in *box*. They are not articulated in a homorganic position, and even though they are associated with alphabet symbols *qu* and *x*, respectively, they are not considered phonemes. The derived affricates are written with separated IPA symbols.

IPA   ʧ
Dictionary   ch, ch̬ Key Words: *chair, such, teacher*
General American ch (tch)

/ʧ/ PRODUCTION—Lingua-alveolar, Lingua-palatal Voiceless Affricate

With the velopharyngeal port closed and the sides of the tongue against the upper molars, the tip of the tongue closes on or just behind the alveolar ridge; air held and compressed in the oral cavity is exploded as audible breath through the broad aperture between the alveolar ridge and front of the tongue, directing the breath stream through and against the slightly open front teeth as audible friction. The position is essentially that for the /ʃ/ except that instead of the steady flow of breath for friction, breath is compressed by the tongue closure slightly farther back on the alveolar ridge than for the /t/, and breath is released more slowly but with greater pressure than for the /t/. This affricate is produced with a single impulse of breath, even though it includes components of both the /t/ and the /ʃ/ sounds.

/ʧ/ SPELLING—*ch* is Primary Spelling

-*tch* as in *watch, match, catch, crutch, kitchen.*
-*t(ure)* as in *fracture, nature, furniture, lecture.*
-*t(ion)* as in *bastion, mention, convention, question.*
-*(n)s(ion)* with an intruded /t/ for [nʧ] as in *mansion, tension, scansion, pension.*
-*t(u)*- as in *virtue, factual, obituary, natural, mortuary.*
Infrequently with *c*- as in *cello*; -*t(eous)* as in *righteous.*

/ʧ/ WORDS

Initial		Medial		Final	
chop	cherry	kitchen	bachelor	watch	each
choose	cheese	nature	fatuous	march	such

change	chase	mention	natural	church	rich
chin	children	mansion	election	branch	latch
chair	check	virtue	capture	lunch	coach
child	chapter	riches	peaches	which	wretch

/tʃ/ SENTENCES

1. The children chose peaches for lunch.
2. Which virtue matches his riches?
3. With a match, he searched for the butcher's chairs.
4. Nature's mansions are thatched by her branches.
5. The bachelor's kitchen was cheerful.
6. The church mouse searched for cheese.

/tʃ/ CONTRASTS

/tʃ/—/dʒ/		/tʃ/—/ʃ/		/tʃ/—/t/	
cheap	jeep	cheap	sheep	chime	time
batches	badges	chip	ship	chin	tin
lunch	lunge	cheek	chic	chew	too
chain	Jane	march	marsh	beach	beat
chin	gin	watch	wash	each	eat
chunk	junk	witch	wish	pitch	pit
choke	joke	ditches	dishes	match	mat
chug	jug	watched	washed	kitchen	kitten

Note: the /tʃ/ is among consonants frequently misarticulated. French speakers are likely to substitute /ʃ/.

IPA   dʒ
Dictionary   j Key Words: *jam, edge, enjoy*
General American   j (-dge)

/dʒ/ PRODUCTION—Lingua-alveolar, Lingua-palatal Voiced Affricate

With the velopharyngeal port closed and the sides of the tongue against the upper molars, the tip of the tongue closes on or just behind the alveolar ridge; with accompanying voice, air held and compressed in the oral cavity is released through the broad aperture between the alveolar ridge and front of the tongue, directing the breath stream through and against the slightly open front teeth as combined voice and audible friction. The position is essentially that for /tʃ/ except that the production is accompanied by voice and given with slightly less force. The affricate is produced with a single impulse of breath, even though it includes components of both the /d/ and the /ʒ/ sounds.

/dʒ/ SPELLING

j is the most common spelling in the initial position with a variety of spellings in the intervocalic and final positions.

j- as in *judge, jail, jealous, jewel, juice.*
-dg(e) as in *edge, lodge, ridge, judge, badger.*
g(i, e, y) as in *tragic, engine; gem, gauge; gypsy, gymnasium.*
-dj- as in *adjust, adjourn, adjoin.*
-d- as in *cordial, gradual, soldier.*
-gg- as in *exaggerate.*

/dʒ/ WORDS

Initial		*Medial*		*Final*	
jam	giant	lodges	adjourn	age	village
jaw	gem	badger	soldier	edge	bridge
joy	gentle	tragic	exaggerate	gauge	cottage
jump	general	agent	gradual	ledge	college
jelly	gene	agitate	enjoy	orange	judge
Jim	gyrate	adjust	angel	urge	strange

/dʒ/ SENTENCES

1. The *judge* and *jury* *gauged* the logic of his ple*dge*.
2. *John* asked *James* for *juice* and *jam* with his oran*ge*.
3. The mana*ger* said the lar*ge* *jet* en*gine* was of avera*ge* a*ge*.
4. Huge pa*ges* of lan*guage* gave an ima*ge* of ma*jestic* le*gends*.
5. *Jack* lo*dged* in the re*gion* of the sol*diers*.
6. *Ginger* and *Jane* just *joked* about the *giant* cabbage.

/dʒ/ CONTRASTS

/dʒ/—/tʃ/		/dʒ/—/j/		/dʒ/—[dz]	
jeep	cheap	juice	use	budge	buds
badges	batches	joke	yoke	rage	raids
lunge	lunch	Jack	yak	siege	seeds
Jane	chain	Jello	yellow	wage	wades

gin	chin	jail	Yale	wedge	weds
junk	chunk	jam	yam	age	aids
joke	choke	jet	yet	hedge	heads
jug	chug	Jew	you	ridge	rids

Oral Resonants

These consonants depend primarily upon alterations of resonating cavities for their production, rather than upon friction or interruption of the air stream. The process of resonation was described in Chapter II. By dropping or raising the mandible, elevating or lowering the tongue, and varying the opening and rounding of the lips while the velopharyngeal port is closed, the sound of phonation produced at the glottis is selectively changed to amplify certain bands of acoustic energy while reducing others. All vowels are resonant sounds, and a number of resonant consonant sounds are sometimes called "semi-vowels," or "vowelized" consonants, because of their similarity. The oral resonant consonant phonemes of American English are /w/, /j/, /l/, and /r/. These consonants are often given a second order designation, based on variations in their manner of production, to distinguish them from vowel sounds. The /w/ and /j/ are referred to as **glides** because of their rapid movement into a following vowel sound. The /l/ is called a **lateral** sound, since its position with the narrowed point of the tongue closed against the alveolar ridge forces emission of the voice laterally around both sides of the tongue. The /r/ may be called a **retroflex** sound when it is produced so that the tongue tip flexes toward the back of the oral cavity.

IPA   w
Dictionary   w Key Words: *we, awake*
General American w-

/w/ PRODUCTION—Lingua-velar Bilabial Oral Resonant Glide

With the velopharyngeal port closed, the lips are rounded for an aperture slightly smaller than for the vowel /u/ and may be slightly protruded. The tongue is elevated in the back of the mouth as for /u/. Voice is directed through the oral cavity and the rounded lips for a brief period, gliding into the position of the vowel that follows. No audible friction is created so that /w/ is not simply the voiced cognate of /ʍ/. Size of the /w/ lip aperture can be sensed in the syllable [wu]. The /w/ is of short duration and is always released into a vowel.

/w/ SPELLING—*w* is Primary Spelling

o- as in *one, once, everyone, anyone,* and *someone.*

-(ng)u- A [w] glide occurs for *u* in *language* [læŋgwɪʤ], *linguist,* [lɪŋgwɪst], *languish* [læŋgwɪʃ]. The [w] intrusion also occurs in *memoirs* [mɛmwɑrz].

-u- A [w] glide may intrude between the rounded high back vowels [u] or [ʊ], and following vowels in connected speech, as in *you all* [juwɔl], *no easy* [nouwizɪ], *now it* [nauwɪt].

w is silent in *who, whole, write, wrinkle, sword, answer.*

/w/ WORDS (The /w/ does not occur in the final position)

Initial		Medial		Clusters
we	wash	away	unwind	dwell
way	weed	always	seaweed	dwarf
were	won	anyone	jewel	dwelling
wet	one	forward	backward	dwindle
wood	would	inkwell	sandwich	Dwight
winter	wise	reward	otherwise	Gwendolyn

/w/ SENTENCES

1. We *w*ent a*w*ay last *w*eek.
2. William a*w*oke *w*et in the *w*indy *w*arm *w*eather.
3. We *w*ent *w*ading in the *w*ater any*w*ay.
4. The *w*est *w*indow *w*as *w*ashed for the *w*inter.
5. Every*o*ne al*w*ays *w*orks *w*ell on the *w*agon.
6. Warren d*w*ells *w*est of the *w*oods.

/w/ CONTRASTS

/w/—/ʍ/		/w/—/r/		/w/—/v/	
wear	where	wed	red	wane	vane
wet	whet	wake	rake	wary	very
watt	what	wade	raid	west	vest
wine	whine	wise	rise	went	vent
witch	which	one	run	we	vee
way	whey	wave	rave	wail	veil
wile	while	witch	rich	wet	vet
weather	whether	wove	rove	waltz	vaults

Note: the /w/ is mastered early by children and is seldom misarticulated.

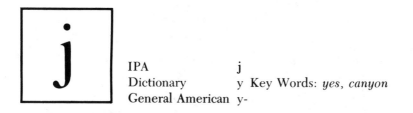

IPA   j
Dictionary   y Key Words: *yes, canyon*
General American y-

/j/ PRODUCTION—Lingua-palatal Oral Resonant Glide

With the velopharyngeal port closed and the tip of the tongue behind the lower front teeth, the front of the tongue is raised high toward the palate and voice is directed through the oral cavity for a brief period as the tongue and lips take the position of the following vowel sound with continued voicing. The lips may be slightly pulled back with the raised tongue. Tongue-palate aperture is slightly smaller and farther back than for the vowel /i/. Note the difference in *ye* [ji]. The /j/ is of short duration and is always released into a vowel.

/j/ SPELLING—*y* is Primary Spelling

-i- as in *onion, pinion, William, union, million, stallion, familiar, view*.
u- blending with [u] for *use* [juz], *union, utilize, cute*.
ew blending with [u] for *few* [fju], *ewe, pew*.
ue blending with [u] for *fuel* [fjul], and *eu* as in *feud*.
Rarely as *-j-* in *hallelujah*, *-g(n)-* as in *poignant*.

The /j/ is often intrusive between words ending in /i/ or /ɪ/ and those beginning with a vowel as in *see it* [sijɪt], *die out* [daɪjaut], and *stay in* [steɪjɪn].

/j/ WORDS (The /j/ does not occur in the final position)

	Initial		*Medial*
yard	young	onion	barnyard
year	yacht	loyal	familiar
yes	yield	minion	canyon
yet	yellow	bullion	few
yolk	use	beyond	cute
yarn	unit	million	William

/j/ SENTENCES

1. The *y*oung *y*eoman from *Y*ork was lo*y*al.
2. The can*y*ons be*y*ond are familiar.

3. Daniel *y*earned to have a *y*ellow *y*acht.
4. *Y*our opin*i*on is pecul*i*ar.
5. *Y*esterday the *y*oungsters were compan*i*ons.
6. Will*i*am's on*i*ons are mixed with *y*east and egg *y*olks.

/j/ CONTRASTS

/j/—/w/		/j/—/ /		/j/—/ʤ/	
yet	wet	yam	am	yam	jam
yoke	woke	year	ear	yell	jell
yield	wield	yearn	earn	yacht	jot
yell	well	Yale	ale	yet	jet
yes	Wes	yoke	oak	yak	jack
yaks	wax	yeast	east	yawn	John
Yale	wail	yawning	awning	yoke	joke
yacht	watt	canyon	cannon	year	jeer

Note: the /j/, when released into /u/, is sometimes considered to form a glide-vowel combination or diphthong [ju], as in *use, cute, you,* and *few.*

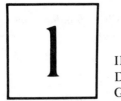

IPA   l
Dictionary   l Key Words: *low, bowl, color*
General American l

/l/ PRODUCTION—Lingua-alveolar Lateral Oral Resonant

With the velopharyngeal port closed, the point of the tongue (see Figure II–4) closes with slight pressure against the alveolar ridge with opening on both sides, as voice escapes around the tongue and out the oral cavity. The mouth opening is that for the preceding or following vowels. The /l/ is voiced when it initiates a syllable and when it is preceded by a voiced consonant ([bl], [gl]) in the same syllable. It is given partially without voice, especially near the point of juncture, when it is preceded by a voiceless consonant in the same syllable ([pl̥], [kl̥], [sl̥], [fl̥]) except in *s-l* clusters (*splash, sclerosis*) where the stop is unreleased.

When /l/ follows homorganic consonants /t/, /d/, or /n/, the tongue tip remains on the alveolar ridge, narrowing to a point as the sides of the tongue pull to center for lateral emission of voice, as in *handle* [hændl̩]. When /l/ is the final consonant following another consonant (*cable* [keɪbl̩], *angle* [æŋgl̩], *bottle* [bɑtḷ], *gavel* [gævḷ]), the /l/ may become a semi-vowel and be produced with the duration of a syllable. As the initial consonant (*lay*) or in a consonant blend (*play*), the /l/ has the very brief duration of a glide.

/l/ SPELLING—*l* is Primary Spelling

ll as in *all, fall, follow, million, llama, Lloyd* has a single /l/ sound.
-le as in *bottle, valuable, little, middle, table, people.*
-el as in *pommel, funnel, gavel, kennel.*
-sl- with silent *s* as in *island, isle, aisle, Carlisle.*
-ln with silent *n* as in *kiln.*
The *l* is silent in *palm, balm, talk, walking, calf, halves.*

/l/ WORDS

Initial		Medial		Final	
lay	loose	tulip	dollar	oil	bell
leaf	lunch	eleven	William	owl	fall
low	lamb	family	yellow	hole	able
like	leg	lily	fellow	school	uncle
lion	lift	always	selling	all	gavel
loud	log	along	teller	mill	motel

/l/ SENTENCES

1. While flying, he will have a cool bottle of milk.
2. Eagles fly aloft easily in glorious splendor.
3. Ronald's dollars were obligated for clothes and blankets.
4. The class wrote well in the middle of the school blackboard.
5. Twelve healthy girls helped build Uncle William's wall.
6. The child sold old pencils as cold bleak snowflakes fell.

/l/ CONTRASTS

/l/—/w/		/l/—/r/		/l/—/n/	
leap	weep	lies	rise	line	nine
leak	week	lair	rare	low	no
led	wed	late	rate	let	net
let	wet	blew	brew	bowl	bone
lake	wake	glow	grow	slow	snow
sleep	sweep	flank	frank	willing	winning
slim	swim	cloud	crowd	towel	town
sleet	sweet	play	pray	tell	ten

Note: the /l/ is mastered late by children, with /w/ substitution common, but it is seldom misarticulated later in life. Europeans may articulate /l/ forward off the upper teeth rather than farther back off the alveolar ridge. Orientals produce a sound [ɭ] with the tongue point touching behind the alveolar ridge giving impression of an /r/ substitution.

IPA   r
Dictionary   r Key Words: *red, bar, oral*
General American r

/r/ PRODUCTION—Lingua-palatal Oral Resonant

The essence of /r/ is intrusion of the tongue high in the oral cavity without contacting the roof of the mouth. There are two prevalent formations for American-English /r/. The tongue tip up position is more common than the tongue tip down position.

Tongue tip up position: with the velopharyngeal port closed and the sides of the tongue against the upper molars, the tongue tip is raised toward the palate just behind the alveolar ridge but without contact; voice escapes between the tongue and palate-alveolar ridge and out the oral cavity. The lips may be slightly protruded similar to /ʊ/ but usually take the position of the surrounding vowels. If the tongue tip is curled back toward the palate, it is referred to as a "retroflex" /r/.

Tongue tip down position: with the velopharyngeal port closed and the sides of the tongue against the upper molars, the front of the tongue is raised toward the palate with the tip neutral or pointing downward; voice escapes between the tongue and palate-alveolar ridge and out the oral cavity. The lips may be slightly protruded similar to /ʊ/ but usually take the position of the surrounding vowels.

The /r/ is voiced when it initiates a syllable and when it is preceded by a voiced consonant ([br], [gr], [dr]) in the same syllable. It is given partially without voice, especially near the point of juncture, when it is preceded by a voiceless consonant in the same syllable ([pr̥], [tr̥], [kr̥], [fr̥], [ʃr̥], [θr̥]) except in *s-r* clusters (*scratch, spring, string*) where the stop is unreleased. Following lingua-alveolar consonants /t/ and /d/ as in *try* and *dry*, the /r/ is produced as a fricative.

/r/ SPELLING—*r* is Primary Spelling

rr as in *barrel, ferry, horrible, burr, whirr, purr* has a single /r/ sound.
wr- as in *write, wrecker, wring, wrought, wren, wrist*.

rh- as in *rhinocerous, rhinology, rhyme, rhythmic, Rhesus.*
Rarely as *-rrh* in *catarrh, -rt-* in *mortgage, -rps* in *corps.*

/r/ WORDS

Initial		Medial		Final *Vowels*	
ran	write	very	marry	car	or
red	wrist	around	terrible	air	dear
rock	wren	orange	berry	four	chair
rub	rhyme	story	arrow	near	are
rake	right	bedroom	carrot	fire	dare
rose	room	already	sorry	hair	bar

/r/ SENTENCES

1. Around the rugged rock the ragged rascal ran.
2. Mary and George are crying.
3. The barbecued ribs brought forth hungry truck drivers.
4. April's strong threatening rains shrank their garments.
5. Three chairs are in the orange room.
6. Sarah wrote for radio about tomorrow's race.

/r/ CONTRASTS

/r/—/w/		/r/—/l/		/r/—/ɝ/ or /ɚ/	
reap	weep	rise	lies	train	terrain
run	won	rare	lair	bray	beret
red	wed	rate	late	dress	duress
rate	wait	brew	blew	crest	caressed
rail	wail	grow	glow	broke	baroque
reek	week	frank	flank	throw	thorough
train	twain	crowd	cloud	creed	curried
trig	twig	pray	play	crowed	corrode

Note: during development of /r/, a /w/ substitution is common among children and may persist as sub-standard speech into adulthood. Some foreign speakers may use a trilled [r̃], or the one-tap trill of British inter-vocalic [ɾ], which may make *very* [vɛrɪ] sound like [vɛdɪ]. Orientals produce a sound /l/ with the tongue point touching behind the alveolar ridge, giving the impression of an /l/ substitution. General American preconsonantal /r/ as in *park* or *first* and final /r/ as in *bar* or *more* are either omitted or replaced by a vowel in New England and Southern speech.

There are two American-English vowels with /r/ quality. They are the accented /ɝ/ as in *fur* and *certain,* and the unaccented /ɚ/ as in *maker* and *caller* (see Chapter IV). These vowels differ from the consonant /r/ (1) by their greater duration, (2) by constituting a syllable, and (3) by tongue movement toward rather than away from the /r/ tongue position.

Nasal Resonants

The nasal resonant consonants of American-English are /m/, /n/, and /ŋ/. Like the oral resonants, they are produced by alteration of the resonating cavities of the vocal tract, but with two important differences. First, the velopharyngeal port is open, permitting open resonation in the nasal cavity. Second, the oral cavity is completely closed off at some point, forcing the flow of breath through the nasal cavity (see Figure II–12). For production of /m/, the resonating tube includes the oral cavity occluded at the lips as well as the open nasal cavity. For /n/, the resonating tube includes the oral cavity behind the lingua-alveolar closure. In addition, there is a resonating cavity in front of the lingua-alveolar closure and between the open lips. Vibration of the hard structures of the oral cavity causes resonation in this supplemental cavity, helping to differentiate /n/ from /m/. Similarly, the oral cavity with open lips in front of the lingua-velar closure for /ŋ/ contributes resonance that helps distinguish it from /m/ or /n/. Figure III–2 shows a schematic diagram of the resonating cavities for the nasal resonant consonants.

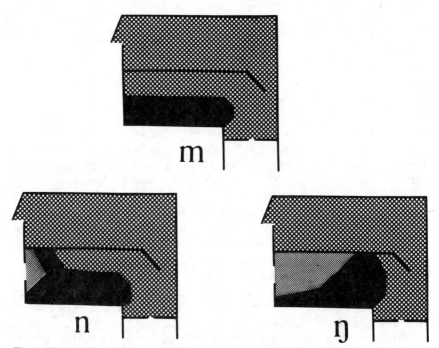

Figure III-2.   Schematic diagram of the resonating cavities for the nasal resonant consonants.

IPA m
Dictionary m Key Words: *my, team, camera*
General American m

/m/ PRODUCTION—Bilabial Nasal Resonant

With the lips closed, voice is directed through the open velopharyngeal port to the nasal cavity and out the nostrils. The tongue lies flat in the mouth or is prepared for the following vowel, providing opening for resonation of the voice in the entire oral cavity closed off by the lips, as well as resonation in the open nasal cavity. The teeth are slightly open. (See Figure III–2.)

/m/ SPELLING—*m* is Primary Spelling

-*mm*- as in *hammer, summer, command, immobile, accommodate* has a single /m/ sound.
-*mb* with silent *b* as in *lamb, comb, dumb, bomb, clamber, climber.*
-*mn* with silent *n* as in *hymn, damned, column.*
-*lm* with silent *l* as in *calm, palm, psalm, balm, salmon.*
-*gm* with silent *g* as in *phlegm, diaphragm.*

/m/ WORDS

Initial		Medial		Final	
me	men	summer	coming	am	storm
may	mount	hammer	camera	whom	realm
meat	might	animal	fireman	time	heroism
miss	mat	among	remember	lamb	diaphragm
more	moon	family	somewhere	hymn	team
must	malt	lamp	smell	palm	roam

/m/ SENTENCES

1. Remember them at Christmas in December.
2. He smiled as his dream of heroism came true.
3. Some animals from the farm may harm him.
4. Mary combed the mother lamb.
5. Firemen have more time at home in summer.
6. My room may not accommodate them.

Note: the /m/ is one of the most frequently occurring consonants in American-English speech.

/m/ CONTRASTS

/m/—/b/		/m/—/n/		/m/—/ŋ/	
mean	bean	mob	knob	sum	sung
make	bake	mow	no	hum	hung
mat	bat	met	net	dumb	dung
match	batch	sum	sun	ram	rang
rum	rub	rum	run	Sam	sang
roam	robe	ram	ran	Kim	king
lambs	labs	coming	cunning	swim	swing
lamer	labor	terms	turns	bomb	bong

Note: the /m/ is one of the first sounds mastered by children and is seldom misarticulated.

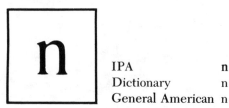

IPA   n
Dictionary   n Key Words: *new, tin, any*
General American n

/n/ PRODUCTION—Lingua-alveolar Nasal Resonant

With the tip of the tongue closed against the alveolar ridge and the sides of the tongue against the upper molars, voice is directed through the open velopharyngeal port to the nasal cavity and out the nostrils. The back of the tongue is down and open to the oropharynx for resonation of voice in the oral cavity behind the lingua-alveolar closure as well as for resonation in the open nasal cavity. In addition, the teeth and lips are open, forming a resonating cavity in front of the lingua-alveolar closure. Tongue pressure at the alveolar ridge is less than for either /t/ or /d/. (See Figure III–2.)

/n/ SPELLING—*n* is Primary Spelling

-nn- as in *inn, cunning, cannot, running, spanned, funny* has a single /n/ sound.
kn- with silent *k* as in *knife, know, knee, knob, knit, knight.*
gn- with silent *g* as in *gnat, gnome, gnu, gnash, gnaw, gnarled.*
-gn with silent *g* as in *align, malign, sign, reign, feign, deign.*
pn- with silent *p* as in *pneumatic, pneumonia.*
mn- with silent *m* in *mnemonic.*

/n/ WORDS

Initial		Medial		Final	
not	nut	banana	snow	can	ripen
knife	north	annotate	snake	align	cotton
gnarled	new	funny	any	sign	kitten
pneumonia	neck	connote	tiny	inn	burn
know	nap	peanut	under	on	learn
name	nice	Indian	only	been	listen

/n/ SENTENCES

1. Nancy knelt with her bananas on the napkin.
2. He knew that nine knives were near the window.
3. The sign next to the barn was gnarled.
4. The knight's knee needed pneumatic panels.
5. Can you run down the green lawn?
6. The queen's reign spanned seven generations.

/n/ CONTRASTS

/n/—/d/		/n/—/m/		/n/—/ŋ/	
no	dough	knob	mob	ban	bang
near	dear	no	mow	fan	fang
none	done	net	met	ran	rang
noun	down	sun	sum	win	wing
den	dead	run	rum	kin	king
ban	bad	ran	ram	pin	ping
bin	bid	cunning	coming	thin	thing
man	mad	turns	terms	sun	sung

Note: the /n/ is one of the first sounds mastered by children and is seldom misarticulated. Foreign speakers may need to learn to make the American-English /n/ off the alveolar ridge rather than off the upper front teeth. The /n/ is one of the most frequently occurring sounds of American-English speech.

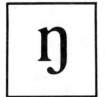

IPA   ŋ
Dictionary   ng, n͡g Key Words: *song, singer*
General American ng

/ŋ/ PRODUCTION—Lingua-velar Nasal Resonant

With the back of the tongue closed against the front portion of the velum or back of the palate, voice is directed through the open velopharyngeal port to the nasal cavity and out the nostrils. The teeth and lips are open and the tip of the tongue rests just behind the lower front teeth, forming a resonating cavity in front of the tongue-palate closure. Tongue pressure at the velum or palate is less than for the /k/ or /g/. (See Figure III–2.)

/ŋ/ SPELLING—*-ng* is Primary Spelling

-n(k) as in *ink, sink, think, bank* in the same syllable; often in adjoining syllables through assimilation as in *income, include, Concord.*
-n(g) as in *single, angry, mingle, bangle, jungle, hunger.*
-n(x) as in *lynx, phalanx, minx, anxious, jinx.*
-ngue as in *tongue, harangue, meringue.*

/ŋ/ WORDS (/ŋ/ does not occur in the initial position)

Medial		*Final*	
singer	finger	sing	along
hanger	longer	long	hang
swinger	younger	sang	singing
donkey	strongest	lung	running
drinks	anger	among	working
thanks	lengthen	bring	thinking

/ŋ/ SENTENCES

1. Among the young donkeys were angry wranglers.
2. Frank thinks playing ping-pong makes him hungry.
3. He sang a song in a lilting language.
4. He sings strongest on spring evenings.
5. I think Hank drank some writing ink.
6. He spent the long evening drinking with swinging singles.

/ŋ/ CONTRASTS

/ŋ/—/g/		/ŋ/—/n/		/ŋ/—/m	
wing	wig	bang	ban	sung	sum
ding	dig	fang	fan	hung	hum
tong	tog	rang	ran	dung	dumb
tongue	tug	wing	win	rang	ram
ringer	rigger	king	kin	sang	Sam
dinger	digger	ping	pin	king	Kim
banging	bagging	thing	thin	swing	swim
longing	logging	sung	sun	bong	bomb

Note: the /ŋ/ is one of the first sounds mastered by children and is seldom misarticulated. In informal speech, the *-ing* ending is frequently pronounced as [ɪn] as in *singing* [sɪŋɪn] and *walking* [wɔkɪn].

REVIEW VOCABULARY

Affricate consonant—a stop released into a fricative position as a single speech sound. Affricate phonemes are /tʃ/ and /dʒ/.

Aspiration—audible release of breath as with the [p] in *pot.*

Closure—oral cavity stop action of voiced consonants /b/, /d/, and /g/.

Coarticulation—influence of one speech sound on the adjacent sound in connected speech.

Consonant—a speech sound used marginally with a vowel to constitute a syllable.

Diphthong—a sequence of two vowel positions taken in a single syllable with one of the vowel positions dominant.

Fricative consonant—a speech sound with audible friction as its primary perceptual feature. Fricatives are /h/, /ʍ/, /f/, /θ/, /s/, /ʃ/, /v/, /ð/, /z/, and /ʒ/.

Glide—referring to a consonant, a very brief sound rapidly blending into the following vowel sound. Glides include /w/, /j/, and, sometimes, /l/ and /r/.

Homorganic—made in the same or very nearly the same place of articulation.

Intruded sound—a sound resulting from coarticulation, as the intruded [t] in *chance* [ʧænts].

Lateral—a sound in which air escapes around the sides of the tongue. The /l/ is the lateral sound of American-English.

Manner of production—the way the speech mechanism modifies the voiced or voiceless air stream in articulation.

Nasal resonant consonant—produced with open velopharyngeal port. The nasal resonant consonants are /m/, /n/, and /ŋ/.

Oral resonant consonant—produced with closed velopharyngeal port. The oral resonant consonants are /w/, /j/, /l/, and /r/.

Place of articulation—those parts of the speech mechanism involved most prominently in production of speech sounds.

Release—opening of voiced stop consonants /b/, /d/, and /g/.

Retroflex—bending backward, as in the tongue position for a retroflex /r/.

Stop consonant—a speech sound with closure or stopping of the air stream as its primary perceptual feature. The /p/, /t/, /k/, /b/, /d/, and /g/ are stop consonants.

Vowel—a speech sound that may constitute a syllable or the nucleus of a syllable.

EXERCISES

1. Write the IPA symbol that matches each of the following brief descriptions.

   (a) Bilabial Nasal Resonant
   (b) Lingua-alveolar Voiceless Stop
   (c) Lingua-palatal Voiceless Fricative
   (d) Lingua-velar Voiced Stop
   (e) Lingua-dental Voiceless Fricative
   (f) Lingua-palatal Oral Resonant Glide
   (g) Labio-dental Voiceless Fricative
   (h) Lingua-alveolar, Lingua-palatal Voiceless Affricate
   (i) Lingua-velar Bilabial Oral Resonant Glide
   (j) Lingua-dental Voiced Fricative
   (k) Lingua-velar Voiced Stop

(l) Lingua-velar Nasal Resonant
(m) Lingua-palatal Voiced Fricative
(n) Bilabial Voiced Stop
(o) Labio-dental Voiced Fricative
(p) Lingua-alveolar Lateral Oral Resonant
(q) Bilabial Voiceless Stop
(r) Lingua-palatal, Lingua-velar Voiceless Fricative
(s) Lingua-alveolar Nasal Resonant
(t) Lingua-alveolar Voiced Stop
(u) Lingua-velar, Bilabial Voiceless Fricative
(v) Lingua-velar Voiceless Stop
(w) Lingua-alveolar, Lingua-palatal Voiced Affricate
(x) Lingua-palatal Oral Resonant

2. Write the brief descriptive terms for the features of place, voicing, and manner of production associated with each of the following consonants. Example: /p/—Bilabial Voiceless Stop.

(a) /v/ /r/ /tʃ/ /m/ /d/ /w/
(b) /n/ /j/ /ʍ/ /l/ /h/ /dʒ/
(c) /b/ /k/ /ð/ /g/ /ŋ/ /z/
(d) /f/ /s/ /t/ /ʃ/ /ʒ/ /θ/

3. Write the IPA symbol that matches each of the following descriptions of speech sound production.

(a) With the velopharyngeal port closed and without voice, the lips close and breath is held and compressed in the oral cavity. Breath is released suddenly as audible aspiration between the lips.   p

(b) With the velopharyngeal port closed and without voice, the sides of the tongue are against the upper molars, the broad front surface of the tongue is raised toward the palate just back of the alveolar ridge, forming a central aperture slightly broader and farther back than for /s/, to direct the breath stream continuously through and against the slightly open front teeth as audible friction.   ʃ

(c) With the tip of the tongue closed against the alveolar ridge and the sides of the tongue against the upper molars, voice is directed through the open velopharyngeal port to the nasal cavity and out the nostrils. The back of the tongue is down and open to the oropharynx. The teeth and lips are slightly open.   n

(d) With the velopharyngeal port closed and with voice, the back of the tongue closes against the front of the velum or back portion of the palate as voicing begins or continues, and air is held briefly in the back of the oral cavity and in the oropharynx. Closure of the back of the tongue and the velum-palate is released as voicing continues.

(e) With the velopharyngeal port closed, the point of the tongue closes with slight pressure against the alveolar ridge with opening on both sides, as voice escapes around the tongue and out the oral cavity.

4. Describe a detailed sequence of voicing, resonance, and articulatory actions for the generalized and isolated production of each of the following speech sounds.

(a) Voiceless fricatives /f/, /θ/, and /ʌ/.
(b) Nasal resonants /m/, /n/, and /ŋ/.
(c) Voiced stops /b/, /d/, and /g/.
(d) Voiced fricatives /v/, /ð/, and /ʒ/.
(e) Affricates /tʃ/ and /dʒ/.
(f) Oral resonants /w/, /j/, and /l/.
(g) Voiceless stops /p/, /t/, and /k/.

SUGGESTED READING

Bronstein, Arthur J.: *The Pronunciation of American English.* Englewood Cliffs, N.J., Prentice-Hall, Inc., 1960.

   Chapters 4, 5, and 6 (pp. 59–130) survey the consonants of American English with numerous diagrams to show positions in the oral cavity.

Griffith, Jerry, and Miner, Lynn E.: *Phonetic Context Drillbook.* Englewood Cliffs, N.J., Prentice-Hall, Inc., 1979.

   This paperback provides for each of the American-English consonants a variety of phonetic contexts in words, phrases and sentences that are used in everyday language. The practice words are selected from among those most commonly used.

Chapter IV

VOWEL AND DIPHTHONG PRODUCTION

- **ANALYSIS OF VOWELS AND DIPHTHONGS**
  - **FRONT VOWELS**
  - **BACK VOWELS**
  - **MIXED VOWELS**
  - **DIPHTHONGS**
- **REVIEW VOCABULARY**
- **EXERCISES**
- **SUGGESTED READING**

Vowels are not classified in the same way as are consonants. American-English vowels, as pointed out in Chapter III, are all made with essentially the same manner of production. They are voiced and are oral resonant sounds. The different sound quality of vowels depends upon variations in the shape of the oral cavity. Shaping for the most part is achieved by the tongue, with important differences also made by jaw opening and lip rounding. Therefore, categorization has traditionally been by place and by height of tongue elevation, with supplementary notation of lip rounding. Tongue height, considered in relation to the palate and velum above it, is measured in tongue-to-palate or tongue-to-velum distance. This measure accounts for the jaw opening as well as for movement of the tongue, since the entire tongue must follow the vertical movement of the mandible.

The three primary classes of vowels, grouped by place of tongue elevation, are **front vowels, back vowels,** and a group usually termed **mixed vowels** which consists of those with central tongue elevation or those that do not fit easily into the first two groups. **Diphthongs** are considered to be a special kind of vowel sound. The front and back vowels, together with the mixed vowels and the two unique positions taken for diphthongs (the /e/ and /o/), may be schematically viewed on the vowel diagram of Figure IV-1. Of course, during actual production, the positions and degrees of tongue elevation are not so neatly symmetrical, especially when one considers individual variability and the influence of adjoining sounds during connected speech.

105

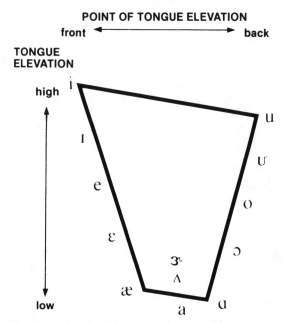

POINT OF TONGUE ELEVATION

front ◄—————————► back

TONGUE ELEVATION

high

low

Figure IV-1. Vowel sounds ordered by tongue elevation and position in the oral cavity.

However, the diagram does serve to relate, visually, one vowel to another for tongue height and the point of highest tongue elevation. Note the shift of the point of tongue elevation toward the center as the tongue is lowered.

Some of the IPA symbols for vowels, as mentioned in Chapter I, can indicate the presence or absence of stress on a syllable. **Stress** refers to the pointing up or drawing special attention to a unit of speech. It is accomplished by a number of speech actions discussed in Chapter VI, including making the selected unit louder or longer. When the stress is on a syllable within a word, we refer to it as **accent**. The /ʌ/ and /ɝ/ symbols are used for accented syllables, as in *utmost* [ʌtmost] and *hurting* [hɝtɪŋ], respectively. The unaccented or reduced counterpart of /ʌ/, made at the same place of articulation, is /ə/ as in *upon* [əpán]. The unaccented counterpart of /ɝ/ is /ɚ/ as in *butter* [bʌtɚ]. Diphthongs /eɪ/ and /oʊ/ also have unaccented counterparts written as [e] and [o], respectively. They are used in transcribing accenting in such words as *rotate* [roútet] and *rotation* [roteíʃən].

ANALYSIS OF VOWELS AND DIPHTHONGS

The vowel and diphthong phonemes of American-English speech are described individually in this chapter. Their written symbols as used in the International Phonetic Alphabet (IPA), in dictionaries, and in the General

American symbol system are listed, along with key words to assist in pronunciation. A typical place of articulation is outlined, using both the conventional descriptors and a step-by-step analysis of their production. Then the most common American-English spellings of the phoneme are presented, along with some irregular spellings. This is followed by words, sentences, and contrast discrimination exercises for each vowel and diphthong phoneme. Notes are added about some of the phonemes.

As with the consonants of Chapter III, the reader should heed this word of caution. These descriptions of the phonemes of our language may suggest there is a single or standard way of producing each sound. This is not the case! The descriptions are generalizations of how most people produce speech sounds. Individual differences are significant.

The individual analysis begins with front vowels, then moves to the back vowels, the mixed vowels, and finally to the diphthongs. Exercises are included at the end of the chapter.

Front Vowels

The front vowels of American-English, in order of their tongue height, are /i/, /ɪ/, /ɛ/, and /æ/. With the tip of the tongue lying just behind and usually touching the inner surface of the mandibular incisors, the front of the tongue is raised toward the palate without touching it, and without approximating it closely enough to cause turbulence resulting in audible friction (Figure IV-2). The tongue-to-palate distance appropriate for each front vowel may be achieved either by differentially elevating the front of the tongue from its base of the stationary mandible or by raising and lowering the mandible while the front of the tongue is steadily posed high. The reader can demonstrate these alternative ways to achieve the same acoustic results by producing the front vowels—/i/, /ɪ/, /ɛ/, and /æ/—in front of a mirror.

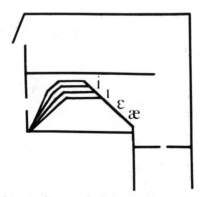

Figure IV-2. Schematic diagram of relative tongue positions for front vowels.

First, place a pencil eraser between the front teeth to maintain a constant jaw opening and produce the front vowels in the foregoing order. One may feel the tongue height dropping. Next, begin with the tongue and jaw opening for producing /i/, then drop the jaw in observable steps to produce /ɪ/, /ɛ/, and /æ/, keeping the tongue posed in the same position. Repeat the sequence several times in order both to feel and see the changes in positions. Note that as the tongue elevation decreases, the point of elevation is also slightly farther back in the mouth. The reader may also examine his pattern of producing front vowels by watching in a mirror as he says the following series of words:

	[i]	[ɪ]	[ɛ]	[æ]
1.	beat	bit	bet	bat
2.	meet	mit	met	mat
3.	peat	pit	pet	pat
4.	lead	lid	led	lad
5.	dean	din	den	Dan
6.	keen	kin	Ken	can

In connected speech, the tongue height for front vowels may be achieved by a combination of tongue and mandible adjustments. Some speakers use one kind of adjustment more regularly than the other. When the front of the tongue is elevated, as the mandible remains steady, there is a tendency for the lips to be pulled back, or retracted, at the corners. For some speakers, front of the tongue raising is accompanied by lip retraction along with an increased separation of the lips. This may be especially marked for the highest front vowel, /i/. The associated lip separation may expose mandibular front teeth or maxillary front teeth or both. This action can provide readily observable visual information for speech reading, a topic discussed in Chapter VIII.

IPA   i
Dictionary   ē Key Words: *eat, seed, be*
General American   ee (ea, -y)

/i/ PRODUCTION—High Front Vowel

With the velopharyngeal port closed and the sides of the back of the tongue closed against the upper molars, the middle to front portion of the tongue is raised high, nearly touching the palate and alveolar ridge, while the tip of the tongue touches lightly behind the lower front teeth, and voice is given. The upper and lower front teeth are slightly open. The lips are not directly involved but are slightly open and tend to retract at the corners as the front of the tongue is raised.

/i/ SPELLING

-e occurs most frequently as in *be, me, she, he, we.*

ee is very consistent for /i/ as in *eel, agree, see, feet, seed, three.*

ea may take other sounds but occurs frequently as /i/ as in *eat, tea, teach, leave, please, east.*

Less frequently and irregular spellings include ey as in *key;* e-e as in *eve;* ei as in *either;* -i as in *ski;* ie as in *chief;* i-e as in *marine;* eo as in *people;* ae as in *aeon;* oe as in *Phoenix;* -is as in *debris;* e- as in *equal;* -i- as in *chic.*

/i/ WORDS

Initial		*Medial*		*Final*	
eat	either	seed	read	be	trustee
eve	Easter	leave	feet	he	free
eel	equal	believe	green	key	knee
east	eager	teach	bead	agree	flee
each	enough	these	chief	plea	tea
even	eagle	lease	sheep	three	see

/i/ SENTENCES

1. These teams seem even.
2. We believe he needs these keys.
3. Jean Green sees three bees.
4. He receives Steve's fees.
5. We'll eat Lee's green beans.
6. She pleases these Eastern trustees.

/i/ CONTRASTS

/i/—/ɪ/		/i/—/ɛ/	
deep	dip	meat	met
deed	did	bead	bed
beat	bit	neat	net
peak	pick	seat	set
bean	bin	mean	men
peach	pitch	teen	ten
eat	it	we'll	well
eel	ill	keep	kept

Note: /i/ has the highest tongue position of the front vowels.

Alternative Pronunciation

-*y* when unstressed is pronounced either /i/ or /ɪ/ in General American as in *candy, lobby, only, very, army, baby, hardly*. This unstressed final sound is also spelled -*ie* as in *cookie*, -*ey* as in *monkey*, and -*i* as in *taxi*. The IPA symbol [ɪ̯] may be used for transcription.

/i/ immediately before /r/ is frequently modified in General American to become /ɪ/ as in *beer, here, near, year, rear, peer*.

IPA   ɪ
Dictionary   ĭ, i Key Words: *if, bit*
General American   -i-

/ɪ/ PRODUCTION—High Front Vowel

With the velopharyngeal port closed and the sides of the back of the tongue closed against the upper molars, the middle to front portion of the tongue is raised toward the palate and alveolar ridge, slightly lower and farther back than for the /i/, while the tip of the tongue touches lightly behind the lower front teeth, and voice is given. The upper and lower front teeth are open, slightly wider than for /i/. The tongue is less tense than for /i/ and the corners of the mouth retract little with tongue elevation.

/ɪ/ SPELLING

i- occurs most frequently as in *it, in, if, bit, sick, lift, fish, mirror*.

-*y*- is frequently /ɪ/ as in *gypsy, syrup, gypsum, myth, gym, hymn*.

ea(r), ee(r), ei(r), and *e(r)e* usually have the /ɪ/ sound as in *hear, sheer, weird*, and *here*, respectively.

Less frequent and irregular spellings include -*ee*- as in *been*, -*u*- as in *busy*, -*ui*- as in *built*, -*ie*- as in *sieve*, -*o*- as in *women*, -*e*- as in *pretty*, and i-e as in *give*.

Unstressing of several vowels, especially in New England and Southern speech, leads to /ɪ/ as in *courage, devote, kitchen, character, Dallas, relate*.

-*y* when unstressed is pronounced either /i/ or /ɪ/ in General American, but more often /ɪ/ in New England and Southern as in *candy, lobby, only, very, army, baby, hardly*.

/ɪ/ WORDS

The /ɪ/ does not occur in final position except for unstressed final -*y* in New England and Southern speech.

Initial		Medial		Final -y	
in	into	his	pill	only	city
it	ignorant	busy	quill	busy	any
if	interest	kitten	written	ready	heavy
id	insect	limb	sit	hilly	bury
ill	idiot	mit	tin	kitty	curry
is	invert	nick	victor	pretty	duty

/ɪ/ SENTENCES

1. The little kitten is pretty.
2. Will the insect sit still?
3. Give him a pill in the gym.
4. The pink crystal is thin.
5. Is it in this tin?
6. Bill spilled his liquor.

/ɪ/ CONTRASTS

/ɪ/—/i/

dip	deep
did	deed
bit	beat
pick	peak
bin	bean
pitch	peach
it	eat
ill	eel

/ɪ/—/ɛ/

mit	met
bid	bed
knit	net
sit	set
tin	ten
will	well
lid	led
hid	head

Note: the /ɪ/ is one the most frequently occurring sounds in American-English speech.

IPA   ɛ
Dictionary   ĕ, e Key Words: *end, bet*
General American -e-

/ɛ/ PRODUCTION—Front Vowel

With the velopharyngeal port closed and the sides of the back of the tongue closed against the upper molars, the middle to front portion of the tongue is raised slightly toward the palate and alveolar ridge, lower and farther back than for the /ɪ/ or /e/, while the tip of the tongue touches lightly behind the lower front teeth, and voice is given. The upper and lower front teeth are open slightly wider than for /ɪ/. The corners of the mouth do not retract with the slight tongue elevation.

/ɛ/ SPELLING

e- occurs most frequently as in *end, ebb, estimate, ten, lent.*

-ea- is frequently /ɛ/ as in *head, meant, bread, dread, steady, breakfast.*

Several vowel combinations associated with /r/ have the /ɛ/ sound including -e(r)e as in *there* and *where*, -eir as in *their* and *heir*, ai(r) as in *air* and *fair*, -ea(r) as in *pear* and *bear*, -a(r)e as in *bare* and *care*, and ae(r)- as in *aerial.*

Less frequent and irregular spellings include a- as in *any*, -ay- as in *says*, ae- as in *aesthetic*, -ai- as in *said*, -ei- as in *heifer*, -ie- as in *friend*, -ue- as in *guest*, -u- as in *bury*, and -eo- as in *leopard.*

/ɛ/ WORDS

The /ɛ/ does not occur in final position

Initial		Medial	
edge	extra	men	head
end	elephant	bed	said
egg	else	get	many
elm	engine	them	friend
every	excel	beg	guest
any	effort	neck	bear

/ɛ/ SENTENCES

1. Many men said Fred would wed.
2. Tell Ben's friend about the ten bears.
3. The pet hen would not be fed any bread. ·
4. Let their bed and chairs stay there.
5. Where was the tent sent Wednesday?
6. Their eggs compare fairly well.

/ɛ/ CONTRASTS

/ɛ/—/ɪ/		/ɛ/—/æ/	
met	mit	bet	bat
bed	bid	net	gnat

net	knit	set	sat
set	sit	ten	tan
ten	tin	head	had
well	will	send	sand
led	lid	end	and
pair	peer	led	lad

Note: the /ɛ/ is one of the most frequently occurring speech sounds in American-English speech.

IPA   æ
Dictionary   ă, a Key Words: *at, bat*
General American -a-

/æ/ PRODUCTION—Low Front Vowel

With the velopharyngeal port closed and the mouth open wider than for the other front vowels, the middle to front portion of the tongue is raised farther back than the other front vowels, while voice is given. The sides of the back of the tongue may move away from the upper molars and the tongue tip may move slightly behind the lower front teeth.

/æ/ SPELLING

a- occurs most frequently as in *at, and, an, bat, rabbit, black*.
Less frequent and irregular spellings include -*ai*- as in *plaid*, -*au*- as in *laugh*, -*i*- in *meringue*, and -*a-e* as in *have*.

/æ/ WORDS

The /æ/ does not occur in final position.

Initial		*Medial*	
at	after	cat	salmon
an	aunt	ham	rather
and	Adam	sand	example
add	absolute	dad	grant
amp	answer	sang	dance
ask	atom	that	laugh

/æ/ SENTENCES

1. Ask the man at that stand.
2. That stamp is an example of bad planning.
3. Dad has had the answer after all.
4. The black cat sat in the grass.
5. The half-back can catch that pass.
6. Master the answer by half past nine.

/æ/ CONTRASTS

/æ/—/ɛ/		/æ/—/ɑ/	
bat	bet	cat	cot
gnat	net	pad	pod
sat	set	Dan	Don
tan	ten	cad	cod
had	head	shack	shock
sand	send	cap	cop
and	end	pat	pot
lad	led	gnat	not

Note: the /æ/ is usually in an accented syllable of a polysyllabic word. A common non-standard production, particularly before nasal consonants, involves raising of the back of the tongue sides to touch the back molars with a resulting [ɛ] sound from tongue elevation and restriction of voice for oral resonance, noticeable in such words as *chance* [tʃɛ̃nts], *camp* [kɛ̃mp], and *can't* [kɛ̃nt].

[ær] is a common alternate pronunciation for [ɛr] in such words as *chair, fare, rare, air,* and *bear.*

[a] is a common alternate pronunciation for [æ] in New England speech for such words as *bath, and, hat, man, tack,* and *laugh.*

Back Vowels

The back vowels of American-English, in order of their tongue height, are /u/, /ʊ/, /ɔ/, and /ɑ/. With the tip of the tongue behind and slightly below the mandibular incisors, or lightly touching the lower gum ridge, the back of the tongue is raised toward the velum near its juncture with the palate (Figure IV–3). The high point of the tongue neither touches the velum nor approximates it closely enough to cause turbulence and audible friction. Like the front vowels, the tongue-to-velum distance appropriate for each back

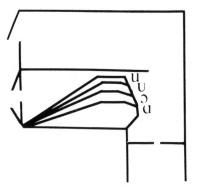

Figure IV-3.   Schematic diagram of relative tongue positions for back vowels.

vowel is achieved by a combination of lingual and mandibular adjustments. As the tongue elevation decreases, the point of elevation is slightly farther forward in the mouth. When the back of the tongue is raised, the lips tend to round. The highest back tongue position for /u/ is accompanied by the tightest rounding and the smallest lip aperture. The /ʊ/ and /ɔ/ have lower tongue positions and wider lip openings. Back tongue elevation and lip rounding are reciprocal. As the lips are rounded even for /w/ or /ʍ/, the back of the tongue also tends to rise so that tongue position influences the sound of both these consonants. The degree of lip rounding for back vowels is variable from speaker to speaker. Some speakers use very little lip rounding for /u/, /ʊ/, and /ɔ/, compensating by tongue positioning. The reader may experience this compensatory tongue action by observing in a mirror as he purposely attempts to produce /ʊ/ with the lips open, unrounded, and relaxed. As with lip retraction for front vowels, lip rounding for the back vowels /u/, /ʊ/, and /ɔ/ can assist the observer in speech reading. The /ɑ/ is also a back vowel, but the lips are not rounded for this sound. This vowel has the greatest jaw opening of all American-English vowel sounds and is formed by slightly raising the back of the tongue and moving it slightly backward into the oropharynx.

The following series of words provide examples of the steps of tongue elevation and lip rounding for the back vowels:

	/u/	/ʊ/	/ɔ/	/ɑ/
1.	cooed	could	cawed	cod
2.	shoe	should	Shaw	shod
3.	who	hook	hawk	hock
4.	Lew	look	law	lock
5.	rue	rook	raw	rock
6.	noon	nook	naught	not

u

IPA   u
Dictionary   o͞o, ü, o͡o Key Words: *ooze, boot, too*
General American oo (ew)

/u/ PRODUCTION—High Back Round Vowel

With the velopharyngeal port closed and the sides of the back of the tongue closed against the upper molars, the back of the tongue is raised high and tense, nearly touching the palate, the lips are rounded and may be slightly protruded for a small aperture, and voice is given. The tongue tip is just behind the lower front teeth, and the upper and lower teeth are slightly open. The aperture of the rounded lips is smaller than for any other vowel and is almost imperceptibly wider than for /w/ (compare in the syllable *woo*).

/u/ SPELLING

-oo occurs most frequently as in *boot, cool, mood, loose, noon, too;* however, the *oo* may often have the sound of /ʊ/.
    -o as in *do, who, to, tomb, whom*.
    -ew as in *blew, crew, chew, grew, drew, brew*.
    -u-e as in *rude, rule, crude, Luke, presume*.
    -ou as in *you, group, troup, soup, ghoul, wound*.
    -ui- as in *fruit, cruise, bruise, recruit*.
    Irregularly and infrequently as *-o-e* as in *lose, whose, move; -oe* as in *shoe, canoe; -ue* as in *true, blue, sue; -iue-* as in *lieu, lieutenant; -ioux* as in *Sioux; -au-* as in *Sault; -ough* as in *through* and *slough; -u* as in *flu, gnu, tulip; -wo* as in *two; -eu-* as in *rheumatism* and *-eue* as in *queue*.

/u/ WORDS

The /u/ seldom occurs as an initial vowel except in slang and in Hawaiian words.

Initial	Medial		Final	
ooze	boot	moon	too	do
oodles	crew	move	who	drew
oops	doom	rude	queue	blew
	fruit	tomb	shoe	through
	group	school	you	flu
	lose	whom	true	canoe

/u/ SENTENCES

1. Ruth's soup soon grew cool.
2. The ripe fruit oozed through the bamboo.
3. Do you approve of the move?
4. Two groups from school went through the zoo.
5. He cleaned the booth in the room with a blue broom.
6. Whose tooth was loosened by a spoon?

/u/ CONTRASTS

/u/—/ʊ/		/u/—/ju/	
pool	pull	boot	butte
fool	full	ooze	use
wooed	would	coot	cute
stewed	stood	booty	beauty
Luke	look	coo	cue
cooed	could	moot	mute
shooed	should	food	feud
kook	cook	whose	hues

Note: a few words are variable in pronunciation by choice with either /u/ or /ʊ/, including *roof, coop, hoof, root,* and *hoop.* Some words are variably pronounced with either /u/ or /ju/, including *new, tune, duke, due, nude, suit,* and *resume.*

U		
	IPA	u
	Dictionary	o͝o, u Key Words: book, *could*
	General American	-oo- [oo(k)]

/ʊ/ PRODUCTION—High Back Round Vowel

With the velopharyngeal port closed and the sides of the back of the tongue closed lightly against the upper molars, the back of the tongue is raised high, but lower and with less tension than for /u/, the lips are rounded and may be very slightly protruded for an aperture larger than for /u/, and voice is given. The tongue tip touches behind the lower front teeth, and the upper and lower teeth are slightly open.

/ʊ/ SPELLING

-oo(k) is almost invariably /ʊ/ as in *look, book, hook, cook.*
-oo- as in *good, wool, wood, hood, stood.*
-u- as in *put, bush, pull, sugar, full, bull.*
-ou- as in *would, should, could.*
Rarely as *-o-* as in *wolf* and *bosom; -or-* as in *worsted.*

/ʊ/ WORDS

The /ʊ/ does not occur in initial or final positions of words.

	Medial	
cook	hood	pull
look	woolen	bush
book	wooden	could
shook	full	should
good	put	would
stood	push	wolf

/ʊ/ SENTENCES

1. He took a cook book from the butcher.
2. He looked at the brook in the woods.
3. The bushel basket was full of cookies.
4. Pull up the woolen hood.
5. He could be good if he would.
6. He should push and pull the wooden cart.

/ʊ/ CONTRASTS

/ʊ/—/u/		/ʊ/—/ou/	
pull	pool	pull	pole
full	fool	bull	bowl
would	wooed	could	code
stood	stewed	should	showed
look	Luke	stood	stowed
could	cooed	good	goad
should	shooed	brook	broke
cook	kook	cook	coke

Note: a few words are variable in pronunciation by choice with either /ʊ/ or /u/, including *roof, coop, hoof, root,* and *hoop.*

IPA ɔ
Dictionary ô, aw Key Words: *awful, caught, law*
General American aw [au, a(l)]

/ɔ/ PRODUCTION—Back Round Vowel

With the velopharyngeal port closed, the back and middle portion of the tongue is slightly raised with elevation similar to /o/ but the mouth is open wider than for /o/, the lips are rounded and slightly protruded for an aperture larger than for /o/, and voice is given. The tongue tip touches behind the lower front teeth. Tense lip rounding and wide mouth opening is the essence of /ɔ/.

/ɔ/ SPELLING

au- occurs most frequently for /ɔ/ as in *auto, audio, taut, applause, vault, haunt, laundry.*
aw occurs very consistently for /ɔ/ as in *awe, awful, yawn, lawn, law, saw, jaw.*
Less frequently but consistently *-augh(t)* as in *caught, fraught, taught, naught;* and *ough(t)* as in *bought, thought, brought, ought.*
Less regularly but frequently *o-* as in *off, loft, wrong, cloth, strong,* and *a(1)-* as in *ball, all, call, talk, altogether, small, already.*
Infrequent and irregular -oa- as in *broad, abroad; -o-e* as in *gone;* and *-ou-* as in *cough, trough.*

/ɔ/ WORDS

Initial		Medial		Final	
awful	always	taut	caught	saw	straw
awning	all	applaud	taught	raw	craw
awl	almost	vault	thought	law	draw
auto	off	yawn	bought	paw	thaw
audio	often	talk	cloth	caw	gnaw
auction	ought	walk	wrong	jaw	slaw

/ɔ/ SENTENCES

1. They *a*ll th*ou*ght they s*aw* him y*aw*n.
2. We b*ou*ght *a*lmost *a*ll the cl*o*th at the *au*ction.
3. He was t*au*ght *a*lways to c*a*ll the l*aw*.

4. *They sought the wrong law officer.*
5. The fawn often walked on the straw.
6. We thought he would fall off the automobile.

/ɔ/ CONTRASTS

/ɔ/—/ɑ/		/ɔ/—/ou/	
caught	cot	fawn	phone
hawk	hock	bought	boat
naught	not	caught	coat
taught	tot	paws	pose
caller	collar	taught	tote
auto	Otto	bawl	bowl
wrought	rot	call	coal
pawed	pod	fall	foal

Note: the /ɔ/ is one of the most inconsistently used vowels in American-English speech. Its acoustic distinctiveness depends upon lip rounding and protrusion, which, with some tongue elevation, is its primary difference from /ɑ/. Speaker variability in the tenseness of lip shaping and dialectic differences in usage lead to a continuum of lip rounding and protusion ranging from speakers using a strongly lip-shaped /ɔ/ in many words to others with almost total absence of the vowel and universal substitution of /ɑ/. The *aw*, *au-*, and *-augh(t)* spellings are most consistently pronounced /ɔ/, but at the extreme of omission for some General American speakers, even these spellings are produced as /ɑ/ so that *awful* becomes [ɑfəl], *law* becomes [lɑ:], *taut* is said [tɑt], *haunt* is [hɑnt], and *caught* is [kɑt]. Apparently the /ɑ/ for /ɔ/ substitution, and the degree of lip shaping, is not phonemically critical for speech intelligibility.

The *o-* spelling is highly variable so that some speakers who say [lɔ:] for *law* may say [klɑθ] for *cloth* and [kɑst] for *cost*. *On* is most frequently pronounced [ɔn] in Southern speech but [ɑn] by most General American speakers and [an] by many in New England. The *-og* words, such as *log* and *dog*, are given a strong /ɔ/ in Southern speech but /ɑ/ throughout the rest of the country. The /ɑ/ for /ɔ/ variability holds for *a(1)* words such as *ball*, *call*, and *all*, with varying degrees of lip rounding and protrusion tension used.

The *o(r)* spelling has very high variability even within a dialect group. In words such as *or*, *for*, *born*, and *origin*, the vowel may be heard as /ɔ/, /o/, /ou/, or /ɑ/. In New England and Southern speech, the *o-* before intervocalic /r/ is often /ɑ/ as in *origin* [ɑrɪdʒən] and *forest* [fɑrɪst], even though *for* is likely to be [fɔə] or [fɔr]. In St Louis, although *coffee* is said [kɔfɪ], *cork* is said [kɑrk], and *born* is said [bɑrn]. Of course, the New England and Southern omission of the preconsonantal and final /r/ adds further variability to *o(r)* pronunciation.

Principally in New England, and following British pronunciation, a slightly rounded /ɔ/ or /ɑ/ of rather short duration is used for some *-o-* spellings. Written /ɒ/, it is especially prominent before voiceless stop consonants as in *hot, not, rock, top,* and *spot.* It may also be heard in New England *coffee, cost, long, lost,* and *song.*

IPA	ɑ
Dictionary	ŏ, ä Key Words: *odd, father, pa, ah*
General American	-o- [ah, a(r)]

/ɑ/ PRODUCTION—Low Mid-back Vowel

With the velopharyngeal port closed, the tongue is relaxed and slightly raised in the back with the tip touching behind the lower front teeth, the mouth is opened wider than for any other vowel as voice is given. The lips are not rounded or protruded, differing from /ɔ/ primarily in this characteristic. The /ɑ/ differs from /ʌ/ in having a wider mouth opening and lower back-of-tongue elevation.

/ɑ/ SPELLING

-o- occurs most frequently as in *fog, top, bother, common, bomb, rod, borrow.*

a(r) occurs frequently whether or not the *-r* is pronounced as in *car, part, barn, bark, yard, arm, are, army.*

-al(m) with silent *-l-* as in *palm, calm, psalm, balm, alms.*

The /ɑ/ occurs infrequently and irregularly as *-a* in *father, mamma, pa, was, watch;* as *-ea(r)-* in h*ear*t and hearth; *-ua(r)-* in *guard; -ow-* in *knowledge; -e-* in *sergeant; -aa(r)* in *bazaar;* and *ho-* with silent *h-* as in *honest.*

The /ɑ/ is popularly written *ah* as an exclamation or to indicate the /ɑ/ in a character's speech pattern.

/ɑ/ WORDS

The /ɑ/ occurs in final position only in slang as *pa, ma,* and *ha.*

Initial		Medial	
art	honest	father	Tom
arm	olive	heart	beyond
are	ominous	bomb	bar
ark	onset	palm	car

| army | oxen | calm | doll |
| honor | onyx | don | psalm |

/ɑ/ SENTENCES

1. Father's car is parked in the barn.
2. Palm trees are arched toward the ark.
3. Mom was calm despite the ominous army.
4. Honesty is the policy for Olive to observe.
5. Tom's honor is beyond need of bonding.
6. The bazaar and arcade are not far.

/ɑ/ CONTRASTS

/ɑ/—/ɔ/		/ɑ/—/ʌ/		/ɑ/—/æ/	
cot	caught	bomb	bum	not	gnat
hock	hawk	calm	come	shock	shack
not	naught	cot	cut	cop	cap
tot	taught	psalm	some	psalm	Sam
collar	caller	pop	pup	knock	knack
Otto	auto	shot	shut	rot	rat
rot	wrought	cop	cup	pot	pat
pod	pawed	dock	duck	cot	cat

Note: the /ɑ/ is quite variable in American-English, often interchanged with /ɔ/ and /æ/. See the discussion of /ɑ/ - /ɔ/ usage as notation in the /ɔ/ section of this chapter. The "broad a" of some Eastern speakers makes *aunt* pronounced [ɑnt], *ask* [ɑsk], and *bath* [bɑθ]. New England speakers may use /ɒ/ for -o-, particularly followed by a voiceless stop as in *top*, *hot*, and *lock*, and may use [a] for *a(r)* in *park* [pa:k], *arm* [a:m], and *car* [ka:].

Mixed Vowels

In the center of the vowel diagram of Figure IV–1 are **mixed vowels** with more central tongue elevation or without any special point of elevation. The /ʌ/ is produced with a relaxed tongue, lying fairly flat in the oral cavity, and is thus called the "natural" vowel. The jaw opening for the natural vowel is minimal so that the tongue-to-palate velum distance is small, and tongue height on the diagram is greater than for the /æ/ and /ɑ/, which have the greatest jaw opening. To gauge the extremes of tongue and jaw positions for American-English vowels, the reader might carry out the following exercises, moving from the natural vowel position to the position for each vowel at the corners of the vowel diagram:

$$[ʌ] \rightarrow [i]$$
$$[ʌ] \rightarrow [u]$$
$$[ʌ] \rightarrow [æ]$$
$$[ʌ] \rightarrow [ɑ]$$

The exercise may be conducted with a brief pause between the vowels or with the vowels smoothed together for [ʌi], [ʌu], [ʌæ], and [ʌɑ], with vocalization or without.

At the bottom center of the diagram is the /a/, a sound limited primarily to New England in the United States. It occurs in New England dialect as described in Chapter VII, with a wide jaw opening and middle tongue elevation in words like *Boston* [bastən], *Harvard* [havəd], *park* [pak], and *car* [ka:]. In stage pronunciation, the [a] is preferred over either [æ] or [ɑ] in such words as *path, ask,* and *bath.*

Inside the vowel diagram is another sound considered a mixed vowel—the /ɚ/. This sound differs from all other vowels in one important aspect of production. Whereas the other vowels are produced with the tongue tip against the lower front teeth or just behind the teeth, the /ɚ/ requires that the tip be raised or pulled back to form a broad front similar to that formed for /ʃ/. Positioning of the tongue tip can be observed in shifting from another vowel to /ɚ/ as in [ɑɚ] and [uɚ]. Note in producing [sɚ] that the tongue tip pulls back considerably for the [ɚ] but that less movement is needed in making [ʃɚ].

IPA   ʌ
Dictionary   ŭ, u Key Words: *up, cub*
General American -u-

/ʌ/ PRODUCTION—Low Mid Vowel

With the velopharyngeal port closed, the tongue lies relaxed in the mouth with slight elevation in the middle to back portion, the upper and lower front teeth are separated similar to the degree of opening for /ɛ/, and voice is given. The tip of the tongue touches lightly behind the lower front teeth. With the relaxed tongue, the /ʌ/ is called the "natural" or "neutral" vowel.

/ʌ/ SPELLING

u- is most frequent and consistent as in *cup, but, up, abut, hundred, under.*

-o-e is frequent but not consistent as in *come, done, above, money, hover.*

-ou- as in *rough, trouble, couple, enough, touch, tough, double.*

-o- as in *ton, son, month, won, tongue, color, compass.*

Infrequently *-oe-* as in *does.*

/ʌ/ WORDS

The /ʌ/ does not occur in the final position of words.

Initial		*Medial*	
upper	usher	cup	flood
upward	utter	tub	blood
under	utmost	hunt	rough
ultimate	oven	but	couple
uncle	ultra-	some	nothing
other	ugly	done	mother

/ʌ/ SENTENCES

1. Some other mothers were at the hunt.
2. The usher led the young couple upward.
3. The buns in the sun oven are done.
4. Come hunt the ugly bug.
5. The bunny jumped in the mud puddle.
6. His son must run through the flood.

/ʌ/ CONTRASTS

/ʌ/—/ɑ/		/ʌ/—/ʊ/		/ʌ/—/ɛ/	
bum	bomb	luck	look	bun	Ben
come	calm	tuck	took	nut	net
gun	gone	stud	stood	but	bet
nut	not	shuck	shook	hull	hell
putt	pot	putt	put	lug	leg
duck	dock	buck	book	mutt	met
cut	cot	cud	could	pun	pen
sum	psalm	crux	crooks	money	many

Note: the American-English /ʌ/ occurs in few other languages and is produced close to /ɑ/ in British-English. It is used for stressed vowels with primary or secondary accent in polysyllabic words. Primary stressing is apparent in such words as *upper, couple, ultimate, nothing, begun*, and *encompass*. Secondary stressing of /ʌ/ occurs with a change in word form when the syllable of the root word would take a primary accent /ʌ/, as in *conduct* (n.) [kándʌkt] and *upset* [ʌpsét] and in words with clear secondary accent on the first syllable as in *úmbrélla, únléss, úntíl*, and *últérior*. Or it may reflect the stressing of a particular speaker, as when in formal speech the word *nation* might be said [neíʃʌn].

The unstressed counterpart of /ʌ/ is /ə/, called the "schwa" vowel. For /ə/, the tongue is more relaxed, and duration is considerably shorter. It is used for very lightly stressed syllables as in the following words:

Initial	Medial	Final
abóve [əbʌv]	lémon [lɛmən]	sófa [soufə]
agáin [əgɛn]	táble [teɪbəl]	cóbra [koubrə]
awáy [əweɪ]	nátion [neɪʃən]	banána [bənænə]

Medial Syllables
télephóne [tɛləfoun]
púrposeful [pɝpəsful]
fúndaméntal [fʌndəmɛntl̩]

The /ə/ is used especially for vowels that are so reduced in stressing that pronunciation is changed to the schwa as in the following words:

	Lightly stressed	Unstressed
pávement	[peɪvmɛnt]	[peɪvmənt]
aménd	[æmɛnd]	[əmɛnd]
crísis	[kraɪsɪs]	[kraɪsəs]
authórity	[ɔθorɪtɪ]	[əθorɪtɪ]
befóre	]bifor]	[bəfor]

The /ə/ can be spelled with any vowel alphabet letter (*a*, alone; *e*, moment, *i*, pencil; *o*, comply; *u*, circus) and with many combinations (*ae*, Michael; *ai*, fountain; *au*, authority; *eo*, pigeon; *ea*, sergeant; *ie*, conscience; *io*, religion; *ous*, dangerous, etc.)

Frequently used, short linking words are often reduced to /ə/ in connected speech so that their former or "dictionary" pronunciations are almost forgotten. Especially noticeable are *was* [wɑz], *from* [frɑm], *of* [ɑv], *a* [eɪ], and *the* [ði]. For emphasis, these typically unstressed words are often "restressed" with /ʌ/ as in "a government *of* [ʌv] the people," or "that's the way it *was* [wʌz]."

/ə/ WORDS

Initial		Medial		Final	
about	appeal	alphabet	relative	sofa	vanilla
above	arouse	chocolate	syllable	soda	camera
another	attach	company	emphasis	tuba	gorilla
away	abate	buffalo	accident	zebra	cinema
awhile	allow	elephant	parasol	quota	arena
alive	amaze	parachute	cinnamon	drama	stamina

Note: the /ə/ is one of the most frequently occurring sounds in American-English speech.

IPA   ɝ
Dictionary   ûr, er Key Words: *urn, burn, fur*
General American ur (er, ir)

/ɝ/ PRODUCTION—High Mid Vowel

With the velopharyngeal port closed and the sides of the tongue closed against the upper molars, the tongue is slightly retracted. As voicing begins, the tip or front of the tongue is raised toward the palate just behind the alveolar ridge but without contact. The /ɝ/ differs from the consonantal /r/ (see Chapter III) in the following ways: (1) /ɝ/ has greater duration, (2) it constitutes a syllable, (3) it has tongue movement toward rather than away from the /r/ tongue position, and (4) it is never given voiceless following voiceless consonants as the /r/ is. The /ɝ/ is the only vowel for which the tongue tip is necessarily raised from just behind the lower front teeth.

/ɝ/ SPELLING

-er most frequently as in *her, herd, stern, merchant, kernel, fern.*
ur very often as in *urn, burn, fur, recur, turtle, curd, murmur.*
-ir frequently as in *fir, bird, first, firm, girl, squirm, girdle.*
ear- as in *earth, pearl, search, earnest, earn, learn.*

Less frequently and irregularly as follows: *-or* as in *worm, word; -urr* as in *purr, burr; -our-* as in *journey; -aur-* as in *restaurant;* and *-yr* as in *myrtle.*

/ɝ/ WORDS

Initial		Medial		Final	
earn	erstwhile	turn	dirt	fir	purr
urn	early	curl	bird	sir	burr
irk	ermine	hurt	first	stir	cur
Ernest	urban	turf	girl	fur	infer
earnest	urge	work	learn	blur	her
earth	herb	worm	heard	spur	recur

/ɝ/ SENTENCES

1. Her bird heard the cat purr.
2. The merchant burned the ermine curtain.
3. Earl learned to do dirty work.
4. The early bird deserves the worm.
5. He turned the earth to grow turf and herbs.
6.. The first girl stirred the burning soup.

/ɝ/ CONTRASTS

/ɝ/—/ʊ/		/ɝ/—/ʌ/		/ɝ/ or /ɚ/—/r/	
shirk	shook	hurt	hut	terrain	train
stirred	stood	lurk	luck	beret	bray
curd	could	shirk	shuck	duress	dress
lurk	look	shirt	shut	corrode	crowed
word	wood	pert	putt	caressed	crest
furl	full	burn	bun	baroque	broke
gird	good	curt	cut	thorough	throw
Turk	took	burrs	buzz	curried	creed

Note: the unstressed counterpart of /ɝ/ is written /ɚ/. For /ɚ/, the tongue is more relaxed and duration is considerably shorter. It is used in very lightly stressed or unstressed syllables as in the following words:

móther	múrmur	revérberate
lábor	terráin	pervért
mártyr	urbáne	fermént

The /ɚ/ is spelled by a number of vowels combined with r, including any combination that spells /ɝ/.

Diphthongs

Diphthongs are considered single phonemes, each having a sequence of two different vowel positions. One of the positions is the dominant **nucleus** (sometimes called the "radical") with greater duration; the other position, the **glide** (or "vanish"), is of reduced duration and stress. Both positions are taken in a single syllable. The diphthongs of American-English are /eɪ/, /ou/, /aɪ/, /au/, and /ɔɪ/. Rather than the static plot of the steady or "pure" vowels shown in Figure IV–1, diphthongs should be represented by movement of the tongue within the oral cavity. Figure IV–4 uses the outline of the vowel diagram to show the direction of movement for the two positions of each diphthong. All diphthong phonemes of American-English move from the nucleus to the glide position. From Figure IV–4, it may also be seen that the diphthongs move from a lower tongue elevation to a higher elevation.

IPA	eɪ
Dictionary	ā Key Words: *able, made, may*
General American	a-e (ai, ay)

/eɪ/ PRODUCTION—Front Diphthong

With the velopharyngeal port closed and the sides of the back of the tongue closed against the upper molars, the middle and front portion of the tongue is raised toward the palate and alveolar ridge, slightly lower and farther back than for the /ɪ/ as voice is given; then the tongue briefly rises toward the /ɪ/ height as voice continues. The tip of the tongue touches lightly behind the lower front teeth. The upper and lower front teeth are open and may move from the /e/ to the /ɪ/ opening. The [e] portion is the longer nucleus and the [ɪ] portion is the shorter glide. For many speakers, the glide portion may have a tongue-mouth position close to /i/ but of short duration.

/eɪ/ SPELLING

a-e occurs most frequently as in *ate, cake, able, paper, grateful, makeshift.*

ai- is frequently /eɪ/ as in *aim, braid, rain, main, braille.*

-ay is also frequently /eɪ/ as in *may, say, pray, maybe, delay, tray.*

Less frequently *-a-(y)* is /eɪ/ as in *baby, lady, shady, navy, wavy.*

When *a-e* is changed to *a-(ing)*, the pronunciation remains /eɪ/ as in *saving, making, bathing, wading, baking.*

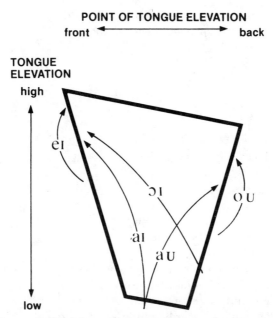

POINT OF TONGUE ELEVATION
front ←————————————→ back

TONGUE ELEVATION
high

low

Figure IV–4.   Movement of diphthongs by tongue elevation and position in the oral cavity.

Initial stressed *a-* in some polysyllabic words has the /eɪ/ sound as in *amiable, aviary, atrium, atheist, Abraham.*

Irregular spellings include *ei-* as in *eight, weigh, freight,* and *neighbor;* *-ea-* as in *steak* and *great; -ey* a in *prey* and *they; -au-* as in *gauge; -e-e* as in *fete; -ee* as in *matinee* and *melee,* and *-et* as in *sachet* and *ballet.*

/eɪ/ WORDS

Initial		*Medial*		*Final*	
age	apex	bake	label	may	neigh
ache	eight	came	baby	bay	weigh
aid	aviary	date	making	say	decay
aim	alien	face	placed	spray	away
able	apron	steak	taper	they	matinee
ape	acre	gain	relation	prey	ballet

/eɪ/ SENTENCES

1. They say the paper may decay.
2. The ape weighed eight hundred and eighty pounds.
3. James and Kate came to play today.
4. The agent placed the tapes on the tray.

5. L*a*bel the b*a*by's pl*ay* p*ai*l and cl*ay*.
6. The *a*miable wh*a*le *spray*ed his n*eigh*bor.

/eɪ/ CONTRASTS

/eɪ/—/ɛ/		/eɪ/—/ɪ/	
mate	met	mate	mit
date	debt	late	lit
bait	bet	tame	Tim
rake	wreck	weight	wit
main	men	bait	bit
gate	get	hate	hit
laid	led	chain	chin
fade	fed	fate	fit

Note: when *ai-*, *a-e*, or other spellings associated with /eɪ/ occur with /r/, as in *air* and *bare*, the vowel may be heard and transcribed as /eɪ/, /e/, or /ɛ/. The *ai-* or *a-e* before /l/, as in *ail* and *bale*, may be transcribed as /eɪ/ or without the glide as /e/, according to listener judgment.

In American-English, the /eɪ/ occurs usually with primary accent in words such as *átrium*, *máking*, and *matinée*. It also occurs with secondary accent as in polysyllabic words with the *-ate* endings of *lúbricáte*, *incórporáte*, and *mítigáte*. But when unaccented, it is produced and transcribed as a pure or monothong vowel /e/. This usually occurs when the sound is in the syllable next to the accented syllable, as can be seen in the form changes of the following pairs of words:

/eɪ/	/e/
nátive	natívity
fátal	fatálity
vácate	vacátion
cháos	chaótic

Note that the unaccented /e/ may also be pronounced /ə/ in some of these words. The unaccented /e/ also occurs in bisyllabic words ending in an unaccented *-ate* such as *dónate*, *órate*, *víbrate*, and *rébate*, immediately following the accented syllable. As the last sound of an utterance, it is usually transcribed as /eɪ/.

European speakers should observe that American-English /eɪ/ is a diphthong and not the monothong /e/ they are used to producing as in the French *les* [le] and the Spanish *se* [se].

IPA   ou
Dictionary   ō Key Words: *own, boat, no*
General American oa (-o, o-e)

/ou/ PRODUCTION—Back Round Diphthong

With the velopharyngeal port closed, the middle and back portion of the tongue is raised toward the palate, slightly lower than for /u/, the lips are rounded and may be slightly protruded for an aperture larger than for /u/ as voice is given; then the tongue briefly rises toward the /u/ height and the rounded lip aperture decreases in size as voice continues. The tip of the tongue touches lightly behind the lower front teeth. The [o] portion is the longer nucleus and the [u] is the shorter glide. For many speakers, the glide portion may have a tongue-lip position close to /u/ but of short duration.

/ou/ SPELLING

o occurs most frequently as in *hold, both, old, go, no, so*.

-o-e is very consistently /ou/ as in *home, note, mole, rose, hope,* and *smoke*.

ow as in *blow, crow, row, owe, own, throw*.

oa- as in *road, boat, moan, oats, oak, whoa*.

-oe as in *toe, hoe, doe, sloe, woe, roe*.

Irregular spellings include *-au-* as in *chauffer, -eau* as in *beau, -ew* as in *sew, -ough* as in *though* and *dough, -eo-* as in *yeoman, -oo-* as in *brooch,* and *-ou-* as in *soul*.

/ou/ WORDS

Initial		*Medial*		*Final*	
oak	ocean	boat	toes	go	toe
oats	over	pole	thrown	no	hoe
only	oaf	code	both	so	woe
opal	odor	showed	rose	row	sew
own	omen	broke	hope	low	dough
open	oval	road	smoke	bow	though

/ou/ SENTENCES

1. The cr*ow* was sl*ow*ly going h*o*m*e*.
2. *The b*oa*t goes *o*ver the *o*cean.

3. Joe wrote the note in code.
4. The doe's bones won't grow.
5. Don't throw snow at the pony.
6. Those roses have their own odor.

/ou/ CONTRASTS

/ou/—/u/		/ou/—/ɔ/	
pole	pull	phone	fawn
bowl	bull	boat	bought
code	could	coat	caught
showed	should	pose	paws
stowed	stood	tote	taught
goad	good	bowl	bawl
broke	brook	coal	call
coke	cook	foal	fall

Note: when o, oa-, o-e, or other spellings associated with /ou/ occur with /r/, as in for, oar, and bore, the vowel may be heard and transcribed as /ou/, /o/, or /ɔ/, and dialectically as /ɑ/. The o, oa-, and o-e, and other spellings before /l/, as in cold, coal, and hole, may be transcribed as /ou/ or without the glide as /o/, according to listener judgment.

In American-English, the /ou/ occurs usually with primary accent in words such as only, emotion, and below. It also occurs with secondary accent in polysyllabic words such as telephone, monotone, and chromosome. When unaccented, it is traditionally transcribed as a pure or monothong vowel /o/. This usually occurs when the sound is in the syllable next to the accented syllable as can be seen in the form changes of the following pairs of words:

/ou/	/o/
rótate	rotátion
lócate	locátion
dónate	donátion
prórate	prorátion

The unaccented /o/ also occurs in words just before the accented syllable as in obey, opinion, omission, and obese, and after the accented syllable as in geode. As the final unaccented syllable in window, polo, pillow, elbow, and potato, the sound may be transcribed either /o/ or /ou/, according to listener judgment. As the last sound of an utterance, it is usually transcribed as /ou/, even when unstressed.

aɪ

IPA aɪ
Dictionary ī Key Words: *ice, mine, my*
General American i-e (igh, -y)

/aɪ/ PRODUCTION—Low Back to High Front Diphthong

With the velopharyngeal port closed and the mouth open as for /æ/, the middle and front portion of the tongue is raised more than for /ʌ/ but less than for /æ/ while voice is given; then the tongue briefly rises in front toward the /ɪ/ height and the mouth opening is slightly decreased as voice continues. The tip of the tongue touches lightly behind the lower front teeth. The [a] portion is the longer nucleus and the [ɪ] portion is the shorter glide. For some speakers, the nucleus may be closer to the /ɑ/ position and the glide close to /i/ but of short duration.

/aɪ/ SPELLING

i occurs most frequently but inconsistently as /aɪ/ as in *child, mild, find, wild, mind, idol, idea, alibi, I.*

i-e occurs less frequently but more consistently as in *ice, ride, file, bike, time, kite, chide.*

-y as in *by, why, my, cry, deny, nylon, psychology, ply, fry.*

-ie as in *die, vie, pie, tie, cried, lie.*

-igh as in *high, fight, light, might, night, right.*

Less frequently and irregularly *-y-e* as in *type, style, Clyde; -ui-* as in *guide, beguile; -ye* as in *rye, dye, lye; -uy* as in *buy, guy; -ei-* as in *height, sleight; -oi-* as in *choir;* and spelled *eye* or *aye.*

/aɪ/ WORDS

Initial		Medial		Final	
ice	item	find	light	by	die
ivy	idea	child	psyche	my	lie
idle	icicle	wild	shine	guy	sigh
iris	eyes	kind	fright	deny	bye
aisle	eyed	pine	type	thigh	buy
ivory	island	hide	height	sky	rye

/aɪ/ SENTENCES

1. *I* tri*ed* to fl*y* the k*i*t*e*.
2. M*y* g*ui*de l*i*kes *i*ce cream.
3. The ch*i*ld's b*i*ke is the r*i*ght s*i*ze.
4. T*i*me has been m*igh*ty kind to Cl*y*de.
5. Wh*y* does the br*i*de wish to b*uy* a f*i*le?
6. M*y* *eye*s are t*i*red from cr*y*ing.

/aɪ/ CONTRASTS

/aɪ/—/ɑ/		/aɪ/—/ɪ/		/aɪ/—/aʊ/	
type	top	ride	rid	dine	down
ride	rod	fine	fin	mice	mouse
pipe	pop	like	lick	nine	noun
like	lock	type	tip	lied	loud
light	lot	sign	sin	by	bow
fire	far	hide	hid	high	how
side	sod	light	lit	file	fowl
hide	hod	bite	bit	spite	spout

Note: the /aɪ/ occurs in stresséd syllables and does not have an unstressed transcription as do /eɪ/ and /oʊ/. When a speaker strongly downgrades stress for an /aɪ/ spelling, the unstressed sound may become either /ɪ/ or /ə/. Note the following possible pronunciations in these stress situations:

	Stressed /aɪ/	Unstressed to /ɪ/	Unstressed to /ə/
psychólogy	[saɪkɑlədʒɪ]	[sɪkɑlədʒɪ]	[səkɑlədʒɪ]
critéria	[kraɪtɪrɪə]	[krɪtɪrɪə]	[krətɪrɪə]
gigántic	[dʒaɪgæntɪk]	[dʒɪgæntɪk]	[dʒəgæntɪk]

The /a/ occurs alone in American-English primarily in New England dialect and in some stage speech, taking the mouth position for /æ/ with the tongue height between /æ/ and /ʌ/, in such words as the following:

	General American	New England
ask	[æsk]	[ask]
path	[pæθ]	[paθ]
park	[pɑrk]	[pak]
car	[kɑr]	[ka:]

IPA   aʊ
Dictionary   ou Key Words: *out, loud, now*
General American   ou (ow)

/aʊ/ PRODUCTION—Low Back to High Back Round Diphthong

With the velopharyngeal port closed and the mouth opened as for /æ/, the middle and front portion of the tongue is raised more than for /ʌ/ but less than for /æ/ while voice is given; then the tongue briefly rises in the back toward the /ʊ/ height, the mouth opening is slightly decreased and the lips are round as for /ʊ/ as voice continues. The tip of the tongue touches lightly behind the lower front teeth and may move back slightly for the /ʊ/ portion. The [a] portion is the longer nucleus and the [ʊ] portion is the shorter glide. For some speakers, the nucleus may be closer to the /ɑ/ position and the glide close to /u/ but of short duration.

/aʊ/ SPELLING

ou- occurs frequently and consistently as in *out, mouse, found, mouth, shout, ground, ouch.*

ow occurs frequently as in *owl, fowl, cow, town, plow, howl, allow.*

Irregularly and infrequently *-ough* as in *bough, drought; -au-* as in *Faust, kraut; hou-* with silent *h* as in *hour.*

/aʊ/ WORDS

Initial		Medial		Final	
out	outlaw	count	town	now	vow
ouch	outline	found	fowl	cow	endow
ounce	outfit	mouse	gown	sow	allow
oust	output	doubt	dowel	prow	somehow
ours	outlet	noun	towel	how	eyebrow
owl	hour	about	brown	bough	thou

/aʊ/ SENTENCES

1. I doubt that the trout is now out of the water.
2. Count us out for about an hour.
3. Our brown cow has been found.
4. The mouth is rounded for the /aʊ/ sound.
5. The scouts are around the outside of the house.
6. A loud shout left no doubt about the cow.

/aʊ/ CONTRASTS

/aʊ/—/ɑ/		/aʊ/—/ʌ/		/aʊ/—/aɪ/	
shout	shot	town	ton	down	dine
spout	spot	down	done	mouse	mice
down	don	gown	gun	noun	nine
cowed	cod	bout	butt	loud	lied
scout	Scott	found	fund	bow	by
gout	got	cowl	cull	how	high
pout	pot	noun	nun	fowl	file
tout	tot	pout	putt	spout	spite

Note: the /aʊ/ occurs in stressed syllables and does not have an unstressed transcription as do /eɪ/ and /oʊ/. The /a/ occurs alone in American-English primarily in New England dialect and in some stage speech, taking the mouth position for /æ/ with tongue height between /æ/ and /ʌ/, in such words as the following:

	General American	*New England*
ask	[æsk]	[ask]
path	[pæθ]	[paθ]
park	[pɑrk]	[pak]
car	[kɑr]	[kaː]

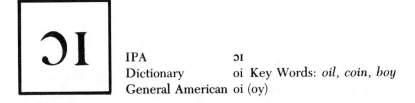

IPA   ɔɪ
Dictionary   oi Key Words: *oil, coin, boy*
General American oi (oy)

/ɔɪ/ PRODUCTION—Back Round to High Front Diphthong

With the velopharyngeal port closed, the back and middle portion of the tongue is slightly raised with elevation as for /ɔ/, the mouth is open for /ɔ/ with lips rounded and slightly protruded as voice is given; then the lip rounding relaxes and the tongue briefly rises toward the /ɪ/ height as voice continues. The lower jaw may move upward from the opening of /ɔ/ to the smaller opening of /ɪ/. The [ɔ] portion is the longer nucleus and the [ɪ] portion is the shorter glide. For many speakers, the glide portion may have a tongue-mouth position close to /i/ but for short duration.

/ɔɪ/ SPELLING

oi- most frequently as in *oil, ointment, voice, coin, foil, Detroit.*
oy frequently as in *oyster, soy, coy, loyal, boycott, boy, toy.*

/ɔɪ/ WORDS

Initial	*Medial*		*Final*	
oil	foil	boycott	boy	toy
oiler	coin	royal	soy	deploy
ointment	voice	mastoid	coy	cloy
oyster	join	appoint	joy	enjoy
	soil	goiter	Roy	destroy
	loin	thyroid	poi	Troy

/ɔɪ/ SENTENCES

1. The royal boy enjoyed his toys.
2. Oysters help avoid thyroid goiters.
3. The ploy was poised to destroy Troy.
4. Roy's noise annoyed the envoy.
5. Boiling oil will foil the spoilers.
6. They deployed a destroyer as decoy for the convoy.

/ɔɪ/ CONTRASTS

/ɔɪ/—/aɪ/		/ɔɪ/—/ɔ/		/ɔɪ/—/ɝ/	
toil	tile	coil	call	oil	earl
poise	pies	foil	fall	loin	learn
toys	ties	toil	tall	voice	verse
loin	line	boil	ball	boil	burl
foil	file	joy	jaw	poise	purrs
boy	buy	cloy	claw	boys	burrs
voice	vice	noise	gnaws	royal	rural
oil	aisle	soy	saw	coil	curl

Note: an /ɔɪ/ for /ɝ/, and an /ɝ/ for /ɔɪ/ substitution occurs in non-standard urban New York pronunciation as in [gɔɪl] for *girl* and [ɝl] for *oil.*

REVIEW VOCABULARY

Accent—stress on a syllable within a word.

Back vowels—vowels with resonance influenced by raising of the back of the tongue (include /u/, /ʊ/, /ɔ/, and /ɑ/).

Front vowels—vowels with resonance influenced by raising of the front of the tongue (include /i/, /ɪ/, /ɛ/, and /æ/).

Mixed vowels—vowels with resonance influenced by raising the middle of the tongue or with no tongue elevation (include /a/, /ʌ/, and /ɝ/.

Round vowels—vowels with resonance influenced by rounding and slightly protruding the lips (include /u/, /ʊ/, and /ɔ/).

Stress—pointing up or drawing special attention to a unit of speech.

EXERCISES

1. Place the following front vowels in order of tongue elevation:

    /ɛ/   /e/   /i/   /æ/   /ɪ/

2. Place the following back vowels in order of tongue elevation:

    /ʊ/   /o/   /ɑ/   /u/   /ɔ/

3. From memory, draw the vowel diagram and fill in static vowel phonemes. Be sure to label the two dimensions. Check Figure IV–1.

4. Pronounce and transliterate into Roman alphabet symbols the following nonsense monosyllabic units:

[gɪf]	[ʌik]	[θɔk]	[stɔɪp]
[mɛŋ]	[saʊp]	[kʌut]	[kɪb]
[ʃɑlt]	[ðæd]	[vɛbz]	[fiʒ]
[zuθ]	[bɑv]	[heɪm]	[æŋk]

5. Pronounce and transliterate into Roman alphabet symbols the following nonsense bisyllabic units, being sure to observe accent where vowel transcriptions indicate:

[teɪdəs]   [haɪskɚ]   [splinod]
[jɚmæb]   [frɔɪθəʃ]   [hɝslɪg]
[wɑvlʌt]   [ðautn̩]   [kʌodʒub]
[tʃoumbet]   [bekɪz]   [priŋed]

SUGGESTED READING

Bronstein, Arthur J.: *The Pronunciation of American English.* Englewood Cliffs, N.J., Prentice-Hall, Inc., 1960

Chapters 7, 8, 9, and 10 survey the vowels and diphthongs of American English (pp. 131–204) with numerous diagrams to show tongue height and positioning.

Griffith, Jerry, and Miner, Lynn E.: *Phonetic Context Drillbook.* Englewood Cliffs, N.J., Prentice-Hall, Inc., 1979

This paperback provides for each of the American-English vowels and diphthongs a wide variety of phonetic contexts in words, phrases and sentences that are used in everyday language. The practice words are selected from among those most commonly used.

Singh, Sadanand and Singh, Kala: *Phonetics Principles and Practices.* Baltimore, University Park Press, 1982.

Chapter 6., "Dynamic Aspects of Speech Production," presents a novel display of sequential photos of mouth positions for vowel sounds in productions somewhat exaggerated for demonstration.

Chapter V

CONNECTED SPEECH AND THE INFLUENCE OF CONTEXT

The previous chapters have analyzed the elements of our speech, treating them as segments to be described and considered individually. This has been necessary to understand the make-up of speech. At the same time, we have warned that such analysis is somewhat artificial, since speech does not actually occur in discrete segments. In normal speech—i.e., real connected speech—speech sounds do not follow one another as separate and distinct units like beads on a string. Rather, the necessary movements of the articulators from the place and manner of one sound to those of the next influence the way each phoneme is produced. The influence of adjoining sounds upon each other is called **coarticulation**. Coarticulation occurs for any unit of connected speech so that even in a simple word like *pin*, the influence of the [ɪ] in the nucleus of the syllable is apparent in both the [p] and the [n] sounds, in how they are formed as well as how they sound. A vowel such as the low front /æ/, with a fairly wide mouth opening. can influence the way two or three or even four other sounds before it are produced.

In some cases, vowels in context do not actually reach the target production described for them in the analyses of Chapter IV, but merely head for that target before merging into the following sound. In instrumental analysis, either physiologic or acoustic, it is often impossible to mark an exact place where one sound ends and the next begins. Since we have over 40 phonemes in American-English and thousands of words, the possible variations caused by phonetic context can be extensive. Here we point out a few of the most significant effects of the context of connected speech, some of which influence phonetic transcription.

INFLUENCES OF CONTEXT

Place of Articulation

The place of articulation of a consonant or a vowel varies with the vowels or consonants that precede or follow it. The specific place where the tongue touches the roof of the mouth to produce /k/, for example, differs depending upon whether the adjoining vowel is made by elevating the front of the tongue (as for /i/) or the back of the tongue (as for /u/). Figure V–1 illustrates these different points of contact for the /k/ phoneme on the palate and on the velum, respectively. This slight difference in place of tongue contact on syllables [kik] and [kuk] results in predictable changes in the acoustic characteristics of /k/. Even though both [k] allophones are recognized as

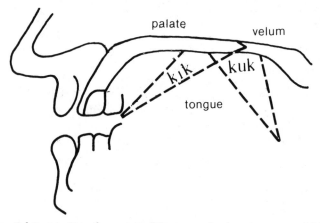

Figure V–1.   Relative positions for contact of the tongue for the stop portion of /k/ associated with the front vowel /i/ and with the back vowel /u/.

representing the phoneme /k/, coarticulation with vowels has made them different acoustically. This slight acoustic difference in the [k] may provide important cues for the listener in distinguishing whether the adjoining vowel sound was [i] or [u]. Similarly, when the consonant sound is different, as in syllables [ik] and [it], the relative position of the tongue contact to produce [k] (on the palate) and to produce [t] (on the alveolar ridge) influences the sound of the adjoining vowel [i] so that it is slightly different in the two syllables.

Voicing

Although phonemes have previously been described as being either voiceless or voiced sounds, the presence of voicing in their allophones is markedly influenced by coarticulation. When a breath sound like /t/ is produced in rapid speech between two voiced sounds (the intervocalic position) as in the word *butter*, it tends to be partially voiced as [bʌt̬ɚ], falling between the sounds of /t/ and /d/. The allophone of /t/ in such a word may be heard with voicing ranging from [bʌtʰɚ] with full aspiration, to [bʌt̬ɚ] with very light aspiration and some voicing, to [bʌdɚ], which is voiced and not aspirated. Similarly, the /r/ and /l/, though usually considered voiced consonants, when blended with a preceding voiceless consonant are produced almost without voicing, especially where they join the preceding voiceless consonant. Note in the following pairs of words that the /r/ and /l/ are produced in the first word with voice and in the second almost without voice:

ray [reɪ]—pray [pr̥eɪ]	lie [laɪ]—ply [pl̥aɪ]
rue [ru]—true [tr̥u]	lay [leɪ]—clay [kl̥eɪ]
rye [raɪ]—fry [fr̥aɪ]	low [lou]—slow [sl̥ou]
row [rou]—crow [kr̥ou]	lee [li]—flee [fl̥i]

The narrow transcription symbols (see Table 1–4) of [ˌ] for voicing and [̥] for indicating voiceless breath are useful when careful transcription of these subtle differences is important.

Duration

Length of vowel sounds is influenced by the manner of articulation of the consonant that follows them. Vowels are typically shorter before a stop consonant or affricate than before a fricative or resonant consonant.

Note that the vowel is of greater duration in the first word of these pairs:

ease — eat
if   — it
us   — up
tame — take

The vowel is also of shorter duration before a voiceless stop or affricate than before its voiced counterpart, made in the same position. Note the difference in vowel duration in the following pairs of words:

edge	— etch	sub	— sup
ad	— at	bag	— back
lab	— lap	sued	— suit

Notice how the vowel duration differs in these sets of words even though the consonant has the same place of articulation:

ad	— an	— at
cub	— come	— cup
lug	— lung	— luck

Double letters in the same syllable as in *butter* and *summer* are produced as a single consonant sound. However, when the same consonants join at the end of one word and the beginning of the other, they are produced as one sound but the duration is usually extended. Compare *summer* [sʌmɚ] with *some more* [sʌmːor], *falling* [fɔlɪŋ] with *fall line* [fɔlːaɪn]. The stop phase of similarly combined stop consonants is also held longer as in *hot time* [hɑtːaɪm], *top pair* [tɑpːɛr], and *black cat* [blækːæt].

Release of Stops

Stop consonants have the possibility of both a stop or closure and an aspiration or release action. An initial voiceless stop followed by a vowel is both stopped and audibly aspirated as in *pie*. But when the stop is preceded by /s/, as in *spy*, it is unaspirated but the breath pressure is released to begin voicing for the vowel that follows. The sound of the [p] in the *sp-* combination may be heard as sounding very close to the /b/ sound but of somewhat greater duration. Compare [spɑ] with [sbɑ], [stu] with [sdu], and [ski] with [sgi]. In considering the similarity of these sounds, it is noteworthy that English does not have [sb], [sd], or [sg] combinations in words, so that the confusion does not influence meaning.

Stop consonants at the end of utterances are frequently not released or are released so gently that they are not audible. In the word *up*, for example, the [p] need not be released because the influence of lip closure on the termination of the [ʌ] vowel presents the listener with sufficient acoustic information about the place of articulation of the final sound to know that the /p/ phoneme was present. If the place of articulation of the adjoining sound is similar, however, the final stop must be aspirated to be distinguished. In the word *amp*, the [m] and [pʻ] are both articulated at the lips. The final [pʻ] must be exploded in order to be heard. Similarly, if the manner of articulation of the last two sounds is the same, that is if they are both stops, the final stop must be exploded to be distinguished. Note that in *at*, the [t] can be unreleased but in *apt* or *act*, it must be released with an audible explosion.

Consonant Blends

When two consonants adjoin within a syllable and the first uses part of the speech mechanism not necessary to produce the second, the position of the two consonants may be taken simultaneously so that they are produced in very rapid succession as a **consonant blend**. For example, in the word *blue*, the position for the [l] with the tongue point against the alveolar ridge can be taken while the lips are still closed for the [b]. When they are released, the [l] is of very brief duration, a glide, between the [b] and [u]. If the [l] position is not taken simultaneously with the [b] position, an /ə/ sound is likely to intrude between [b] and [l]. The combinations of [br] as in *breeze*, [pɹ̥] as in *pray*, and [pl̥] as in *play* are other examples of such blends. The [kl̥] combination as in *clay* can also be a blend as the back of the tongue can make a closure on the palate for the [k] position, while the point of the tongue simultaneously touches the alveolar ridge in anticipation of the [l̥]. The [gl], [kɹ̥], and [gr] combinations are other examples of this kind of consonant blend.

Abutting Consonants

When two stops occur successively but in separate syllables, as the [tp] in *footpath* or the [db] in *hardball*, instead of closures and releases for each of the stops, there is a lingua-alveolar closure, followed immediately by a bilabial closure, and a single release from the latter position. Note the closures and single release in *woodcraft*, *black tie*, *football*, and *lab coat*. When the stops are made in the same position, as in *hotdog*, *hip bone*, and *black gown*, only a single closure and release is needed with an appropriate change in voicing and aspiration. When the same stops abut as in *black cat*, *mad dog*, and *big girl*, a single stop is closed and released but the closure period is usually held for a longer time, as in *black key* [blæk:i].

When a stop is followed immediately by a fricative, an affricate-like sound is derived. Note, however, that the secondary affricate formed in producing *white shoe* [ʍaɪtʃu] is different from the primary affricate in *why chew* [ʍaɪtʃu], in that the closure of [t] in *white shoe* is held longer to give it identity, whereas the [tʃ] in *why chew* is produced on a single impulse. Other secondary affricates may be formed as [kʃ] in *makeshift*, [ts] in *hot stove*, [pf] in *hop farm*, [df] in *headfirst*, and [ks] in *backside*. Among these, only [ks] and [kʍ] have associated alphabet letters, the *x* and the *qu*, respectively.

Syllabic Consonants

Resonant consonants in the final position may take the full durational value of a syllable, without an associated vowel, when they follow a consonant made in essentially the same position, or in positions that permit a consonant blend. In the word *kitten* [kɪtṇ], the homorganic [t] and [n] have a common lingua-alveolar place of articulation so that the tongue need not move when the /t/ stop is released as a nasal /n/. Note the syllabic final consonant in *ridden* [rɪdṇ], *stop 'em* [stɑpm̩], and *bottle* [bɑtl̩]. In the blends of *uncle* [ʌŋkl̩] and *eagle* [igl̩], the syllabic /l/ can also be formed.

Intrusion

When nasal resonant consonants /m/, /n/, and /ŋ/ immediately precede a voiceless fricative such as /s/ or /θ/, a voiceless stop sound with closure in the same position as the nasal consonant is likely to intrude. Note that in the word *chance*, a [t] stop is produced between the [n] and [s] sounds to form [ʧænts], as though the word were spelled *chants*. During the closure of the [n], some breath pressure is necessarily built up in preparation for the fricative [s] that follows. Release of that pressure into the [s] creates the sound of the aspiration of a lingua-alveolar voiceless stop, or /t/. In the word *length*, the intruding stop takes the lingua-palatal position for /k/ to produce [lɛŋkθ]. A [p] may similarly be created at the juncture of [m] and [θ] in *something*.

The glides [w] and [j] are sometimes intruded in order to separate vowels that end one word and begin another. Following /u/ as in *to eat*, a glide [w] may bridge between [u] and the following [i] to form [tuwit]. Note the same intrusion after lip rounded vowels as in *go on* [gouwɑn], *New England* [nuwɪŋglənd], and *bow out* [bauwaut]. Following the high front vowels /i/ or /ɪ/, a [j] sound may intrude as in *see it* [sijɪt], *die out* [daɪjaut], and *stay in* [steɪjɪn].

Assimilation

To simplify the motions of articulation, one adjoining consonant may partially or completely conform to the manner or place of articulation of the other. Nasal resonant consonants are especially susceptible to accommodation or partial assimilation, taking the place of articulation of the following sound. For example, the /n/ before a /k/ sound takes the place of articulation of the /k/, that is, the back of the tongue against the palate or velum, changing the nasal from /n/ to /ŋ/ as in the words *ink, thank, think, bank, sunk, income,* and *pancake*. The /n/ also changes to an /ŋ/ position before /g/ as in *single* or *finger*. The /m/ may change, too, toward the /k/ and /g/ position as in the word *pumpkin*, often becoming [pʌŋkɪn]. Note the assimilation as *handkerchief* becomes [hæŋkɚʧɪf].

Complete assimilation may take place when the manner and place of articulation of adjoining sounds are very similar, as is shown in dropping the [s] in *this show* [ðɪʃou] and *horseshoe* [horʃu], while producing the dominant [ʃ] sound. The words *cupboard* and *kiln* are examples of equalization or complete assimilation, where omission of the /p/ before /b/ and the /n/ following /l/ are so common as to have become standard pronunciation.

Omission

A number of speech sounds are omitted in connected speech. The most apparent of these is the vowel sound in *not* when that word is unstressed. The omission from speech of this sound in *can't, wouldn't, didn't,* and *haven't* is marked by an apostrophe in writing. The /h/ and /ð/ are also frequently dropped in rapid connected speech as *Where is he?* becomes [ʍɛrɪzi], and *Stop them!* becomes [stɑpm̩]. Final consonants of words are occasionally omitted during rapid speech as *Let me go!* becomes [lɛ mi gou]. Whole syllables may be omitted in the phenomenon called "haplology" when two very similar syllables occur in close succession. *Mississippi*, for example, is often pronounced [mɪsɪpi] by natives of that state rather than [mɪsəsɪpi]. *Coca Cola* may similarly become [koukoulə]. When a different sound occurs between two sounds that are essentially the same to cause a difficult articulation, as in *-sts*, the intervening sound may be omitted and the first sound is elongated. Examples are the *-sts* in *guests*, which is often pronounced [gɛs:], or the *-sks* in *asks*, which may become [æs:]. Similarly, when a final /ɚ/ follows an /r/ as in *mirror* or *bearer*, the words may be said as [mɪr:] or [bɛr:]. To say "5/6," one encounters [sɪksθs] in the last syllable, which regularly becomes [sɪks] or [sɪkts].

The Glottal Stop

In addition to the voiceless stops /p/, /t/, and /k/, produced by the lips, tongue, and palate in the oral cavity, an abrupt hiatus of voicing can be produced at the glottis by closing the vocal folds tightly and then releasing them to continue voicing. This **glottal stop** is written as /ʔ/ in the IPA. It is often used in General American to separate two words when the first ends and the next begins with a vowel. The glottal stop is especially needed to separate /ə/ or /ʌ/ and any following vowel as in *the uncle* [ðəʔʌŋkl̩], *the only* [ðəʔounlɪ], and *the apple* [ðəʔæpl]. In the phrase *he eats*, two [i] sounds adjoin and when produced together might be confused with the word *heats*. The simple elongation of [i:] leaves the meaning ambiguous so that it is helpful to stop voicing very briefly between the words for them to be distinguished as in [hiʔ its] and *we even* [wiʔ ivən]. Of course the speaker may, instead, insert a [j] glide to separate the vowels as in *he eats* [hijits], described previously in the section on intrusion. The glottal stop also occurs in [i] and [ɪŋ] sequences such as in *being* [biʔɪŋ].

In conversational General American speech, the glottal stop is sometimes substituted for /t/ between the homorganic /n/ and /n/ as in *mountain* [maʊnˀn̩], *sentence* [sɛnˀn̩ts], *Denton* [dɛnˀn̩], *Scranton* [skrænˀn̩], and *Benton* [bɛnˀn̩]. A similar substitution may be made between /l/ and /n/ as in *Hilton* [hɪlˀn̩] and Skelton [skɛlˀn̩]. Some New York City speakers habitually substitute the /ˀ/ for /t/ in such words as *bottle* [bɑˀl̩] and *little* [lɪˀl̩]. Hawaiian words, with their heavy use of vowels, make extensive use of the glottal stop for separation as in *nuuanu* [nuˀuɑnu] and *Hawaii* [hɑwɑiˀi].

Influence of /r/ and /l/ Sounds

The /r/ and /l/ have very strong influence on adjoining speech sounds. As resonant sounds, they are like vowels but with the tongue intruding more into the oral cavity. Following a pure or monothong vowel, movement of the tongue toward the point-upward /r/ or /l/ position during continued voicing creates a diphthong sound. The word *eel*, which appears to have just the two sounds [i] and [l], actually sounds like [iəl], [iɪl], or [ijl]. Similarly, in *school* and *poor*, movement of the tongue creates an /ə/ following the vowel. By convention, this /ə/ sound between the vowel and the /r/ or /l/ is not transcribed unless very prominent. It is an understood influence of the /r/ and the /l/ sounds.

When spelling suggests the /i/ before /r/ as in such words as *beer, here, year, peer,* and *rear,* positioning of the tongue in anticipation of the /r/ makes the vowel much closer to /ɪ/. Even though *bean* would be transcribed [bin], *beer* would be transcribed [bɪr], unless the vowel were especially emphasized as [i]. Similarly, the /eɪ/ before /r/ is difficult to distinguish. Although the vowel in *bake* is clearly /eɪ/, the vowel in *bare* may be heard as either /ɛ/ for a transcription of [bɛr], as /e/ for a transcription of [ber], or as /eɪ/ for a transcription of [beɪr]. If the /e/ is diphthongized for a full /eɪ/, the word *bare* might sound like [beɪjɚ], suggesting two syllables and the name *Bayer.* The words *care, dare, fair, hair, pear, heir,* and *mare* offer similar difficulty. Again, the /oʊ/ before /r/, articulated as a diphthong, would create a triphthong sound for *ore* to become [oʊɚ] or [oʊwɚ]. It is more appropriately transcribed as [or], but it may be pronounced [or], [ɔr], [ɑr], or [oʊɚ] in the United States. The same would be true for the words *core, for, door, port, course, court, four, forest,* and *orange.* For General American, the following transcriptions are recommended:

> beer   [bɪr]
> bare   [bɛr]
> bore   [bor]

The listener should use the alternative transcriptions to indicate subtle differences in pronunciation by a speaker or group of speakers.

The diphthongs /eɪ/ and /ou/, when they immediately precede an /l/ sound, may similarly be transcribed without their glide, unless the speaker emphasizes the glide portion. The words *pale* and *bail* may be written [pel] and [bel] unless the speaker gives obvious emphasis to the glides for [peɪl] and [beɪl]. Similarly, the words *bowl* and *hole* may be transcribed [bol] and [hol] unless heard as [boul] or [bouwəl], and [houl], respectively.

DIFFICULT ARTICULATIONS

Articulating speech sounds is a skill. Some speech sounds require greater skill and are more difficult to master than others as we are learning speech. Certain sequences and clusters of speech sounds in words also seem more difficult to articulate than others. Consonants (C) separated by vowels (V) seem easiest, as in words like *bee* (CV), *cap* (CVC), *above* (VCVC), and *relate* (CVCVC). Consonants in clusters are more difficult in words like *desks* (CVCCC), *scream* (CCCVC), *spliced* (CCCVCC), *pharynx* (CVCVCCC), and *sixths* (CVCCCC). People with otherwise accurate articulation occasionally stumble over difficult or unfamiliar words with clusters of consonants. Many words with such clusters are habitually mispronounced by a large portion of American-English speakers. Among these are the following:

Word	Desirable Pronunciation	Common Mispronunciation	Articulation Change
library	[laɪbrɛrɪ]	[laɪbɛrɪ]	omit second consonant
arctic	[ɑrktɪk]	[ɑrtɪk]	omit third consonant
athlete	[æθlit]	[æθəlit]	insert vowel
diphthong	[dɪfθɔŋ]	[dɪpθɔŋ]	change consonant
realtor	[riltɚ]	[rilətɚ]	insert vowel
nuclear	[nukliɚ]	[nukjulɚ]	insert vowel
asterisk	[æstɚɪsk]	[æstɚɪk]	omit second consonant
guests	[gɛsts]	[gɛs:]	omit medial consonant
mirror	[mɪrɚ]	[mɪr:]	omit syllable

Other words commonly mispronounced include *chimney, larynx, ophthalmologist, subsidiary, exorbitant, liaison, jeopardy, recognize, suggest,* and *temperature.*

Especially difficult sequences of words are called "tongue-twisters." Children verbally wrestling with "she says she sells sea shells" is a common part of American-English culture. Peter Piper and his proverbial "peck of pickled peppers" has been traced to an English grammar* published in London in 1674, but it was probably around by word of mouth much earlier. Rapid repetition of the apparently simple name "Peggy Babcock" is reputed to be one of the most difficult tongue-twisters in the language.

What makes these particular sequences so difficult? Seldom are the words difficult by themselves. There are no difficult clusters of consonants in a phrase like *she says she sells*. It is apparent that the problem comes from the sequence of consonants that are highly similar in some aspects of articulation but different in another. The difficulty is in our ability to control the anticipation of sequences to come, or our "feed forward" mechanism. For example, two fricatives made with turbulence against the front teeth, but with the slight difference in tongue position of /s/ and /ʃ/, are placed in a sequence of /ʃ/-/s/, /ʃ/-/s/ (*she says she sells*) and then reversed /s/-/ʃ/ (*sea shells*), changing the pattern slightly but apparently beyond the ability of our physiologic speech mechanism to manage with rapid repetitions. To test this, the reader should try repeating the following sequence rapidly without vowels: [ʃsʃssʃ], [ʃsʃssʃ], [ʃsʃssʃ]. *Peggy Babcock* is loaded with stop consonants (/p, g, b/) made at different places of articulation and in clusters. The simple combination of *Greek grapes* loads the system with lingua-velar stops (/g, k/) and throws a bilabial stop (/p/) into the sequence to break the rhythm. The word *lemon* can be repeated rapidly with little trouble and *linament* can be repeated with only a little more difficulty. But combine the two and repeat *lemon linament* rapidly, and the best articulator will be helpless. Here are a few other twisters, notable for their brevity and simplicity, for the reader to say or repeat rapidly and to analyze:

> We surely shall see the sun shine soon.
> Which wristwatches are Swiss wristwatches?
> Toy Boat
> Unique New York
> His shirt soon shrank in the suds.
> Shave a cedar shingle thin.
> A cup of coffee in a copper coffee pot.
> Thirty-three free throws.
> Soldiers' shoulders.

ANALYSIS OF CONNECTED SPEECH

Speech can be analyzed and described at a variety of phonetic levels. The important effects of coarticulation, just pointed out, make it clear that a static phoneme-by-phoneme view of speech is a great over-simplification. It is a useful starting place, but stopping at that level of analysis would overlook the important allophonic differences as well as the transitions from one

---

*Wallis, John: *Grammatica Linguae Anglicanae*. Oxford, 1674.

sound to another. We speak only in connected coarticulated speech and we apparently depend upon the normal flow of speech in order to understand it. On the other hand, because of the immense complexity of speech—the neurologic innervation, the sequences of muscular action, the movements of structures, and the aerodynamic variations that must occur—some very sophisticated equipment and hours of careful measurement would be required to delineate exhaustively all that occurs in producing a simple utterance like [kæt]. Instrumental physiologic phonetics is concerned with the study of just such phenomena.

However, it is also possible to describe the actions that occur more briefly and in general terms. Such descriptions of the sequences involved in connected speech may serve both as an introduction to further study of speech dynamics and for the immediate uses of practical or applied descriptive phonetics. We can begin to describe units of connected speech using the tools we have at hand: phonetic symbols (Chapter I), basic knowledge of the speech mechanism and processes (Chapter II), vocabulary and understanding about the place of articulation and manner of producing consonant and vowel sounds (Chapters III and IV), our personal ability to analyze the tactile (touch) and kinesthetic (muscle stretching) information fed back to us as we produce speech, and perhaps the assistance of such homey apparatus as a mirror and flashlight. Certainly the literature of instrumental phonetics provides a continuing, invaluable resource for clarification, correction, and confirmation of our judgments.

We begin with simple units that form familiar words, first briefly describing the sequence of actions, then analyzing the movements and conditions in more detail. Then, for further analysis, we consider some of the errors that might have a high probability of occurrence during production. Bracketed numerals relate sections of these descriptions.

Analysis of meat [mit]

Description

With the velopharyngeal port open and the oral cavity closed at the lips, voicing begins (1). As voicing continues, the front of the tongue elevates (2) with the tip against the lower front teeth, and almost simultaneously (3), the lips open slightly and the velopharyngeal port closes. The front of the tongue is very high, nearly touching the palate (4). The tip of the tongue begins to move upward, voice terminates abruptly (5), and the tip of the tongue moves upward rapidly from behind the lower front teeth to press against the front (6) of the alveolar ridge, closing off the flow of air (7). The tongue front and tip relax, and the air held and compressed in the oral cavity is released as breath flow ceases (8).

Analysis

1. Resonance for [m] involves the nasal cavity open at both ends and the oral cavity open at the pharynx but closed at the lips.
2. The tongue begins to move toward the [i] position during the production of [m].
3. Opening of the lips and closure of the velopharyngeal port must be almost simultaneous for the transition from [m] to [i].*
4. Resonance for [i] involves the nasal cavity closed at the velopharyngeal port and the oral cavity open at both ends, but the size of the oral cavity is reduced by the high front tongue position, and the opening at the lips is narrow.
5. Before voicing terminates, the tongue tip is already moving upward, influencing the acoustic characteristics of the end of the [i] sound.
6. Closure for the [t] is forward on the alveolar ridge, almost to the upper front teeth, because of the front tongue position for the preceding [i]. Compare to the position of the [t] closure back on the alveolar ridge following [u] as in [mut].
7. As voicing terminated, the glottis remained open and breath continued to flow into the oral cavity, closed off at the tongue and alveolar ridge, and compressing air in the oral cavity.
8. Depending upon the situation, the release can be very soft and almost silent, or it can be produced with an audible explosion or aspiration.

Error Implications

Consider the misarticulations that might have taken place during production of [mit] at each of the moments numbered above:

1. Had the velopharyngeal port been closed, a sound like /b/ would have been produced, changing the meaning of the word to *beat*.
2. If the tongue does not begin moving toward the [i] position before oral resonance begins, an [ə] sound may intrude for [məit].
3. If the lip opening and velopharyngeal port closure do not occur almost simultaneously, the [i] will be hypernasal and have the sound of [ĩ]. †
4. If the front of the tongue is not high enough, the vowel resonance may sound like [ɪ] or [ɛ], so that the word would be heard as *mit* or *met*.
5. Had the voicing continued too long while the tongue tip was moving upward, an [ə] might have intruded to form [miət].
6. Closure farther back on the alveolar ridge might have permitted intrusion of [ə] or a lingua-alveolar fricative between [i] and [t].

---

*Instrumental studies reveal that the velopharyngeal area moves more slowly than the tongue and lips so that closure may actually follow lip opening slightly.
†The usual lag in velopharyngeal closure does make the beginning of the vowel somewhat more nasal than the same vowel would be in a syllable such as [pit].

7. If the flow of air had not continued to produce an abrupt closure, the final consonant might have been heard as the less tense [d].
8. If the [t] is aspirated and breath flow continues with the tip of the tongue opened only slightly and grooved, the final sound may be heard as [s] so that the word becomes [mits].

It is obvious from this analysis and description of articulation that the simple speech unit we produce for the word *meat* is really very complex. It involves changes in resonance from primarily nasal to primarily oral, changes from voicing to voiceless breath, fine tongue adjustments within the oral cavity to create just the right resonance for a particular vowel sound, and a stoppage and release of the breath stream. Positions for any subsequent speech sound are anticipated during production of preceding sounds, and positioning of the tongue for closure of the breath stream is influenced by tongue position of the previous sound. A number of misarticulations are possible in producing this short but complicated speech unit.

Next, we analyze an utterance that forms the word *fence*. Note that this speech unit has an intruded [t] sound, which is not reflected in its spelling.

Analysis of fence [fɛnts]

Description

With the velopharyngeal port closed, breath is forced through the oral cavity (1), and the lower lip approximates the maxillary front teeth so that air flow is constricted through the narrow opening (2) to cause turbulence and audible friction. During the friction (3), the front-to-mid part of the tongue moves up slightly toward a position between /e/ and /æ/ (4). Simultaneously (5), voicing begins and the lower lip is dropped (6). Voicing continues (7) as the tip of the tongue closes against the middle (8) of the alveolar ridge, closing off the flow of air through the oral cavity, and almost simultaneously (9), the velopharyngeal port opens (10). The tongue remains in the lingua-alveolar position but increases muscular tension, as simultaneously (11), voicing ceases and the velopharyngeal port closes. Breath pressure (12) is built up briefly behind the tongue. The tongue releases the breath pressure as it pulls rapidly (13) but slightly away from the alveolar ridge and forms a narrow groove. The breath stream is directed through the narrow aperture between the alveolar ridge and the grooved tip of the tongue (14) against the closely approximated front teeth (15) to form turbulence with audible friction, as breath flow ceases.

Analysis

1. Sufficient breath pressure must come from the lungs to force the stream of air through the oral cavity.

2. The slight separation or approximation of the lower lip and upper front teeth is critical to form a narrow opening for developing turbulence with audible friction.

3. While the friction for [f] is being produced, the tongue is already advancing toward the position of [ɛ].

4. The position for [ɛ] involves raising the front of the tongue to the exact position that will create the resonant formants for this vowel.

5. The beginning of voicing and moving away of the lower lip is simultaneous.

6. The moving away of the lower lip is achieved by relaxation of lip muscles; the lower jaw need not move for the following [ɛ] position.

7. Resonance for the [ɛ] involves the nasal cavity closed at the velopharyngeal port,* and the oral cavity open at both ends but restricted at the mid-to-front by the elevated tongue.

8. The point of [n] closure is determined by the tongue position of the preceding vowel [ɛ], farther back than that for the [i] and farther forward than for the [u].

9. Opening of the velopharyngeal port to the nasal cavity is almost simultaneous with closure of the oral cavity by the tongue.*

10. Resonance for the [n] involves the nasal cavity open at both ends, and the oral cavity closed by the tongue at the alveolar ridge. Another resonance cavity is formed in front of the tongue and between the lips, which must be open for this sound.

11. Termination of voice and closure of the velopharyngeal port must be simultaneous.

12. Breath pressure sufficient for the fricative [s] must be built up behind the tongue which has previously (10)–(11) increased muscular tension in order to hold and compress the breath.

13. Lingua-velar closure and rapid release of the breath pressure creates an aspirated [tʻ] sound before the [s], like a fricative [ts].

14. Grooving narrows the aperture necessary for the fricative sound specific to [s].

15. Breath turbulence around the front teeth is necessary for the friction sound of [s].

Error Implications

Consider the misarticulations that might take place at each of the moments numbered above:

1. Insufficient sub-glottal breath pressure will not create audible friction so that the initial sound may be perceived as a weak [v].

---

*Instrumental studies reveal that the velopharyngeal port actually opens during the last portion of the vowel [ɛ], anticipating the nasal resonant [n], and begins its gradual closure as the tongue tip begins to close on the alveolar ridge.

2. If the opening is too wide, friction will not be created at the labio-dental position so that the initial sound may be heard as [h] or may seem to have been omitted.
3. If the tongue does not advance toward the [ɛ] position until friction terminates, an [ə] sound may intrude between [f] and [ɛ] to form [fəɛnts].
4. Positioning of the tongue too high or too low will create a vowel near /e/ or /æ/, respectively.
5. If voicing begins before the lip is dropped, a [v] sound may intrude between [f] and [ɛ] for [fvɛnts].
6. If the jaw is dropped to pull the lower lip away, the tongue will have to compensate by rising higher to form [ɛ]. Its rise during voicing may cause intrusion of a [ə] sound before the [ɛ] position is achieved for [fəɛnts], giving the impression of a two-syllable word.
7. If the velopharyngeal port should open too soon, the vowel will be a nasal [ɛ̃] sound.
8. The position of the front of the tongue for [ɛ] places the tip of the tongue just below the middle of the alveolar ridge. In order to make closure of the oral cavity almost simultaneous with opening of the velopharyngeal port, the tongue tip must close at the closest position on the alveolar ridge. Otherwise, the ending of the [ɛ] may have excessive open nasal resonance.
9. If the velopharyngeal port should be delayed in opening, the voiced stop [d], homorganic with [n], may intrude for [fɛdnts].
10. Resonating cavities to produce [n] require that the lips be open in front of the lingua-velar closure. If not, the bilabial nasal resonant [m] will be heard instead.
11. Should the velopharyngeal port remain open as voicing ceases, breath would escape from the nasal cavity, leaving insufficient oral breath pressure for the [s].
12. Unless the breath is compressed briefly behind the tongue, not enough pressure will be built up for the [s].
13. If the tongue were to move too slowly or too far away, breath pressure necessary for [s] would be dissipated, possibly giving the listener perception of a final [z].
14. If the front of the tongue were too broad, a [ʃ] sound would replace the intended [s].
15. The teeth must be fairly close together to create necessary turbulence for audible friction.

It is readily apparent that the simple one-syllable word *fence* involves a number of very complex articulatory movements. For example, voicing and resonance change from the first breath sound to the vowel with oral resonance, to the nasal resonant [n], to the voiceless sounds that terminate it. The position of the tongue for the vowel sound must be anticipated during production of the initial fricative consonant. Position of the tongue on the alveolar ridge for [n] was determined by the vowel [ɛ] that preceded it. The first three phonemes are continuants that flow easily into each other, but the intruded [t] stops the flow of breath briefly. This stop is necessary to give a clear [s] sound or the unit might sound like *fens* [fɛnz]. Note that nearly simultaneous articulatory movements are required at three moments, numbered 5, 9, and 11 in the analysis.

Other units of connected speech may be analyzed with descriptions such as those used for [mit] and [fɛnts], considering coarticulation effects noted earlier in this chapter. The reader may begin with the unit of *spoon* [spun]. Consider how the [p] would be different were it not preceded by [s], and how the [n] would differ if the vowel before it were [i] instead of [u]. What would probably happen to the *n* if it were followed by a [k]? Other suggested words to analyze are listed in the exercises at the end of this chapter.

TRANSCRIPTION OF CONNECTED SPEECH

Accurate phonetic transcription of how another person says a speech unit requires a good deal of skill and discipline. We not only need to know the IPA symbols well and to listen carefully, but we need to inhibit some of our habitual thinking about speech, spelling, and language. We must guard against thinking of how we believe it should be said "correctly," how we might have said it, how it is spelled, how we would typically segment language into units of words, phrases and sentences, and what the speech unit means. Our auditory-perceptual system is tuned to ignore subtle phonetic differences, such as allophonic or speaker variations, in favor of focusing on the meaning of spoken language. Because we cannot always hear all speech sounds well, we have developed effective use of a mental catalogue of probabilities based on other perceptual cues. These cues are available from **redundant** phonetic, linguistic, and contextual information. Redundancy refers to the presence of more information than is absolutely necessary for understanding. Redundancy permits us to use other available cues to guess what an unheard or poorly heard speech sound most probably was. We have developed the habit of hearing only enough speech to get the meaning and of ignoring the rest.

To retrain the auditory perceptual system, we may begin by attending to spoken nonsense syllables or larger nonsense units. In a bisyllabic unit such as [sprutʃɪŋ], we do not have the meaning of the word to help us fill in or remember sounds. However, the consonant cluster of [spr] is a familiar one in American-English and the [ɪŋ] ending makes the unit sound like a word, so that it is fairly easy to hear and transcribe. If we create a bisyllabic unit like [ts3˞htuʌ], which contains the same number of phonemes as [sprutʃɪŋ], we encounter difficulty because of some unfamiliar sequences. The [ts] affricate does not occur except in compound words, the [ʍ] does not occur at the end of a word, and the [h] is always followed by a vowel in American-English. Here, our well learned catalogue of probabilities can give us misinformation. There is little phonetic information available except by listening to each sound in the sequence. The student may wish to have a friend create similar nonsense units or use unfamiliar foreign words, and read them to him for practice in transcription. Unfamiliar American-English words may also be helpful.

A second step in retraining our auditory-perceptual system is to transcribe speech in connected units just as it is spoken. We do not speak with a string of separated words anymore than we say words with distinct and separate phonemes. In the printed phrase, *he wore a white tie,* we see the words as distinct linguistic units, each contributing something special to the thought conveyed by the sentence. But when the sentence is spoken in normal conversational speech, it is usually a single phonetic unit, [hiworəʍaɪtːaɪ]. The temptation to transcribe this sentence [hi wor ə ʍaɪt taɪ] is strong, but note how this would overlook that only a single [t] sound was produced at the end of *white* and beginning of *tie.* Compare a word-by-word transcription of the phrase, *this surely evened Dick's score,* with that of a connected transcription:

Word-by-Word	[ðɪs ʃurlɪ ivənd dɪks skor]
Connected	[ðɪʃurlɪʔivəndɪksːkor]

The "word" transcription above ignored many coarticulation effects: the assimilation of the [s] in *this* before the [ʃ] sound of *surely,* the glottal stop between vowels, the single [d] joining *evened* and *Dick's,* and the single lengthened [sː] between *Dick's* and *score.* To practice connected transcription, the reader may have a friend say short phrases in a natural, conversational manner. If necessary, the speaker may repeat the phrase but must do so exactly as said the first time. The transcriber should then read the phrase back aloud from his transcription to see if the original speaker agrees that it matches his production. The following phrases may be helpful practice transcribed as single units of speech:

around the rock	*say it isn't so*
not that time	*pick up a couple of bucks*
play it again	*you lost your chance*
nobody knows him	*let me at him*

For increased familiarity with connected transcription, the student may read aloud this passage from *Charlotte's Web* by E. B. White:

[əspaɪdɚzwɛb ɪztrɔŋgɚðænətluks].
[ɔlðouɪtsmeɪdəv θɪn],
[dɛləkətstrændz], [ðəwɛbɪz
nɑtizəlɪbroukən]. [hauwɛvɚ],
[əwɛbgɛtstorn ɛvrɪdeɪ baɪðəʔɪnsɛks
ðætkɪkəraundɪnət], [ændəspaɪdɚ
mʌstribɪldɪt ʍɛnətgɛtsfuləholz].
[ʃɑrlət laɪktəduɚwɪvɪŋ
dɝɪŋðəleɪtæftɚnun],
[ændfɝn laɪktəsɪtnɪrbaɪŋwɑʧ].

There are a number of ways the listener can help himself with the difficult task of phonetic transcription. When confronted by unfamiliar words or nonsense units, the transcriber will unconsciously seek additional speech information through lipreading. This supplementary visual information, discussed in Chapter VIII, can be very helpful in discriminating slight differences within speech units. The rate of transcribing speech is considerably slower than the rate of producing speech, so that the listener will have to remember a number of sounds in a particular sequence. He will need to "record" the live signal in his auditory perceptual memory system and possibly "play it back" several times as he completes the transcription. This process is called **re-auditorizing**—that is, listening by memory to something over and over again. The strength of the recalled auditory signal will fade quickly unless reinforced by the motor memory of producing the speech unit. In listening to difficult words, the transcriber may find himself unconsciously moving his tongue or lips as he re-auditorizes, "getting his tongue around the word," so to speak. If developed with care, so as not to substitute the transcriber's pronunciation for that of the speaker, this motor memory for perceived speech can help the transcriber both discriminate the sounds and remember them. Motor aspects of speech perception are discussed in Chapter VIII.

Of course, for units of speech of several phrases or paragraphs, the transcriber will need a magnetic tape or other recording device. An audiotape recording provides long-term storage and the possibility of playing a unit of speech back as often as needed. A video-tape recording can provide lipreading information as well as the acoustic signal. An important consideration in recordings and in live listening is the acoustic environment. Of special concern is high background noise, which may establish a disadvantageous signal-to-noise ratio. Keeping the recording microphone close to the speaker's lips will help, but care must be taken to see that air flow of speech against the microphone does not distort the acoustic signal.

As we move to longer units of speech, we shall see in the next chapter that features of speech rhythm also influence the production of speech sounds and their coarticulation.

REVIEW VOCABULARY

Abutting Consonants—consonants joined in coarticulation but in separate syllables. The [tb] in *football* is an example.

Assimilation—conforming of one sound to the manner of production or place of articulation of a neighboring sound. The *n* in *ink*, for example, takes the same place of articulation as the final [k], to be pronounced [ŋ] for [ɪŋk].

Coarticulation—any influence of one speech sound upon the manner of production or the place of articulation of a neighboring sound.

Consonant blend—a sequential combination of consonants within a syllable in which the positions of the two may be taken simultaneously. The [bl] in *blue* is an example.

Glottal stop—an abrupt hiatus of air at the glottis during connected speech as in *he eats* [hiʔits].

Intruded consonant—a consonant not included in spelling but phonetically present with coarticulation as the [t] in *chance*.

Re-auditorize—to recall the sound of a unit of speech.

Redundant—having more information that is absolutely necessary for intelligibility.

Syllabic consonant—a consonant that serves the function of a vowel as the nucleus of an unaccented syllable. The [l̩] in *bottle* [bɑtl̩] is an example.

EXERCISES

Using the narrow transcription symbols of Table I–4, transcribe the following speech units as you would say them in conversational speech.

1. Voicing [̥], [̬]

three	crew	behind	somewhere
pray	splash	sitting	little
slim	clean	butter	scratch
please	fry	ahead	thrill

2. Lengthening [ː]

soon know	about time	bad days
some men	big girl	cub bears
full load	black car	ripe pears
spare ribs	tap pins	this service

3. Syllabic consonants [ˌ]

little	ridden	bread 'n butter
kitten	bottle	riddle
cattle	Eden	cuddle
digging	slap 'em	eaten

4. Intrusion [t], [p], [k], [w], [j]

chance	something	go out	we each
Samson	transcribe	no older	the east
length	fancy	two hours	panther
suspense	comfort	to eat	else

5. Follow the sequence of production below and transcribe, with three IPA symbols, the speech unit that matches the description.

> With the velopharyngeal port closed and without voicing, the lips are closed and the teeth slightly open. As breath flow begins, the front of the tongue begins moving upward in anticipation of the next sound as air held and compressed in the oral cavity is audibly exploded between the lips, and as the mandible drops slightly. Voicing begins, after lip opening and aspiration, as the front tongue height just lower than that for [ɛ] is achieved (resonation condition—oral cavity open at lips, nasal cavity closed at velopharyngeal port). Voicing is continued as the tip of the tongue begins moving upward and forward, anticipating the next sound. Then voicing ceases as breath is directed between the broad, thin tip of the tongue and the maxillary incisors, where they are closely approximated to cause turbulence and audible friction. Breath flow ceases.

6. Describe what went wrong if a speaker, intending to produce the word, *plunk* [pl̥ʌŋk], instead produced each of the following units:

[pl̥ʌnt]   [pl̥ʌk]

[blæŋk]   [pʌŋk]

[blʌŋk]   [pəlʌŋk]

7. Write out descriptions of the sequences involved in producing each of the following words as you would say them.

better	glass	smooth
twist	pleasure	mixed
whole	gentle	catch

8. Transcribe each of the following phrases in connected IPA transcription as you would say them in conversational speech. Each is a single phrase.

    a. the easy way out
    b. this seems okay
    c. big girls don't cry
    d. under the yumyum tree
    e. better safe than sorry
    f. the days of wine and roses

SUGGESTED READING

Dew, Donald, and Jensen, Paul: *Phonetic Processing: The Dynamics of Speech.* Columbus, Ohio, Chas. E. Merrill Publishing Co., 1977.

Chapter 5, "Coarticulation," emphasizes the coordination of various parts of the speech mechanism in producing speech sounds and the influence of context upon the production of neighboring sounds (pp. 109–130).

Malmberg, Bertil: *Phonetics.* New York, Dover Publications, Inc., 1963.

Chapter VII, "Combinatory Phonetics," deals clearly with some of the important influences of context and coarticulation (pp. 56–73). The syllable is described as it relates to several languages. This book, by a famous Swedish phonetician, is good basic reading for the beginning student.

Chapter VI

SPEECH RHYTHM AND SUPRA-SEGMENTAL FEATURES

- **ACCENT**
- **EMPHASIS**
- **PHRASING**
- **INTONATION**
- **RATE**
- **REVIEW VOCABULARY**
- **EXERCISES**
- **SUGGESTED READING**

One of the first things we notice when hearing a foreign language is a kind of "melody" or rhythmic variation in the flow of speech. This is especially apparent when we do not understand the language and listen just for its sound pattern. We refer to the "lilt" of Irish speech, we note the constant falling and rising pitch and the long resonant consonants of Scandinavian languages, and we are conscious of a regular cadence in Spanish. But we are often surprised when foreign speakers comment on the rhythm of American-English. Listening as we usually do primarily for the meaning, we are often unaware of the rhythmic patterning in the sound of our own speech. Of course, individuals and dialect groups develop differences in their speech patterns, but in this chapter we are interested in those features general to American-English, and those influencing meaning and understanding rather than contributing primarily to aesthetic effect.

The general term used here for this phenomenon is **speech rhythm.** One also finds in the phonetic and linguistic literature such terms as speech "melody" or "patterning," "prosodemes," and the "prosodic" or "temporal" features of speech. Because these features occur in longer connected units, as compared to the segments of phonemes or individual speech sounds, they are often called the **supra-segmental features** of speech. The word "rhythm" has musical and poetic connotations that may be somewhat misleading, since the rhythm of natural connected speech bears only distant resemblance to the more orderly rhythmic structures of music and poetry, but it is nevertheless a serviceable generic term for our use.

The basic unit of speech rhythm is the **syllable.** It is usually described as a cluster of coarticulated sounds produced on a single speech impulse. We recognize in speaking the following words, for example, single impulses or syllables in *go, cat,* and *stretch;* two syllables in *apple, going,* and *pleasant;* three syllables in *terminate, radio,* and *microphone;* and four syllables in *America, tabulation,* and *celebrating.* Our intuitive judgment about how many syllables are present, and thus our notion of what constitutes a syllable, has not satisfactorily been confirmed by instrumental studies. This is true for both physiologic studies of the production of syllables and for acoustic studies of the results of their production. A continuing problem has been in determining spoken syllable boundaries. The spoken or phonetic syllable is not necessarily the same as the written syllable and does not always follow the written segmentation recommended by dictionaries and writing guides. This is primarily because our connected speech does not observe word boundaries. Note that in writing, we would segment the syllables in the phrase, "not even an apple," as *not-ev-en-an-app-le,* whereas for natural connected speech, we might recognize the syllables as [nɑ-ti-və-nə-næ-pl̩].

The syllable is a cluster of coarticulated sounds usually with consonants bordering a vowel. Syllables terminating in a vowel are called "open" syllables, and those ending with an arresting consonant are called "closed." The essential nucleus or central element of the syllable is a vowel or diphthong sound. Consonants may either initiate or terminate a syllable but cannot function as its nucleus, except for the syllabic consonants mentioned in Chapter V. A syllable may consist entirely of a vowel, as in the case of the *a* in "find a boat." In American-English, the most common syllable cluster is a consonant-vowel (CV) combination as in the *-ly* of *lovely.* Almost as common is the consonant-vowel-consonant (CVC) as in the *-ton* of *Washington.* A VC pattern as in the *up-* of *upset* is less common. (Refer to the section on Difficult Articulations in Chapter V for other syllable patterns.) Consonants may be compounded in a single syllable, as in the CCVCC cluster of *stems,* but different vowels do not cluster in a syllable. Each pure vowel or diphthong forms its own syllable nucleus. In the word *being,* for example, the syllables are *be-* (CV) and *-ing* (VC), compared to the single syllable of the word *bing* (CVC). Note that *being* and *bing* would sound very similar were it not for the bisyllable-unisyllable distinction. Speakers verbally mark the syllable boundary in words such as *being* in a number of ways. A /j/ may be intruded to separate the two vowels for [bijɪŋ], the duration of [i] may be extended to point up its difference as in [bi:ɪŋ], a very brief hiatus or glottal stop may separate the vowels for [biʔɪŋ], or a sudden change in fundamental voice pitch may accompany the slight change in tongue position to distinguish the two vowels. Note similar verbal markings for the short but bisyllabic words *eon* and *boa*. Such verbal markings contribute to the listener's discrimination of the number of syllables and thus the intended word.

Syllable clusters influence coarticulation and relate to the timing of speech. American-English syllables average about two-tenths of a second with variations according to individual speaker differences and patterns of stressing. When given equal stress by a speaker, syllables are of roughly equal duration, regardless of their phonetic complexity. Thus *ram* and *scram* may be produced in about the same period. Similarly, *buy* and *bite* may be forced into the same time frame, primarily by reducing the duration of the [aɪ] in *bite*. The compression of a number of phonemes into the single, brief speech impulse of a syllable forces the compact or intrinsic coarticulation of those sounds within the syllable. Phonemes are thus presented to the listener not haphazardly but coarticulated in syllable clusters. Such clusters help in our recognition of each phoneme because of the transitional characteristics of consonant-vowel and vowel-consonant junctures, which give listeners important perceptual information. Of course, coarticulation effects also extend beyond or are extrinsic to syllable boundaries, as pointed out in Chapter V. We shall see in the following pages how the syllable also contributes to speech rhythm.

The sound of American-English speech rhythm results from a very complex combination of **accent, emphasis, phrasing, intonation,** and **rate.** What we hear is the interaction of variations in loudness, pitch, and duration of syllables, occurring in series of connected phrases and pauses. The product provides the listener with information that influences meaning, assists in listening and understanding, and may give aesthetic interest to speech.

ACCENT

Accent is one form of speech stress. **Stress** points out, sets apart, focuses on, or otherwise gives vocal prominence to a unit of speech. Accent refers to the stress given a syllable within a word compared with its other syllables. For example, the *work-* syllable in *working* is given greater stress than the *-ing* syllable, and the *-cause* in *because* is stressed above the *be-*. It is characteristic of English that every word of more than one syllable have a syllable stressed above the others, and that stressed syllables be audibly different from those of lesser stress. English is, therefore, called a "stress-timed" language. Many other languages, which do not observe this variable stressing pattern but have a more regular beat, are referred to as "syllable-timed." American-English uses less difference between heavily stressed and unstressed syllables than does British-English (see Chapter VII).

American-English observes three basic levels of accent with "primarily accented," "secondarily accented," and "unaccented" syllables. The levels differ relative to each other for a particular speaker, in a specific word at a given moment, and they have no absolute acoustic values that can be specified. It is generally the nuclear vowel of the syllable that undergoes change for accent rather than its consonants. The accented syllable is made with greater physiologic force, resulting in (1) greater loudness, (2) greater duration, and (3) a rise in pitch. The accented-unaccented ratio can and often is achieved by reducing force of production on the unstressed or de-accented syllable, giving it reduced loudness, reduced duration, and a lowered pitch in relation to the standard syllable, which now seems to be stressed by virtue of not having been reduced. In connected speech, most persons use a combination of expansion of the stressed syllable and reduction of the unstressed to produce accenting. Because of the resulting acoustic variability, the unreliability of listener judgments, and the vagary of specifying absolute levels of stress, it is possible to argue for four, five, or even more levels of accent. However, it is unlikely that such proliferation of levels beyond the basic three would serve any but the phonetician bent upon the study of fine accent differences.

There are several ways to indicate accent graphically. The International Phonetic Association uses a vertical mark /ˈ/ above and before the syllable with primary accent, a mark of the same size and shape /ˌ/ below and before the syllable with secondary accent, and no mark for unaccented syllables. Thus the word *above* is marked [əˈbʌv], *hotdog* is marked [ˈhɑtˌdɔg] to show secondary accent, and *absolute* is marked [ˌæbsəˈlut] with no mark before the unaccented middle syllable, [sə]. These marks have the advantage of international usage in the literature but the disadvantage of suggesting a separation of phonemes: in [ˈhɑtˌdɔg], the secondary accent mark intrudes between the [t] and [d], which are actually closely coarticulated. Dictionaries frequently use a heavy mark (ˈ) above and just after the syllable of primary stress, and a lighter mark of the same position and length (ˈ) just after the syllable with secondary stress. Another system places directly above the vowel nucleus an acute accent mark (´) for strong or heavy stress, a caret [kɛrət] (ˆ) for secondary stress, a grave [greɪv] accent mark (`) for tertiary stress, and a breve [briv] mark (˘) for the unstressed syllable. A simpler demonstrative system frequently used in teaching or improving speech is the use of a strong acute mark (´) directly above the vowel nucleus of the syllable with primary accent, a weaker and shorter mark (´)directly above the nucleus of the syllable with secondary accent, and no mark above an unaccented syllable.

This latter system has some advantages where teaching or improving speech are concerned. It is visually simple with no angles or positioning to learn. The intensity and durational differences between stronger and weaker stressing are readily apparent, illustrated through the visual analogy of combined darkness (or thickness) and length of the accent marks. The marks placed directly above the syllable nucleus focus attention upon the vowel as the primary phoneme of change, and the succession of letters or phonetic symbols are not interrupted by intervening marks. Still another advantage is that the therapist, teacher, or transcriber may indicate several levels of stress if he wishes to by making the accent marks relatively longer or darker by degrees. This simple system of accent marking will be used throughout this book.

Which syllable should be given strong or weak accent? In American-English, there is a strong tendency for bisyllabic words to have their accent on the first syllable, especially for the vocabulary used in reading books of young children. The accented syllable usually precedes suffixes such as *-ing*, *-er*, *-est*, *-cious*, *-y*, and *-tion*, which are rarely stressed themselves. But the accented syllable frequently follows unaccented prefixes such as *a-, be-, re-, de-, ad-*, and *ex-*. Note the following words:

mák*ing*	hápp*y*	*re*plý
fást*er*	ná*tion*	*de*táin
quíck*est*	*a*bóve	*ad*míre
delí*cious*	*be*wáre	*ex*tént

It is difficult to establish hard and fast rules for applying accent in American-English words. Deciding which syllable to accent is largely a matter of following conventional usage. Our listening, in expectancy of hearing the conventional stressing patterns, is so attuned that we may actually not understand familiar words when the accent is transposed. Pronounce the following words, strongly accented as indicated, and note how unfamiliar they sound:

América	enérgetic	dependént
syllåble	emotiónal	intensíty
intéresting	intónation	catégorize
foundatión	secretarý	cónsider

One reason these words seem to sound so unfamiliar is that pronunciation changes almost automatically as we change accenting. Unstressed syllables tend to have a /ə/ nucleus. Note how the *-i-* in *America* becomes [ə] in *América*, and [ɪ] or [i] when it is stressed in *América*. In the word *syllable*, the *-a-* changes from [ə] to [eɪ] or [ɑ] when it is given unconventional stress. Accented syllables are likely to follow their usual vowel spelling pronunciation, as described in Chapter IV, whereas those unaccented often change. Diphthongs /eɪ/ and /oʊ/ become pure vowels /e/ and /o/ when unstressed, except in final open syllables. The /i/, /æ/, /u/, and /ɑ/ tend to become /ɪ/, /ɛ/, /ʊ/, and /ʌ/, respectively, when reduced, and, if deaccented further, become /ə/. This change in pronunciation with accent is reflected in the spelling of some words as in *pronounce-pronunciation, maintain–maintenance*, and *sustain-sustenance*.

For some pairs of words that have the same spelling, differences in accent and the resulting changes in pronunciation give information that influences meaning. Accent in this regard may be considered to be **phonemic**. Note how the syllable accented determines meaning in the following pairs of words:

pérfect	(adjective)	—	perféct	(verb)
prógress	(noun)	—	progréss	(verb)
rébel	(noun)	—	rebél	(verb)
cónflict	(noun)	—	conflíct	(verb)
ábstract	(adjective)	—	abstráct	(verb)
cómplex	(noun)	—	compléx	(adjective)

Note the change in meaning with movement of the primary accent from the first to last syllable in the following words: *survey, suspect, torment, transport, subject, reject, produce, digest, escort, insult, exile, content, recess.* Although there are standards of conventional accent usage for most words, some words are produced with alternative accented syllables without influencing meaning. For example, *adult* is said both as *ádult* and as *adúlt.* Compare accenting patterns with friends on the following words: *automobile, cigarette, concrete, contrary, defense, dictator, gasoline, illustrate,* and *locate.* For such words, accent is not **phonemic**.

The presence or absence of secondary accent also changes the meaning of a number of words, especially those with an *-ate* suffix. Compare the following and note also that the *-a(t)e* in these words changes pronunciation with stressing from /ə/ to /eɪ/.

No Secondary Accent		**Secondary Accent Present**	
delíberate	(adjective)	delíberáte	(verb)
affíliate	(noun)	affíliáte	(verb)
délegate	(noun)	délegáte	(verb)
gráduate	(noun)	gráduáte	(verb)
móderate	(adjective)	móderáte	(verb)

Secondary accent is usually present in words compounded from two other words. *Aírpláne, hótdóg, cówbóy,* and *básebáll* are examples in which the second syllable is almost never reduced to /ə/.

In some phonetic contexts, reduction of the unstressed syllable may lead to omission of the /ə/ when a following resonant consonant is homorganic with the previous consonant. In *cattle,* for example, both the [t] and [l] have a lingua-alveolar place of production. The final syllable may be reduced from [kǽtəl] to use of the syllabic [l̩] in [kǽtl̩] when the tongue does not move from the alveolar ridge in coarticulation. This reflects a great reduction of stress in which the resonant consonant /l/ takes the function of a syllable nucleus, as [ḷ]. Note similar reduction in *kitten, button,* and *little.* The ultimate extreme of stress reduction is complete omission of the unstressed syllable. The British have a particular tendency to omit and telescope unstressed syllables, as noted in Chapter VII. In American-English, there are a number of words that commonly have syllables omitted in conversational speech. Note the following examples:

	Formal	**Conversational**
annual	[ǽnjuəl]	[ǽnjul]
evening	[ívənɪŋ]	[ívnɪŋ]
family	[fǽməlɪ]	[fǽmlɪ]
miniature	[mínɪətʃɚ]	[mínɪtʃɚ]

Other words that frequently have omitted syllables include *reference, several, temperature, toward, valuable, veteran, difference, diamond, favorable,* and *interest.*

EMPHASIS

Emphasis refers to the stressing of a word or words within a phrase or sentence. Like accent, emphasis is produced primarily by greater physiologic force resulting in increased loudness and duration of syllables within the stressed word, with an accompanying change in pitch. Some words may be de-emphasized by reduction in force, thus making other words stand out. Emphasis may also be achieved by pauses surrounding words or by unusual elongation of duration of a selected syllable. Levels of emphasis are even more variable and difficult to specify than levels of accent. Graphic marking of emphasis should ideally be separate from and not interfere with accent markings. The simple expedient of <u>underlining</u> the stressed words will accomplish this, reserving <u>double underlining</u> for very heavy emphasis. Single and double emphasis underlining may be translated into printed material as *italics* and **bold type,** respectively.

Unlike accent, emphasis is not applied according to recurring patterns or conventional usage. Its application is personal and relates to a speaker's intent. Of course, emotional state may be transmitted by exaggerated emphasis on exclamations, but here we are more interested in how language information is transmitted. Each speaker includes a pattern of emphasis in his formulation of phrases, which adds information over and above the string of phoneme segments, their grouping into syllables, and the syllable accent pattern. For example, he may choose to label something, as in "The next to the last syllable is called the <u>penultimate</u> syllable," drawing special attention to the label word. He may wish to reiterate or stress a fact such as, "I say we <u>can't</u> make it." He may seek to compare or contrast parallel thoughts, as "We

<u>drove</u> home but they <u>walked</u> home." A common use of emphasis is in response to situational context. As an example, try saying the sentence *My house is five miles down the road* several times with each of the words given emphasis in turn. Imagine the context in which emphasizing a particular word might be relevant. For example, emphasizing *my* would indicate "I don't mean your house or his house." Emphasizing *miles* could suggest, "and that's a long distance, possibly too far to go." Try the same exercise for the sentence *That baby is crying again.*

Emphasis may also serve to distinguish in speech a single compound word from an adjective and noun word combination. Compounds such as *hotdog, cowboy, airplane, baseball,* and *blackbird* usually have their primary accent on the first syllable, the modifier portion, with secondary accent on the second noun portion. In some situations, it is useful to clarify that two separate words are intended, for example, to differentiate "a blackbird" from "a black bird." The difference, designated by a physical separation in script, is marked in speech by reversing the stress, placing emphasis on the second word—"bláckbírd" compared with "black <u>bird</u>." Note how this is useful in such pairs as *highchair—high chair, greenhouse—green house, bearskin—bare skin, hotdot—hot dog.*

De-emphasis creates phonetic changes similar to reduction of unaccented syllables. Frequently used short connective words are almost never emphasized and tend to be reduced toward /ə/. Such words as *was, of, the,* and *a,* are so commonly produced in connected speech with /ə/ that, when restressed for special emphasis, they are usually produced with /ʌ/ rather than their original pronunciations. Words like *to, you,* and *my* may also be reduced to /ə/ but usually return to their original vowel when given special emphasis.

PHRASING

A speech **phrase** is defined phonetically as a continuous utterance bounded by silent intervals. In the phrase, syllables, which themselves are clusters of segmental phonemes, are linked together in coarticulated clusters. The intervals between phrases are called **pauses**. Speech **phrasing** is related to breathing but does not necessarily reflect breathing patterns. All inhalations during connected speech occur between phrases, that is, during pauses, but inhalation does not always occur with each pause. A speaker may say two or three or more phrases on the same breath. Note in the familiar quotation "I came, I saw, I conquered" that the three phrases can easily be said with a single breath. Figure VI-1 illustrates some relations between phrasing and breathing.

Some pauses are marked in writing by such punctuation marks as commas, periods, semi-colons, colons, question marks, and exclamation marks.

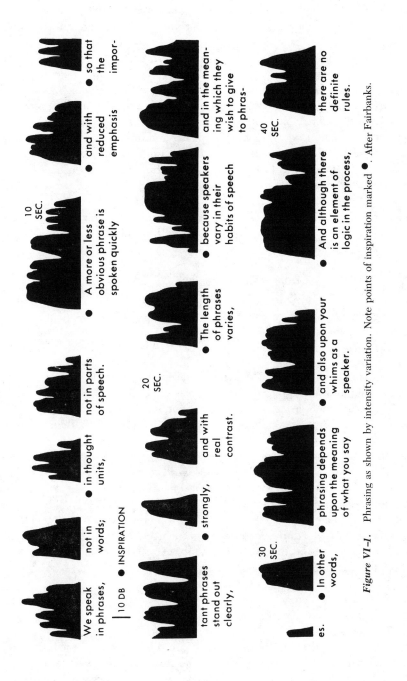

Figure VI-1. Phrasing as shown by intensity variation. Note points of inspiration marked ●. After Fairbanks.

171

However, speech phrasing and written punctuation do not correlate exactly. Note that in the phrase "the red, white and blue," although a comma is present, the speaker may say the passage as a single phrase [ðərɛdʌaɪtn̩blu]. Conversely, the speaker may use a pause for emphasis where no punctuation exists as in "today (pause) is the last day (pause) of vacation." A conventional visual marking for speech phrasing that points up the grouping of words into a phrase is a ligature [lɪgətɚ] or a curved underlining, as for example in "today is the last day of vacation." This marking has the drawback of possible interference with underlining for emphasis and does not give any indication of the relative length of pauses. Another helpful system of visual marking is the use of vertical lines at pauses, using more lines for longer pauses. Usually one, two, or three lines are sufficient to mark the range of pauses used in speech. For example, in *I'll go* ||| *but I expect to return* | *sooner or later*, the vertical lines mark the boundaries of phrases and indicate the relative duration of pauses. This system may be used with regular spelling or IPA symbols. Note the following:

I think	|||	*therefore*	||	*I am*
[aɪθɪŋk]	|||	[ðɛrfor]	||	[aɪæm]

knife			*fork*			*and spoon*
[naɪf]			[fork]			[ændspun]

In transcribing with IPA symbols, accurate phonetic transcription requires that a phrase be written with consecutive symbols, without interruption for word boundaries. This indicates junctures that are coarticulated. The large spaces between symbols, therefore, mark phrase boundaries so that vertical line markers are not necessary unless the transcriber wishes to show the relative duration of a pause. Some transcribers prefer to transcribe word-by-word with spaces left between words to facilitate reading from transcription. In this case, the vertical markers are essential, not only to show duration but to mark phrase boundaries.

The speaker determines which and how many words to link together in a phrase, and the duration of pauses, in order to facilitate the listener's understanding of the intended message. He may use phrasing patterns for the following purposes:
1. To group the words of a thought into a unit
2. To create emphasis
3. For parenthetical comments
4. To accommodate to difficult listening situations

A very important use of phrasing is in presenting units of meaning to the listener. In the sentence "We went to the store | because we were hungry," two different but related thoughts are presented to the listener in two phrase units. Note how an inappropriate phrasing would interfere with meaning if we said the sentence as "we went to the | store because we | were hungry." Series items may also be separated with pauses as in "knives | forks | and spoons." Emphasis is created by setting apart the word or phrase to be emphasized; for example, "I want to go ||| now || without delay." Such pause emphasis is usually accompanied by loudness and pitch rise to indicate stress further. An aside or parenthetical comment, sometimes referred to as an "apostrophe," is set apart with pauses as in "The weather | I believe | is going to get better." The aside phrase is usually de-emphasized with lowered loudness and pitch. The sensitive speaker takes into account difficulties his listeners might have in understanding speech. He may use shorter phrases and longer pauses when his subject matter is complex or unfamiliar to the listener, when the listener is very young or may have a disability in understanding, or when speaking in a noisy background or to large audiences.

A speaker uses some pauses for formulating the next phrase or future phrases during extemporaneous speech, especially in explanatory discourse. Although we do not fully understand the process of rapidly formulating speech as in fluent conversation, pauses may figure very prominently. Some speakers use extensive pauses associated with "filler words," while apparently formulating what they will say next. Such patterns as "Well, ||| uh ||| I suppose ||| that || all things considered, || you know, | uh..." give the speaker considerable time to think and to formulate phrases that carry real meaning. Listeners can note the irregularity of phrasing and pause duration in conversational or extemporaneous speech, compared with the more regular pattern of oral reading. It is indeed amazing that speech can be formulated so rapidly when one considers that the speaker must accomplish the following:

1. Select the appropriate words
2. Place them in an appropriate order
3. Change their forms and endings to agree with the conventions of American-English syntax
4. Select segmental phonemes to produce the words orally
5. Prepare the pattern of syllables and coarticulation
6. Apply accent, emphasis, intonation, and phrasing patterns.

All these tasks and more are accomplished at an average conversational rate of 200 words per minute or more.

INTONATION

Whereas accent reflects changes in the syllables within a word, and emphasis reflects changes in the words in a phrase, **intonation** involves changes over an entire phrase. The nature of the change is primarily in the rising and falling of pitch. These pitch inflections provide audible **intonation contours**, which can give a level of meaning over and above the string of phonemes, the pattern of accent, and the application of emphasis. This is an added meaning rather than a change in meaning. In several languages, notably Chinese, the pitch of syllables does actually change meaning so that a single CVC syllable may have several different meanings, depending upon pitch level.

Important in describing intonation contours are (1) the degree of pitch change, (2) the direction of change, and (3) the rate of change. Varying as we do in fundamental voice pitch, speakers do not seek a target of absolute pitch levels for intonation but use contrast of relative levels. Four relative pitch levels are conventionally recognized in American-English intonation. Level 2 is a standard or baseline for a phrase from which the speaker drops to 1 or rises to 3. Level 4 is reserved for expressions of surprise or high emotional outburst. The levels may be shown by using the respective numbers for each word or syllable, as in the following:

$$
\begin{array}{cc}
(3) & (3) \\
\text{Hurry up!} & \text{He's coming.} \\
(2) & (2) \\
& \qquad (1)
\end{array}
$$

With this system, one can refer to "He's coming" as having here a 2-3-1 intonation contour. Levels may be more graphically marked by lines drawn under and over parts of the phrase at the relative heights as follows:

Hurry up! He's coming.

Direction of pitch change can be inferred from left-to-right positions, and the rate of change may be illustrated by connecting the pitch levels with slanting lines at varied angles. Note the following markings:

Hurry up! He's coming

My goodness!

For most purposes, these connected contour lines, observing target levels of 1, 2, 3, or 4, with the lines sloping to show rate of change, will be sufficient for marking intonation. At best, they or any system will correlate only roughly with measured variations in fundamental voice frequency.

Many intonation patterns result, in part, from pitch changes caused by application of accent and emphasis. For example, note the following sentence:

I lost my ruler.

The word *ruler* is a key word to be emphasized above the rest of the sentence by greater intensity and duration, and by a rise in fundamental voice frequency. Normally, the **accent** pattern of *ruler* would be *rúler*, with the second syllable unaccented. As a final word of this phrase, *ruler* has the final syllable greatly de-accented, not only with intensity and duration reduction but with an unusual audible drop in pitch to relative level 1, below the rest of the phrase. **Emphasis,** in order to aid meaning, determines that intonation will change primarily on *ruler*, the emphasized word. These parts of the intonation contour are dictated by accent and emphasis. The unusual drop in pitch on the final syllable, however, is a product of **intonation** that tells the listener something new. Here, it says "the utterance is completed." Compare the intonation contours in these sentences:

I lost my ruler.

I lost my ruler, my pen and my pencil.

In the second sentence, the rising intonation on ruler, with the help of appropriate phrasing, tells the listener "keep listening, there's more to come." In a sentence such as "We brought knives, forks, dishes, and spoons," note how the rising pitch on *knives, forks,* and *dishes* signals the listener that there is more to come in a series, whereas the dropping pitch on *spoons* indicates the end of the series and the utterance. In this case, the end of the series is also marked by the word *and,* occurring just before the last word, so that *and* and the intonation contour provide complementary and redundant information to aid the listener. Try this sentence again without *and* but with the appropriate intonation, and then again with *and* but with the same intonation rise on *knives, forks, dishes,* and *spoons.* Note that the meaning can be carried by either *and* or the intonation contour, but that the sentence is more easily understood with both.

Indication of a series and of termination of an utterance are just two uses of intonation. Signalling a question is another important use. The phrase "they will," for example, is declarative-interrogative ambiguous. That is, it could be a statement, "They will," or a question, "They will?" Whereas in writing we differentiate with punctuation marks, in speech the difference is marked by intonation contour. The rising intonation here is that which is associated with a question, telling the listener that a response is expected of him. In this case, the intonation contour strongly influences meaning and may be considered to be **phonemic.** If the order of the words in the phrase were reversed for "will they," the word order itself indicates a question so that intonation of "Will they?" provides redundant information.

The purest form of phonemic intonation in American-English is with the expression "oh" [ou]. The syllable does not have a meaning of its own but can serve as a vehicle for conveying meaning through intonation. Note these common intonation messages:

Carrier	Intonation Message
o̲h̲	"I'm still listening to you."
oh\	"I understand."
oh\	"Now I finally understand it."
oh/	"Really, are you sure?"
oh\oh	"Now you're in trouble."

    Some speakers use many intonation carriers in conversation, especially when they wish to signal another speaker that they are listening and do not want to interrupt the speaker's flow of discourse. Such carriers as *uh huh* [ʌhʌ], *mmm* [m:], and *yeah* [jɛə] are common. The signaller may use a nasalized form of *uh huh* [m:m̃:] to avoid opening his mouth during listening. Note how intonation contours carry information with these carriers:

Carrier	Information
uh huh	"I'm still listening."
uh/huh	"I understand."
uh/huh	"I didn't know that," or "That's really interesting."

Carrier	Information
mmmmmm	"I'm still listening."
mmmmmm	"Is that so?"
mmmmmm	"I didn't know that." or "That's really interesting."

Note also how the standard greeting of "hello" can convey a message with intonation:

	Intonation Message
hello	"I am pleased to meet you"
	"I am very pleased to meet you"

hello   "What do you want with me?"
         (telephone)

A great variety of intonation contours may be identified, influenced by accent and intonation patterns, length of the phrase, linguistic intent of the message, and emotional affect of the speaker. Three contours recur that may be considered conventional usage of American-English intonation. These are as follows:

Falling Intonation (2 or 3 to 1)

A falling intonation pattern signals the termination or completion of an utterance, suggesting that no verbal response is required of the listener. It is most often found at the end of a phrase, and it is accompanied by decreased intensity and syllable duration, with vowels reduced to their unaccented pronuciation or to /ə/. Note the falling intonation in the phrases, "That's all" and "its over."

Rising Intonation (2 to 3)

A rising intonation pattern signals an unfinished situation in which something is needed from the listener or something more is to come from the speaker. It marks a series of items as in "the knife, fork, dishes, and spoon." It indicates a question that is likely to take a "yes" or "no" answer as in "Are you coming home?" or "Is that all there is?"

Rising-Falling Intonation (2 to 3 to 1)

A pattern that first rises and then falls is one of the most common intonation contours, the one commonly used when making a simple statement of fact, or giving a command. Note the contour in "The store is closed now" and in "Come here." This pattern is also used for questions that require an answer of information other than "yes" or "no." Note the pattern in "What's the trouble?" and "Where are you going?" These questions usually begin with *where, when, how, why,* or *what.*

A special use of intonation is to indicate saracasm by using a declarative statement word order with the intonation pattern of a question. Note the conflicting pattern in the following:

That's a good idea.

Here the speaker tries to convey "you may think that is a good idea but I really doubt it, myself," without saying so in words.

RATE

The **rate** at which speech is produced is usually measured in the number of words or syllables per unit of time. An average syllable's duration is 0.18 seconds, yielding about 5 to 5.5 syllables/second. Most adults read orally from 150 to 180 words/minute and produce 200 or more words/minute in conversational speech. Individuals vary, of course, in the rate at which they talk. Maximum rate of producing speech appears to be limited by articulatory control. With simple repetitive articulatory movements, speakers reach maximum rates of about 8 syllables/second but cannot exceed this even with practice. Although the time it takes to produce different speech sounds varies greatly, it is interesting to note that speakers average a rate of 10·sounds/second in conversation. At faster rates, it is difficult to coordinate articulation and errors begin to occur. At the rate of 15 sounds/second, errors are frequent and speech is distorted. Comprehending speech, on the other hand, occurs much faster, as does silent reading and thinking in general. While we typically produce speech at 10 sounds/second, we can understand it at as much as 30 sounds/second when paying careful attention.

A speaker's rate is influenced by a number of factors. The duration of pauses and the number of pauses contribute to rate, as does the use of extended vowel duration for stressing accented syllables and emphasized words. Of course, stressed syllables have greater duration than unstressed syllables so that either habitual heavy stressing or great reduction on un-stressed syllables influences overall rate of speech. In normal conversation, the number of syllables in a phrase influences rate. A speaker who says "My name is John" as a single phrase is likely to say "My name is John Brown" in the same time period, cramming in an additional syllable. The other syllables must be spoken more rapidly to accomplish this. As was pointed out in the discussion of phrasing, in difficult listening situations, speakers are likely to reduce rate by using more and longer pauses. They may also articulate more accurately, slowing down the rate of syllable production within a phrase, particularly in public speaking. Emotion or mood is also indicated by rate. For example, "The lawn is green and soft and cool" invites the speaker to slow the rate so that the listener can see and feel the situation as the speaker does. Excitement, on the other hand, is indicated by rapid rate with syllables crammed together in short phrases.

There is no conventional way to mark rate visually. Some writers bunch words such as "sonofagun" to indicate rapid production as though the phrase were a single word. When using IPA symbols, the curved underlined ligature may be used to show unusually rapid production as in [sʌnəvəgʌn]. Compare the phrase "Let's pick up a couple of bucks" when said at a normal rate and then very rapidly.

normal rate   [lɛts pɪkʌpəkʌpələvbʌks]

rapid rate   [ləts pɪkəpəkəpl̩əbʌks]

Combined simultaneous transcription of broad and narrow IPA symbols, together with the markings of accent, emphasis, phrasing, intonation, and rate of connected speech would be a formidable task. It is likely that repeated listening to recordings would be necessary for complete and accurate description of a passage of speech. Even if a trained listener could recognize, recall, and transcribe all these aspects of descriptive phonetics during an extended utterance, the resulting composite of markings would make difficult reading. Fortunately, the usual task of transcribing and marking would require only one or two dimensions of speech description. Whether used singly or in combinations, though, the markings for phonemes and for aspects of speech rhythm are especially useful to describe non-standard and dialectic speech, as described in the next chapter.

REVIEW VOCABULARY

Accent—stress applied to a syllable in a word.

Emphasis—stress applied to a word in a phrase.

Intonation—pitch variations within a phrase.

Intonation contours—the pattern of pitch variations of intonation, including the degree, direction, and rate of pitch change.

Pause—silent intervals between phrases.

Phonemic—having the characteristic of a phoneme, influencing the meaning of speech.

Phrase—a continuous utterance bounded by silent intervals.

Phrasing—organizing flowing speech into phrases.

Rate—the number of syllables or words per unit of time.

Speech rhythm—the general term referring to the combined aspects of accent, emphasis, phrasing, intonation, and rate.

Stress—pointing up or drawing special attention to a unit of speech.

Supra-segmental features—features of speech over and above phoneme segments, especially aspects of speech rhythm.

Syllable—a cluster of coarticulated sounds with a single vowel or diphthong nucleus, with or without surrounding consonants.

EXERCISES

1. Transcribe the following words in IPA symbols as you would say them, and mark the primary accent in each word:

   revolver   suspect (verb)   radio
   inflation   suspect (noun)   reward
   obese   insult (verb)   tedious
   natural   insult (noun)   consenting

2. Say the following sentence seven times, emphasizing a different word each time. Describe the context in which the emphasis would be appropriate.

   "I am the captain of my fate."

3. Transcribe the following speech units in connected IPA symbols as you (or another speaker working with you) would say them, observing coarticulation effects, and marking phrasing and pause duration using |, ||, and ||| symbols.

   a. I don't believe it. I got an A.
   b. Well, sure enough. It's time to go.
   c. No longer, my friends, can we sustain this hard, difficult effort.
   d. My God, what terrible thing have you done?
   e. 'Tis the East and Juliet is the sun.

4. Mark the following paragraph from "The Bathtub Hoax" by H. L. Mencken as you would read it, using markings for accent, emphasis, and phrasing with relative duration of pauses.

   On December 20 there flitted past us absolutely without public notice one of the most important profane anniversaries in American history to wit: the seventy-fifth anniversary of the introduction of the bathtub into these states. Not a plumber fired a salute or hung out a flag. Not a governor proclaimed a day of prayer. Not a newspaper called attention to the day.

5. Transcribe in IPA symbols the following section from "Jabberwocky" by Lewis Carroll as you would say it. Observe coarticulation effects of phrasing and mark relative duration of pauses.

   'Twas brillig and the slithy toves
   Did gyre and gimble in the wabe:

All mimsy were the borogoves,
And the mome raths outgrabe.
Beware the Jabberwock, my son!
The jaws that bite, the claws that catch!
Beware the jubjub bird, and shun
The frumious Bandersnatch!

SUGGESTED READING

Lehiste, Ilse: *Suprasegmentals*. Cambridge, Mass., The MIT Press, 1970.

A well written basic book on speech rhythm with numerous references to research in the field.

MacKay, Ian R. A.: *Introducing Practical Phonetics*. Boston, Little, Brown & Co., 1978.

Chapter 9, "Word Stress," and Chapter 13, "Sentence Stress, Timing and Intonation," give a brief but good overview of some aspects of speech rhythm.

Chapter VII

STANDARDS, DIALECTS, AND DEFECTIVE SPEECH

There are many variations in speech among those who speak American-English. Some of the differences in pronunciation have been pointed out in previous chapters. These and other variations have been the subject of considerable study and description by phoneticians and have prompted numerous attempts to establish standards for speech. However, standards suggest arbitrary value judgments, and controversy always erupts when we judge one way of speaking to be better than another. So personal is speech that even the suggestion that our speech may not be "good," may not be "correct," or may sound "funny" to someone else can cause great embarrassment and even threaten self- or group-image. This causes us to view the variability of speech in different ways, as reflected here in describing deviations from suggested **standards** and **dialects** held in common by groups of speakers, and how these variations differ from **defects** of disordered speech, which call for professional intervention. It is especially relevant for persons who seek to change or influence the speech of others (classroom teachers, speech/language pathologists, and instructors of public address, elocution or drama) to have a frame of reference for considering, first, whether a speech variation merits change, and second, whether direct intervention is appropriate.

STANDARDS

Standards are concerned with what speech ought to be. What is correct pronunciation? What is good speech? Who sets the standards? These questions have plagued phoneticians, teachers, and those who strive for propriety, elegance, and a systematic order of things. A number of the criteria that have been suggested for standards of pronunciation are presented here.

Criteria for Standard Pronunciation

What Most People Say

This criterion of the popular mode suggests that the standard pronunciation should be that which is used most. In other words, the speech pattern that calls least attention to itself is best because it is so common. Without attention called to habits of speech, there is little interference with transmission of the content or message to be conveyed. Television and radio commercials appear to respect this reasoning with their predominance of General American announcers and performers. It has at least the appearance of a democratic solution to the problem of standards but is not entirely consistent with our traditional respect for minority rights and differences.

What Educated People Say

The standard called "The King's English" has been accepted throughout most of England. Sometimes called "Received (accepted) Pronunciation," it is defined as the English spoken by graduates of the large private schools (Eton, Harrow, Rugby) of England; that is, by the Royal family, Members of Parliament, British professionals, industrialists, and bankers. Accordingly, it is strongly associated with an elite social class. It is this style of pronunciation that Henry Higgins taught the cockney girl, Liza Doolittle, in Bernard Shaw's *Pygmalion*, in order to pass her off as an English "lady." It has become the Standard English adopted for the British and often the American stage.

In the United States, however, educated persons in Boston, Atlanta, and Omaha are likely to speak quite differently. But in our mobile society, since "educated" increasingly means "traveled," the speech of well educated persons is becoming more alike, regardless of native dialect. Another "elite" standard in America is the speech of famous, popular, or highly respected persons—folk heroes, athletes, and adventurers—regardless of their social class or education.

What the Media Say

National network broadcasting of radio and television presents a fairly uniform speech pattern to millions of listeners. Reports on listening and viewing habits suggest that these media have an important influence on speech, especially on developing a national standard of pronunciation. They present predominantly a General American pattern of what people throughout most of America speak. Moving pictures present a wider variety of dialects to represent different locales, but blending of the American television and cinema industries is a move toward more unified pronunciation. Live stage speech, particularly in the East, is still likely to reflect "Standard English" (southern British) pronunciation used on the British stage.

What Dictionaries Say

The chicken or the egg, the pronunciation or the dictionary, which came first? Of course, dictionaries are intended to reflect speech as it is commonly used. Webster's Unabridged Dictionary reports that its standard of pronunciation is "the usage that now prevails among the educated and cultured people to whom the language is **vernacular.**" However, dictionary pronunciation has also become the common American "school standard" for correctness, a written static record of the educated pronunciation of one generation to be learned in turn by successive generations. In this sense, dictionaries may act as a conservative and stabilizing influence, actually retarding changes in pronunciation. To account for obvious dialect differences, American-English dictionaries often present more than one possible pronunciation with the most frequent (or preferred) given first. Common variations in pronunciation associated with different patterns of stressing, however, are often overlooked so that *of* is to be pronounced [ɑv] when it is most often pronounced [ʌv] or [əv], and *was* is typically listed as [wɑz] even though it is usually said as [wʌz] or [wəz].

How Words Are Spelled

Chapter I describes the disparate relationship between spelling and pronunciation. Yet spelling has a strong influence upon pronunciation in our culture in which reading is important. Until the 17th and 18th centuries, for example, the initial *h-* was rarely pronounced in English. But with popular

availability of printed books and periodicals, and the influence of Latin pronunciation, the initial *h-* became pronounced as /h/ more frequently in a
process that still continues. Note the use of /h/ in the following words:

Silent h-	Inconsistent	h- pronounced
heir	herb	hospital
honest	homage	heretic
hour	humble	host

A more recently developed word that is likely to be encountered first in
print, *herbicide,* is almost universally pronounced with the initial /h/, even
though its root word *herb* is mixed in its pronunciation. The attraction of
spelling pronunciation can also be seen in the mixed pronunciation of *often*
as [ɑfən] or [ɑftən].

Historical Precedence

This criterion, like dictionary pronunciation and spelling pronunciation,
suggests a static standard. Correctness would be based on the origin of the
word. The standard pronunciation of foreign words, such as the Latin *data*
and *ad hoc,* would be the way Romans pronounced the words centuries ago.
Place names, such as *Los Angeles* and *New Orleans,* would also be pronounced as they would have been in the country of their origin. Except
among scholars of languages, this criterion seems not to be well observed. In
fact, some areas of the country seem to delight in pronouncing names in their
own contrary style. In the Missouri-Illinois area, for example, there are the
towns of New *Athens,* pronounced [eíθənz]; New *Madrid,* said as [mædrɪd];
Cairo, commonly pronounced [keírou], and *Nevada,* which is pronounced
[nəveɪdə].

The historical criterion is too static to survive a dynamic language. It
does not permit the many changes in pronunciation that have taken place
and will continue to take place. Then too, new words are being added to our
language every day. It is estimated that there are now over 600,000 different
words in English, compared with about only 140,000 in Shakespearean
times.

The Situation

This criterion recognizes, realistically, that we do not speak the same
way in all situations. In addition to stage speech, three levels of speech are
often considered. The first is a "formal" or literary level, in which we speak
in sentence structure as we write, pronouncing words with great care. It is
sometimes referred to as "careful" or "citation" form. Vowels are usually
given their full stressed spelling value. For example, *what* would be pro-

nounced [ʍɑt] instead of the more common [ʍʌt]. The endings of words would be clearly enunciated, with stop consonants often audibly released so that *lap* would be said as [læpʻ] with full aspiration rather than [læp] without release. In its extreme, some politicians, attorneys, and other public speakers lend formality to their speech by over-emphasizing the endings of words so that *end* becomes [ɛndə]. Even continuant consonants may be released as though they were stops. For example, as the final words of phrases, *dollars* may be said [dɑlɚzʌ], *some* pronounced as [sʌmʌ], and *due* given as [duʌ] or [djuʌ].

The second level is called "cultivated **colloquial,**" a level of "well educated ease." Pronunciations are in the **vernacular,** that is, the native common usage of educated persons who have learned them as children. Such speech would be suitable for a wide range of situations from academic seminars to business transactions to everyday commerce with persons both familiar and unfamiliar. Here the speaker would use the dialect of his region.

The third level is often called "everyday informal." It reflects somewhat less distinct enunciation, more rapid speech, and the influence of unstressing on vowels in connected strings of words. Running words together and occasionally omitting some syllables is characteristic. This level is usually reserved for "small talk," speaking to a very familiar person or to a younger person in an informal situation when one's linguistic "hair is down." Indistinctness of enunciation is compensated for by familiarity, which enhances intelligibility.

Intelligibility

Here the criterion is whether speech is understood, regardless of how words are pronounced. However, speech **intelligibility** is likely to vary considerably with such factors as familiarity with the speaker, dialect of the listener, noise background, complexity of subject content, level of message redundancy (phonetic, linguistic, and environmental), and rate of message transmission. The standard would need to change with each situation. This criterion by itself also overlooks the important impressions listeners infer about the speaker in addition to receiving the message.

Beauty

Pronunciation and speech habits that are most pleasing to our ear are best. Such a criterion creates two major problems: first, it overlooks the importance of intelligibility, and second, the desirable aesthetic standard is very difficult to describe. We cannot deny that some people have speech patterns that are particularly pleasing, hold our interest, or seem to lend importance to themselves and their messages. Voice quality and intonation patterns are heavy contributors to such impressions. Unfortunately, our judgments about what is impressive and pleasant are very subjective, and a universal standard based on aesthetic qualities of speech is almost futile to define.

None of the Above

One might reach the conclusion that since no single criterion is completely satisfactory, there should be no standards of pronunciation at all. This reasoning is individualistically and democratically appealing, but it is unrealistic. So long as people strive for something better, standards will be developed as practical targets. While we as Americans may reject the concept of a single universal standard, we probably have in the back of our minds a number of the criteria just cited when we seek to improve our speech. We may shift somewhat from one criterion to another as the situation changes, but we are likely to fall back upon one or more criteria when we seek correctness.

Non-Standard Speech

Even though absolute standards are difficult to identify and describe, we recognize that some speech habits are so divergent as to be considered "non-standard" or far outside the range of acceptable American-English speech. The following types of non-standard speech are common.

Non-English Speakers

What is commonly referred to as a foreign "accent" is made up of a number of variations in intonation patterns, stressing differences, and pronunciations. For example, notable among many continental Europeans is difficulty in pronunciation of the lingua-dental consonants /θ/ and /ð/. Either /t/ or /s/ is frequently substituted for the breath /θ/, so that *thing* becomes [tɪŋ] and *something* may become [sʌmpsɪŋ]. Treatment of the /θ/ in Chapter III includes lists of words for contrasts of /θ/-/t/ and /θ/-/s/ for practicing the difference in articulation. Substitution for the voiced /ð/ may be either /d/ or /z/ so that *these* may be said as [diz] and *this* may be pronounced [zɪs]. Chapter III compares words with such /ð/-/d/ differences. In addition, the foreign student may profit from a comparative exercise such as the following:

	Standard	*Non-Standard*	
the	[ðʌ]	[dʌ]	[zʌ]
this	[ðɪs]	[dɪs]	[zɪs]
that	[ðæt]	[dæt]	[zæt]
those	[ðouz]	[douz]	[zouz]
then	[ðɛn]	[dɛn]	[zɛn]

Another especially difficult pronunciation, particularly for Spanish and Italian speakers, is the English vowel /ɪ/ which falls between the /i/ and /ɛ/. The substitution is likely to be /i/ so that *this* becomes [ðis] or [zis] and *it* may be said [it] to be confused with *eat*. In the section on /ɪ/ in Chapter IV, there are lists of words contrasting the /i/-/ɪ/ sounds. The foreign student may also profit from exercises that compare vowels adjoining on the vowel diagram of Figure IV–1 as follows:

Practice saying speech units from left to right, then right to left.

[i]	[ɪ]	[e]	[ɛ]	[æ]
[mi]	[mɪ]	[me]	[mɛ]	[mæ]
[ki]	[kɪ]	[ke]	[kɛ]	[kæ]
[di]	[dɪ]	[de]	[dɛ]	[dæ]
[bit]	[bɪt]	[beɪt]	[bɛt]	[bæt]
[mit]	[mɪt]	[meɪt]	[mɛt]	[mæt]

Many Europeans do not produce voiceless stops with as much force or aspiration as do Americans. This results in reduced duration and different acoustic frequency characteristics so that the voiceless stops sound like their voiced cognates to the American listener. The student may be helped by first practicing exaggerated production of voiceless syllables [pʌ], [tʌ], [kʌ]; [pl̥ʌ], [kl̥ʌ]; and [pr̥ʌ], [tr̥ʌ], [kr̥ʌ], and then practicing comparison of /p/-/b/, /t/-/d/, and /k/-/g/ words listed for these phonemes in Chapter III. A common non-standard pronunciation for Germans is the substitution of the labio-dental /v/ for both /w/ and /ʍ/. *We* may be heard as [vi] and *water* as [vatɚ], and *what* becomes [vɑt] while *when* becomes [vɛn]. This substitution is especially noticeable because the /w/ and /ʍ/ occur so frequently in American-English speech. Sections treating /w/ and /ʍ/ in Chapter III include lists of words contrasting these phonemes with the substituted /v/.

Many Europeans produce the /eɪ/ in all words as a pure vowel [e], whereas in English it is usually a diphthong, /eɪ/, especially in stressed and final open syllables. The foreign student might begin by practicing production of the diphthong as [ei], with equal stress and duration of the two familiar components, and then reduce stress on the second component as [i], rather than try to produce [ɪ] as the second component. Reduced stress on the [i] glide will achieve the same result. Practice in comparing the following pairs of syllables may be helpful:

A	[eɪ]	[e]
take	[teɪk]	[tek]
name	[neɪm]	[nem]
late	[leɪt]	[let]
safe	[seɪf]	[sef]

Japanese has a speech sound similar to both American-English /l/ and /r/. The sound, written as /ɭ/ in IPA script, is produced with the tongue point briefly touching the roof of the mouth on the palate just behind the alveolar ridge. The tongue shaping is similar to /l/ with manner of production like a brief flap (such as the [t] in *city*), while the place of articulation is farther back on the palate and close to the place of articulating /r/. As a result, when an American listener expects to hear /r/, acoustic information from the tongue touching the palate with lateral emission suggests the lingua-alveolar /l/, making *rice* sound like *lice*. Similarly, when one expects to hear /l/, information from the tongue position well behind the teeth and alveolar ridge suggests the lingua-palatal /r/, so that *low* sounds like *row*. The non-standard production is not a simple /l/–/r/ substitution, as our hearing suggests, but substitution of a single sound, native to Japanese, for either.

After studying the positions of American-English /l/ and /r/ as described in Chapter III, the Japanese student might practice vocalizing while moving the tongue from the /l/ position (well forward on the alveolar ridge) back and not touching the palate for the /r/, then back to /l/, alternating positions as voicing continues. Practice on word lists and sentences with /l/ and /r/ in Chapter III might also be helpful.

Immature Speech

Immature speech consists of those patterns, different from the prevalent speech patterns of adults within a dialect group, that an individual uses because of lack of experience and/or maturation. Such speech in children is normal and not considered to be defective or to require special intervention for improvement. With normal opportunity, the immature patterns will fade and be replaced by more adult ones. Improvement toward mature speech comes with (1) the natural process of physical, mental, and social maturation, (2) adequate exposure to the adult speech patterns of the dialect group, and (3) satisfactory experience in using spoken language.

Psychologists, linguists, and speech pathologists have studied progressions from the absence of speech in the baby through the developing speech of the young child to the achievement of mature speech patterns in the older child and young adult. Understanding of the phonologic system and rhythm patterns of a child's native language apparently begins in the early weeks of life. The articulation of consonants and vowels in connected speech starts during the first year and is usually mastered by the eighth or ninth year of life. Figure VII–1 shows the range of ages at which children with normal hearing and speech first master production of English consonant phonemes in connected speech.

Some learning of sophisticated speech rhythm patterns and, of course, new vocabulary continues into later life, but speech is expected to mature within the first decade. If it does not, some special attention is indicated to direct the person toward more mature speech patterns or to determine the cause of the persistent immature pattern.

Considering the order in which production of consonant phonemes are mastered, as described in Figure VII–1, many of the "errors" of young children as they are learning the American-English phonologic system (see Table VII–1) can be seen as evolutionary. That is, earlier learned and mastered consonants will be used in place of newly emerging consonants that have a similar place or manner of production until the child can easily distinguish critical differences and feels confident in producing the new sound.

An example of a common speech phenomenon encountered in young children is the /f/ for /θ/ substitution. These dental, voiceless fricative consonants differ only in the labial/lingual place of production. They are acoustically very similar. The /f/ is mastered early, usually by age 3 or 4 years, whereas /θ/ is seldom mastered before 6 or 7. By his third birthday, the child, now somewhat aware of numbers, will likely respond to a question about his age as [fri] for *three*. The /f/ will usually occur whenever /θ/ is expected so that *thin* becomes [fɪn] and *thank you* is [fæŋk ju]. As the child grows older, /θ/ will begin to appear, at first inconsistently alternating with /f/, and then more regularly, except in seductive phrases such as *free throw*, which is likely to persist for some time as [fri froʊ], and *forty-three* as [fortɪ fri]. Finally, the older child will master the appropriate use of these two consonants, so very similar in manner (voiceless fricative) and place (dental) of articulation.

The /l/ and /r/ sounds are notoriously difficult for some children to develop, and their non-standard productions sometimes persist into adult speech. A frequent pattern is substitution toward /w/, /j/, or /ʊ/ in place of /l/ in the intervocalic, preconsonantal, or final positions, so that *dollars* becomes [dɑwɚz], *William* becomes [wɪjəm], *million* may become [mɪjən], *salt* may be [sɑʊt], and *tell* may become [tɛʊ]. The /w/ for /l/ in the initial position is more obvious and likely to be treated as an adult speech defect. The /r/ shares a similar pattern of lip-rounding substitutions with some dialect variations camouflaging preconsonantal and final non-standard articulations.

Mispronunciations

Some mispronunciations occur from reading words we have never heard spoken, making our best guess from the spelling. It is unlikely, for example, that many young readers will know how to pronounce *chic* as [ʃik], *bade* as [bæd], or *brooch* as [broʊtʃ] the first time they are read. Their spellings contradict the pronunciation rules they have subconsciously learned.

A source of frequent mispronunciation comes from reference to a simpler, more familiar form. The [aʊ] in *pronounce* [pronaúnts], for example, is likely to lead to *pronunciation* being said [pronaʊntsieíʃən] rather than [pronəntsieɪʃən]. The [eɪ] in *nation* [neɪʃən] may influence *national* to be said as [neɪʃənl] rather than [næʃənl]. A reference mispronunciation may occur even when the familiar form is more complex, as, for example, the verb *orient* being said [orɪəntet], influenced by the more familiar noun *orientation*.

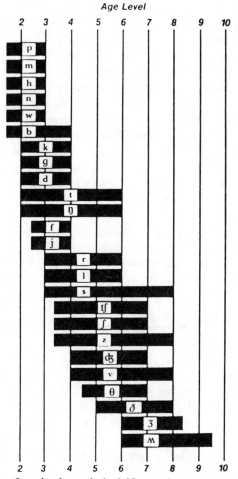

Figure VII–1. Range of age levels at which children with normal hearing and speech first master production of English consonants in connected speech. (Adapted from: Sander, E.: When are speech sounds learned? Journal of Speech and Hearing Disorders, 37:55–63, 1972.)

Another frequent cause of mispronunciation is avoidance of a difficult articulation cluster. *Picture* [pɪktʃɚ] may be simplified to [pɪtʃɚ], undifferentiated from *pitcher*. *Arctic* [arktɪk] is frequently simplified to [artɪk], and *sentence* [sɛntənts] may be said [sɛnəts] or [sɛnənz]. Note the reduction of articulatory complexity in the following pronunciations:

	Non-standard pronunciation	*Complex cluster*
government	[gʌvɚmənt]	[ɚnm]
surprise	[səpraɪz]	[ɚpr]
governor	[gʌvənɚ]	[vɚn]
library	[laɪbɛrɪ]	[brɛr]

TABLE VII–1 FREQUENT CONSONANT SOUND SUBSTITUTIONS
BY FIRST-GRADE CHILDREN WITH NORMAL HEARING
AND SPEECH

TARGET PHONEME	CHILD SOUND	TARGET PHONEME	CHILD SOUND
/l/	[w]	/ŋ/	[n]
/r/	[w]	/θ/	[f]
/ʌ/	[w]	/v/	[f]
/v/	[b]	/ʃ/	[s]
/ð/	[d]	/z/	[s]
/ð/	[v]	/θ/	[s]
/ð/	[θ]	/ʒ/	[dʒ]

Akin to simplification of a cluster by omission is the insertion of a vowel to separate a difficult cluster. The following are common mispronunciations:

	Non-standard pronunciation	*Complex cluster*
athlete	[æθəlɪt]	[θl]
realtor	[rɪlətɚ]	[lt]
chimney	[tʃɪmənɪ]	[mn]
poplar	[pɑpələˈ]	[plɚ]

Omission of unstressed syllables in connected speech has also been considered less than standard for careful articulation. Note the very common mispronunciations of these words:

	Careful preferred	*Common non-standard*
every	[ɛvɚɪ]	[ɛvrɪ]
separate (adj.)	[sɛpɚɪt]	[sɛprɪt]
chocolate	[tʃɑkolət]	[tʃɑklət]
vegetable	[vɛdʒətəbəl]	[vɛdʒtəbəl]
interested	[ɪntɚɛstəd]	[ɪntrəstəd]
federal	[fɛdɚəl]	[fɛdrəl]
national	[næʃənl̩]	[næʃnl̩]
reasonable	[rizənəbl̩]	[riznəbl̩]

Yet the non-standard usage is so prevalent, even among well-educated people, that for such words, either pronunciation has become acceptable. What has been "non-standard" has become, or is becoming, "standard," and the former standard will begin to sound awkward and pretentious, or perhaps be limited to more formal, literary style.

Still another form of mispronunciation is reversal of consonant order, a phenomenon called **metathesis** [mətǽθəsɪs]. Note these changes in /r/ and /ɚ/:

	Standard	*Reversal*
perspiration	[pɚ·spɚ·eɪʃən]	[prɛspɚ·eɪʃən]
hundred	[hʌndrɛd]	[hʌndɚd]
children	[tʃɪldrɛn]	[tʃɪldɚn]
pronounce	[pronaʊnts]	[pɚnaʊnts]
professor	[profɛsɚ]	[pɚfɛsɚ]

Such reversals also occur for /v/ and /l/ as in [rɛvələnt] for *relevant* and [kælvɚɪ] for *cavalry*.

Omission of the final consonant of a cluster of either breath consonants or of voiced consonants is generally considered non-standard even though it is a characteristic of Black American-English dialect. Note the following examples:

	Standard	*Non-standard*
last	[læst]	[læs]
next	[nɛkst]	[nɛks]
end	[ɛnd]	[ɛn]

Sometimes the omission is of a medial consonant or vowel with compensatory extension of duration, as in the following:

	Standard	*Non-standard*
lists	[lɪsts]	[lɪs:]
nests	[nɛsts]	[nɛs:]
mirror	[mɪrɚ]	[mɪr:]
error	[ɛrɚ]	[ɛr:]

These omissions are especially noticeable when they influence syntax, as in the following words:

	Standard	*Non-standard*
cracked	[krækt]	[kræk]
shaved	[ʃeɪvd]	[ʃeɪv]

The /r/ is a non-standard intrusive sound for some speakers as in [wɑrʃ] or [wɔrʃ] for *wash*. Some New Englanders intrude /r/ between words ending and beginning with vowels in connected speech. Note the following phrases:

	Intrusive /r/
law in	[lɔrɪn]
saw at	[sɔræt]
Canada as	[kænədɚ æz]
area of	[ɛriɚ əv]

The habit persists in some final words of phrases such as idea as [aɪdiɚ] and *data* as [deɪtɚ].

The [iə] or [ɪə] sound after /d/ in connected speech may degenerate to [djə] or further with friction to [dʒə] in such words as the following:

	Standard	[djə]	[dʒə]
medium	[midiəm]	[midjəm]	[midʒəm]
Indian	[ɪndiən]	[ɪndjən]	[ɪndʒən]
tedious	[tidiəs]	[tidjəs]	[tidʒəs]
Canadian	[kəneɪdiən]	[kəneɪdjən]	[kəneɪdʒən]

This common degeneration led to calling Arcadians [arkeɪdiənz] in Louisiana "Cajuns" [keɪdʒənz].

Imprecise Enunciation

In addition to standards for pronunciation, we have standards for the clarity of speech, referred to as **enunciation** or diction. As our articulators move from position to position in coarticulated running speech, they achieve more or less accurately the formations necessary to produce each phoneme. The range of accuracy can vary from careful, crisp, and sharp enunciation to approximated, sloppy productions. When enunciation is so casual, slurred, and imprecise that it affects **intelligibility,** it is considered non-standard. Enunciation also suggests personal attitudes, abilities, and intelligence, and it may be considered non-standard if it evokes negative impressions about the speaker. We are familiar with the obviously non-standard enunciation that we exhibit after dental anesthesia, and with the slurred barely intelligible speech of the drunken person. At the other extreme is the professional speaker, actor, or announcer who seems to form, effortlessly, each vowel and consonant so accurately that there is little or no ambiguity. Between these extremes there is a range of precision influenced by the following factors: (1) physiologic control over the articulators, (2) the model from which one has learned speech, (3) attitudes toward the speaking situation, and (4) the speaker's awareness of the value of good enunciation for either speech intelligibility or a favorable impression.

Unless one has significant impairment of physiologic control, it is possible to improve one's enunciation by a conscious effort. Demosthenes (384–322 B.C.) placed pebbles in his mouth to improve his speech. These impediments forced him to articulate speech sounds consciously and with great care. When the pebbles were removed, his deliberate practice apparently improved his natural speech. It is not necessary to speak with a mouth full of pebbles, but the principle of making oneself consciously aware of the mechanics of speech production is as sound today as it was in ancient Greece. Relearning habitual motor skills, such as is involved in improving the precision of one's speech enunciation or diction, is generally facilitated by a sequence beginning with analysis of component parts of the action to effect more precise production and to bring them to the level of consciousness. Then the components are placed into increasingly larger and more complex action units, while the speed of production is gradually increased with practice, maintaining the precision of the relearned components. Feedback about the success of relearning completes the sequence.

For the reader who wishes to improve his enunciation, the following exercises are based on the Demosthenean principle:

1. Review formation of individual speech sounds in Chapters III and IV. Follow slowly with your own speech mechanism the sequence of articulatory movements for each phoneme.
2. Produce each phoneme in syllables of CV (Consonant-Vowel), VC, CVC, and VCV, taking care to produce each phoneme slowly and consciously.
3. Read aloud the words listed for each phoneme in Chapters III and IV with phonemes in the initial, medial, and final positions, and in clusters where appropriate. Produce each speech sound clearly and carefully.
4. Read aloud the pairs of contrast words as listed for phonemes in Chapters III and IV, taking care to feel and hear the difference in producing the key phonemes.
5. Read aloud the following section from Lewis Carroll's "Jabberwocky," reading slowly at first and taking care to produce all sounds accurately, including giving full value to all vowels, stressed or unstressed:

> Twas brillig, and the slithy toves
> Did gyre and gimble in the wabe:
> All mimsy were the borogoves,
> And the mome raths outgrabe.
> 'Beware the Jabberwock, my son!
> The jaws that bite, the claws that catch!
> Beware the Jubjub bird, and shun
> The frumious Bandersnatch!'
> He took his vorpal sword in hand;
> Long time the manxome foe he sought-
> So rested he by the Tumtum tree,
> And stood awhile in thought.

6. Now, reread at a faster pace but be careful to maintain clear enunciation of all words. Read more rapidly until you reach a comfortable and natural pace but with crisp and accurate enunciation. Use a listener to help judge progress.
7. Select familiar prose passages to read aloud, following the sequences of steps 5 and 6.
8. Extemporaneously, describe pictures to a listener, maintaining improved enunciation as much as possible.
9. These exercises, which may take several weeks to complete, may be recorded to provide self-feedback, or they may be monitored by a critical listener for external feedback.

Irregular Voice and Rhythm

We observe a very broad latitude for acceptable speaking voice. The processes of phonation and resonation, described in Chapter II, create a remarkable variety of fundamental frequency and overtone relationships we call **voice quality**. Without pathology of the vocal tract, some persons unconsciously develop voices that are habitually nasal, breathy, or harsh. They encounter a range of listener reactions from acceptance to repulsion.

Greater open nasal resonance in vowels, sometimes referred to as "nasal twang," is generally present in the northern Midwest more than in other parts of the country. Hypernasality is also prevalent in some rural areas of the Midwest and Southwest and in some urban centers of the West Coast. Newsboys [ɛ̃kstrɔ̃], [ɛ̃kstrɔ̃], [ɛ̃kstrɔ̃] and carnival barkers [hɝ̃ɪ], [hɝ̃ɪ], [hɝ̃ɪ] habitually relax the velum and increase nasal resonance. Other talkers with hypernasal voice quality often have habits of speaking with the tongue raised in the back of the mouth, with a very relaxed velum, or with little movement of the jaw and lips. Any of these habits may contribute to the perception of undesirable nasality. A change to more oral resonance may be achieved by taking steps to change such habits. For example, in producing vowel sounds, the bunching of the back of the tongue may be avoided by care in touching the tongue tip against the back of the mandibular incisors during production.

Breathy voices result from excess air escaping from the glottis during phonation. Breathiness occurs naturally during excitement or exertion, and some people effect a breathy voice to evoke interest. If persistent breathiness affects speech intelligibility or fluency, the speaker may want to consult a laryngologist or a speech/language pathologist. For moderate breathiness, the student may benefit from such exercises as extending duration of vowels to gain efficient use of breath pressure at the glottis, then practicing syllables first with voiced consonants adjoining a vowel and later with voiceless consonants. This may be followed by slowly counting aloud ("one-and-two-and-three-and . . .") with continuous voicing, maintaining sufficient volume for a listener six feet away, and extending the count longer with each trial.

"Harsh" voices suggest the negative impression they give listeners. Descriptive adjectives such as "rough, strident, metallic, and grating" reflect common attitudes of listeners. In the absence of apparent pathology, muscular tension or vocal abuse may be the cause. Reference to a laryngologist or speech/language pathologist is suggested if harshness persists.

A Summary View of Speech Standards

It is clear that we do observe some standards for speech. They are implicit and generalized from usage rather than explicitly stated in order to shape usage. The standards are based on several criteria, which change with the situation. Non-standard speech is easier to define than is the standard. When intelligibility is reduced or when the listener receives a negative impression of the speaker, the speech pattern is generally considered to be non-standard.

DIALECTS

"Then said they unto him, 'Say now *Shibboleth*': and he said 'Sibboleth': for he could not frame to pronounce it right" (Judges xii–6). The unfortunate Ephraimite whose language did not include the /ʃ/ sound revealed his nationality by his speech when he pronounced it [sɪbolɛθ], for then the Gileadites of the Old Testament "took him, and slew him at the passages of Jordan." Though the consequences are not always so drastic, we are each marked by how we speak—where we grew up, where our parents were born, how we were educated, what religious or racial groups we represent, how extensively we have traveled, where we have lived, our occupations, even our ambitions. Phoneticians have *shibboleths*, or key words that can identify important things about us. For while our written language may be fairly uniform, our speech is variable and idiomatic.

Dialects are the words, language forms, pronunciations, and speech habits peculiar to people of a specific geographic region who are part of a larger group using the same language. American-English, for example, is a dialect of the English language, as is Australian-English, Canadian-English, South African-English, and that of other countries in which the people are native speakers of English. Even though there are recognized differences in the speech of these various countries, a person from one English speaking country can understand persons from another. In popular usage, dialect has also come to mean the speech patterns associated with any ethnic or other group with different language habits. Thus, Black American-English is considered a dialect of American-English, identified by certain habits of language usage and speech. Dialects occur because of ethnocentric convergence of a group for a common cause, or because of isolation—either geographic or social, either forced or by choice. Easy and rapid transportation, migrations, and pervasive mass media reduce dialect differences, but so long as groups of people have special common interests or are isolated, dialects are likely to persist.

American-English

For our purposes, American-English is that English spoken within the United States. Although some have argued as early as the Revolutionary War that "American" should be considered a different language, there is too much in common with the language used by the natives of the British Isles and of other English dialects in far flung parts of the world to accept this argument, except on political or patriotic grounds. American-English is different from the language of England because of the great distance by which the countries are separated, and because of different patterns of migration and expansion. The differences include vocabulary (truck—lorry, elevator—lift, vacation—holiday), spelling (generalization—generalisation, spelled—spelt), and pronunciation ([bɪn]—[bin], [nu]—[nju], [læf]—[laf]). Another major difference is in rhythm, especially the pattern of stressing and unstressing. American-English is spoken at a slower rate with less varied intonation, and a secondary stress is given to syllables of long words. British-English is more animated with greater intonation variations. The British give heavy stress to the selected syllable, obscuring or even telescoping unaccented vowels. Thus *Worchestershire* becomes [wʊ́stəʃɪə] and *waistcoat* becomes [wɛ́skət]. Such telescoping is historically responsible for "Bedlam," derived as the familiar name for London's famous Bethlehem Hospital. This pattern of stressing is especially noticeable on words with *-ary* suffixes so that British *dictionary* becomes [díkʃənrɪ], *secretary* is said [sɛ́krətrɪ], and *ordinary* is pronounced [ɔ́rdnrɪ]. This habit gave rise to the story that a British gentleman visiting the United States referred to Niagara Falls when he returned home as "Niffles."

Within the major dialect of American-English, there are numerous sub-dialects. Here, "sub-" is used in the sense of smaller, rather than inferior. Dialect areas are not distinct, sharply defined entities with patterns consistently different from their neighbors. Rather, there is considerable overlapping, and one small dialect area may be part of one or more larger areas. For example, the pronunciation of the ice cream sundae as [sʌndə] is peculiar to natives of a very small area centered in the city of St. Louis, whereas the St. Louis area is part of a larger dialect area of the Mid-West in which *born* is commonly pronounced [bɑrn], and this larger area in turn is part of a still larger Southern dialect area in which the word *greasy* is pronounced [grizɪ] and *on* is said [ɔn]. Yet, St. Louis is borderline for

Figure VII–2. The three major dialect areas of the United States

pronunciation of the word *drought* where some people pronounce it [draʊt] and others pronounce it [draʊθ]. As one moves north toward Chicago, [draʊθ] is prevalent, but if one moves west or south, [draʊt] is more common.

American-English is conventionally divided into three major geographic areas of marked dialect differences. These are New England, Southern American and General American (Figure VII–2). If we were to consider slight dialect differences, such as the pronunciation of *sundae* around St. Louis, we could divide the country into literally hundreds of minor dialect areas with extensive overlapping of boundaries. But here we are interested primarily in major variations, particularly in different pronunciations that are systematic and common to more than a few words. In addition to the three major areas, two of the smaller dialect areas, a state and a city, as well as the cultural-racial dialect of Black-English, will be described as examples of less general dialects.

New England

This dialect area includes the states of Maine, New Hampshire, and Rhode Island, and the eastern portions of Connecticut, Massachusetts, and Vermont (see Figure VII–2). The early colonists who settled this area came from the South of England and brought with them dialects of the area around London. Many were well educated and emigrated for reasons of religious freedom. In the new world, they resumed their livelihood as artisans and merchants, creating the character of the Yankee trader who was to be active in the shipping trade of the world. Their commerce and their location on the seaboard kept the colonists in frequent contact with England, so that their speech patterns changed essentially as those of England changed. The area was aptly named "New England."

So successful were the early colonists in dominating the economy that when later settlers with different English dialects came from the northern parts of England and from Scotland and Ireland, they found it necessary to move on to seek their fortune, and they went westward into upper New York and Ohio and toward Iowa and the great plains.

The most common characteristic pronunciation of Southern England that persists in the New England dialect area is omission of /r/ in the final position of words and just before consonants. With -r in the final position, the preceding stressed vowel is either elongated or is diphthongized with a /ə/ off-glide. Note the following examples:

	General American	*New England*
car	[kɑr]	[kɑː]
were	[wɝ]	[wɜː]

poor	[pʊr]	[pʊə]
fear	[fɪr]	[fɪə]
bear	[bɛr]	[bɛə]
four	[for]	[foə]

With the final unstressed /ɚ/, the /r/ quality is omitted so that *after* becomes [æftə] and *better* becomes [bɛtə]. In the preconsonantal position, the -r- is similarly treated as in the following examples:

	General American	New England
third	[θɝd]	[θɜ:d]
cursed	[kɝst]	[kɜ:st]
farm	[farm]	[fa:m]
park	[park]	[pa:k]
fort	[fort]	[foət]
fired	[faɪɚd]	[faɪəd]

The initial *r*-, and the -*r*- between vowels in such words as *arrow, borrow, around,* and *erase* are given full /r/ quality however.

A second pronunciation persisting from its southern English origin and attributed to New England is that called the "broad *a.*" In some words, the /æ/ of General American is pronounced /ɑ/ so that *ask* becomes [ɑsk] and *bath* becomes [bɑθ]. The broad *a* as /ɑ/ is especially prevalent in and around the city of Boston, but in much of New England the /a/ is more often used for General American /æ/. Note the following pronunciations:

	General American	New England /a/	Broad a /ɑ/
class	[klæs]	[klas]	[klɑs]
ask	[æsk]	[ask]	[ɑsk]
path	[pæθ]	[paθ]	[pɑθ]
rather	[ræðɚ]	[raðə]	[rɑðə]

The broad *a* pronunciation is sometimes used in other parts of the United States on the stage, for pedantic or fashionable purposes, or by Anglophiles.

Another pronunciation more typical of New England than of General American is the use of [ju], or sometimes [ɪu], in such words as *new, duty, student, tune,* and *duke.* This residual of Southern England compares with the General American use of /u:/ or /u/. New Englanders also use a slightly rounded /ɑ/ of brief duration in words such as *hot, not, rock, top,* and *spot.* This sound, written phonetically as /ɒ/, is close to a partially rounded /ɔ/ but of shorter duration, used in such words as *coffee, cost, long, lost,* and *song.* Still another typical New England pronunciation is [aɪðə] and [naɪðə] for *either* and *neither.*

These characteristic pronunciations are becoming less common now in

New England, for although the early seaboard colonists could avert the waves of new immigrants from abroad, present day New Englanders can hardly resist infiltration from the rest of the United States, nor can they control the speech of network radio and TV performers that influences their pronunciation inexorably toward General American.

Southern American

The Southern American-English dialect area is designated roughly as the area south of a broad border line that could be drawn from east to west through the southern half of Maryland; northern West Virginia; the southern parts of Ohio, Indiana and Illinois; through southeastern Missouri and the northwest corner of Arkansas, curving southward through the eastern quarter of Texas to the Gulf of Mexico (see Figure VII–2). The dialect is most prevalent in the "deep South" states of North Carolina, South Carolina, Georgia, Florida, Alabama, Mississippi, and Louisiana. It is variable in the border states, including Kentucky and Tennessee.

Early settlers of Virginia came from southern England at about the same time (1607) as New England was being colonized (1620). Although the Massachusetts and the Virginia colonies had a common linguistic origin, there was a virgin wilderness and often hostile Indians between them. This permitted less exchange with each other than with their common mother country, England. The Virginia colonists, with a plantation economy, had less commerce with England, and thus tended to change their speech less to parallel the changes taking place in England. In order to have enough land for their plantation crops, the families and descendents of the planters of tidewater Virginia moved southward and westward into the Florida peninsula and to the Gulf of Mexico. They took their early southern England dialect inland with them, further separating it and themselves from the influences of changes taking place in England. The Southerners who moved into the remote mountain regions of Kentucky, Tennessee, and West Virginia were even more isolated, and retained some of their Shakespearean English well into the 20th century.

Later immigrants to the South found much of the land already occupied by large plantation holdings and accordingly moved westward to find land of their own. An exception is the southern part of Louisiana, which was dominated by French influence and received immigration of the Arcadians (Cajuns) of Canada. A major group of immigrants into the South in the latter part of the 18th century were the Black slaves brought from Africa. They learned and adapted the Southern dialect, and shaped it by "Africanisms" of their own.

Southern dialect reflects its common heritage with New England in the characteristic omission of final and preconsonantal /r/. The vowel before -r or

-r- is often elongated and sometimes simplified, rather than diphthongized as is common in New England. Note the following examples:

	General American	New England	Southern
four	[for]	[foə]	[fo:]
fort	[fort]	[foət]	[fo:t]
fired	[faɪəd]	[faɪəd]	[fɑ:d]
flowers	[flauəz]	[flauəz]	[flɑ:z]

However, *fear* becomes [fɪə], and *four* sometimes is pronounced [foə]. The broad *a* is commonly used in place of the New England /a/ before *-r-* as in these examples:

	General American	New England	Southern
car	[kɑr]	[ka:]	[kɑ:]
farm	[fɑrm]	[fa:m]	[fɑ:m]
large	[lɑrdʒ]	[la:dʒ]	[lɑ:dʒ]
park	[pɑrk]	[pa:k]	[pɑ:k]

Stressed /ɝ/ and unstressed /ɚ/ of General American are pronounced /ɜ/ and /ə/ in words like *third* [θɜ:d] and *sister* [sɪstə], as they are in New England.

Simplification of diphthongs can also occur in Southern Speech without *-r-* as in the following words with /aɪ/:

	General American and New England	Southern
I	[aɪ]	[ɑ:]
my	[maɪ]	[mɑ:]
nice	[naɪs]	[nɑ:s]
time	[taɪm]	[tɑ:m]

Southern pronunciation favors [ju] or [ɪu] in other words as *new, tune,* and *student.* There is a tendency toward use of /ɔ/, for example in *on* as [ɔn] compared with [ɑn] farther north. The South pronounces *-og* words as a well rounded /ɔ/ in such words as *log, frog,* and *dog,* compared with a less rounded /ɔ/ in General American and /ɑ/ or /a/ in New England

The "drawl" that is attributed to Southern speakers is not universal but is characteristic of some speakers. The rate of articulation, contrary to popular belief, is not slower than in General American. Rather, it is the result of a combination of an increased range of pitch change for intonation and diphthongization of some simple vowels. Characteristic of the drawl is the intrusion of /j/ and /w/ glides followed by the /ə/. The following pronunciations of words are examples that contribute to the drawl sound.

sit	[sɪjət]	*cord*	[kɔwəd]
less	[lɛjəs]	*board*	[bouwəd]
class	[klæjəs]	*good*	[guwəd]

A special pronunciation of Southern speech is the use of /ɪ/ rather than /ə/ in some unstressed syllables, as in the following words:

salad	[sælɪd]	*respect*	[rɪspɛkt]
kitchen	[kɪtʃɪn]	*believe*	[bɪliv]
palate	[pælɪt]	*dispose*	[dɪspouz]
bracket	[brækɪt]	*predict*	[prɪdɪkt]
lettuce	[lɛtɪs]	*debate*	[dɪbeɪt]
wanted	[wɔntɪd]	*relate*	[rɪleɪt]

A peculiar single word pronunciation throughout the South is [grizɪ] for *greasy*, compared with [grisɪ] in most of the rest of the country. The /ɛ/ sound is frequently replaced with other vowels or diphthongs as *cent* may become [sɪnt] and *ten* becomes [tɪn], *bed* becomes [bɛəd] or [bɛjəd], and *get* becomes [gɛət]. Before intervocalic /r/, the [ɛ] in General American *dairy* [dɛrɪ] is frequently said [eɪ] as [deɪrɪ], and *Mary* is pronounced [meɪrɪ].

Industrialization, migrations, and easy travel, as well as pervasive public media, are influencing Southern American-English dialect toward General American pronunciation. In such major cities as Atlanta, Birmingham, Charleston, and Houston, one is likely to hear General American almost as commonly as Southern dialect. This is especially true in colleges, universities, and the headquarters of national businesses. However, because of the greater portion of rural area in the South, its dialect is likely to change more slowly than is that of New England.

General American

The second and successive waves of English settlers came from northern England, Scotland, and northern Ireland. Their dialects were different from those colonists who emigrated earlier from southern England and had settled on the seaboard. The southern English colonists so dominated both the Massachusetts and the Virginia areas that the later immigrants felt compelled to move beyond the coast in order to realize their dream of owning their own land and making their fortune. The settlers of western New England moved into upper New York state and westward by the Great Lakes to Ohio, Indiana, Illinois, and Iowa. Those Scottish and Scotch-Irish immigrants who first settled in western Pennsylvania and southern New Jersey migrated south into the Shenandoah valley, the southern mountains, and on to Texas and the cattle country of the northern plains. Those who could not find land in Maryland and Virginia moved westward through the Cumberland Gap into Kentucky and Tennessee and north into Illinois, Missouri, and Kansas. Their dialects moved with them as they migrated westward through the Ohio Valley, across the Mississippi, on to the Great Plains and eventually to the Pacific Coast. These immigrants came in great numbers, fanned out over a broad area into the central and western United States, and established their prevalent speech habits as the basis of today's General American dialect.

The word lists and exercises of Chapters III and IV and the pronunciations in this book reflect the author's General American dialect. General American is marked by pronunciation of *r* wherever it is included in spelling. Not only the initial glide as in *red* and the cluster glide as in *green*, but the intervocalic *-r-* in *very*, the final *-r* in *bar*, the preconsonantal *-r-* in *barn*, and the unstressed *-er* in *farmer* are produced with /r/ quality. The *a* in such words as *ask*, *last*, *bath*, *can't*, and *rather* is pronounced /æ/, compared with the New England /a/ or /ɑ/. In nearly all unstressed suffixes, vowels reduce to /ə/ as in the following words:

surface	[sɝ·fəs]
salad	[sæləd]
pocket	[pɑkət]
bunches	[bʌntʃəz]

Either and *neither* are pronounced [iðɚ] and [niðɚ], compared with the New England [aɪðə] and [naɪðə].

Other vowel sounds are somewhat variable over the vast area of General American. The *-o-* vowel, for example, varies with the consonant that follows. General American *on* is usually pronounced [ɑn] compared with [ɔn] in Southern, and sometimes [an] in New England. *Doll* is pronounced [dɑl] compared with the New England [dɔl], and *-og* words such as *log*, *dog*, and *frog* are usually pronounced [ɔg] in General American and Southern, compared with [ag] or [ɑg] in New England. The *-or* words such as *for*, *more*, and *horse* vary with [ɔr], [or] and [ɑr] pronunciations heard.

Comparison of the Major Dialects

For comparison of the three major dialect areas of the United States, the following short passage is word transcribed in each dialect:

> "Give your doll her bath," Aunt Mary said, placing a bar of soap on the stand near the sink. "Her hair is dirty and greasy." Neither the older woman nor the little girl noticed the new kitchen curtain blowing as the first sign of the rising storm.

**General
American:** [gɪv jɚ dɑl hɚ bæθ], [ænt mɛrɪ sɛd], [pļeɪsɪŋ ə bɑr əv soup an
ðə stænd nɪr ðə sɪŋk]. [hɚ her ɪz dɝ·tɪ ænd grɪsɪ]. [nɪðɚ ðə
ouldɚ wumən nor ðə lɪtļ gɝ·l noutəst ðə nu kɪtʃən kɝ·tņ
blouɪŋ æz ðə fɝ·st saɪn əv ðə raɪzɪŋ storm].

**New
England:** [gɪv jɜə dɔl hɜ: baθ], [ant mærɪ sɛd], [pļeɪsɪŋ ə ba: əv soup an
ðə stand nɪə ðə sɪŋk]. [hɜ: hɛə ɪz dɜtɪ and grɪsɪ]. [naɪðə ðə
ouldə wumən nɔə ðə lɪtļ gɜl noutəst ðə nju kɪtʃən kɜtņ blouɪŋ
az ðə fɜ:st saɪn əv ðə raɪzɪŋ stɔəm].

Southern: [gɪv jɜ: dɑl hɜ: bæjəθ], [ænt meɪrɪ sɛjəd], [pļeɪsɪŋ ə bɑ: əv
soup ɔn ðə stæjənd nɪə ðə sɪŋk]. [hɜ: hɛjə ɪz dɜ:tɪ ænd
grɪzɪ]. [nɪðə ðə ouldə wumɪn nowə ðə lɪtļ gɜəl noutɪst ðə nju
kɪtʃɪn kɜ:tɪn blouwɪŋ æjəz ðə fɜ:st sɑ:n əv ðə rɑ:zɪŋ stɔwəm].

Immigration of various groups of non-English speaking Europeans,
especially Swedes, Italians, and Germans, throughout the General American
area during the 19th and 20th centuries has added a variety of speech habits
and pronunciations in different communities. Other important migrations
involved the Mexicans moving to the American Southwest and the Orientals
moving to the West Coast. By and large, these groups have become linguistically acculturized, moving away from their native language toward a General American with their own peculiar pronunciations and intonation patterns in the second (Creole) generation, and by the third generation becoming nearly indistinguishable from the General American around them.

For the future, General American pronunciation appears to be the
dialect most likely to predominate throughout the United States. It is the
largest dialect in both geographic area and in population. In a very mobile
society, where people frequently move from one part of the country to
another for vocational advancement, the surviving dialect is likely to be that
which is most common. Announcers on network TV and radio are mostly
speakers of General American, bringing this dialect daily into nearly every
Southern and New England Home. Moving pictures, similarly, are largely
dominated by General American speech, even though live stage productions
are likely to reflect New England or Southern English dialect. Some blending of the three major dialects is likely for the future, with small areas of
dialect differences recognized, such as those that follow.

Hawaii

It is not surprising that one finds different sounding speech in the
Hawaiian Islands, often called the "melting pot" of the Pacific. Hawaii is

thousands of miles from the mainland, it became the 50th state of the Union only comparatively recently in 1959, and it has a history of migrations unlike the rest of the United States. New England missionaries and Yankee sailors in the early 19th century brought English to the native Hawaiians, who spoke a Polynesian dialect. Then came waves of "sugar immigrants" imported to grow cane and pineapple. Between 1875 and 1930, over a quarter-million workers (mostly men) were brought to the Hawaiian Islands, which totaled an area of only 6435 square miles. Each group spoke its own language. They came in successive waves of Chinese, Portuguese, Japanese, Puerto Ricans, Koreans, Spaniards, and the last and largest group, the Filipinos, who spoke three different languages themselves.

While each group kept its native language at home and in close social affairs, they needed a "business" language for broader communication. Some simple and universal oral language was especially necessary in dealing with the plantation overseers, for buying and selling with other groups, and just in order to be able to talk to their fellow worker who may have been born on a different continent. They adopted and adapted the dialect called "pidgin" English, a name that probably came from a Cantonese pronunciation of the English word "business."

Although the native Hawaiians had their own language, they eagerly learned English in the mission schools. With the flood of immigrants, the common intermarriage of Hawaiians with these groups, and a steady decrease in the number of pure Hawaiians, the original Hawaiian language has had little chance to survive except in place names. Hawaiian has only seven consonants (/h, p, k, w, l, m, n/) and five vowels (/i, ɛ, ɑ, u, o/), remarkably consistent in pronunciation. Intervocalic *w*, as in *Ewa* and *Hawaii*, inconsistently becomes the labio-dental fricative /v/. There are no consonant clusters and no word ends with a consonant. Hawaiian makes frequent use of the glottal stop to separate like vowels as in *Hawaii* [hɑwɑiʔi], *Nuuanu* [nuʔuɑnu], *alii* [ɑliʔi], and *muumuu* [muʔumuʔu]. To make the strange English words conform to their consonant-vowel sequence, Hawaiians placed a vowel between clustered consonants, and a vowel was added to the end of words. They freely substituted consonants of their own language for English consonants lacking in Hawaiian, so that, for example, the name *Fred* became *Peleke*. The Hawaiians also substituted for consonants of other languages so that the Chinese pidgin word for *food*, "chowchow," became the common Hawaiian word "kaukau."

Pidgin emerged from its early development with plantation terms to its **creole** stage as second generation Islanders learned it as babies. It contained only content words and very few function words, it usually omitted the verb *to be*, and it had little or no inflection—"can do," "bumby" (by and by), "mobetu" (more better), and "savvy" (sabe). At present, citizens of Japanese ancestry and "haoles" (Caucasians) are the largest ethnic groups on the Islands. English is the official language with a mixture of General American and New England pronunciations, but pidgin can still be heard, particularly among non-Caucasian men. Remnants of the immigrants' native languages are still spoken at home and in shops. Original Hawaiian has largely become an artifact in songs and for tourist events.

New York City

This dialect area, which has one of the most concentrated populations on earth, includes the city of New York and its adjoining boroughs, most of Long Island, the eastern portion of New Jersey, the southern end of the Hudson River valley, and southeastern Connecticut. There is almost nothing left from the Dutch heritage of New Amsterdam except here and there an anglicized place name like *Harlem*, where now Puerto Rican Spanish and Black American-English is most likely to be heard. Thousands upon thousands of European immigrants entered the United States through Ellis Island and the Port of New York during the 19th and early 20th centuries. Many stayed in the area from choice because they had relatives or found friends there who spoke their language, or because they either had no money to move away or no desire to move farther into the strange new country. The public schools took responsibility for acculturation of the immigrants, teaching their children the English language as spoken in America. A fine school system and the intense desire of the immigrants to become Americans wrought a linguistic and cultural miracle that, although never since matched, is seldom recognized or appreciated.

The speech of the people of New York City is extremely varied. What is commonly attributed to New York as its dialect is really one among its many dialects that has persisted and has been prominent in drama and public media representations of New York. Here we point out a few prominent characteristics. New York shares the omission of final and preconsonantal *r* with most of the rest of the Atlantic Coast. In some words where /ɔ/ is found in Southern, General American, and New England, a diphthongized [ɔə] is used in New York so that *all* becomes [ɔəl], *law* becomes [lɔə], and *taught* becomes [tɔət] with pronounced lip-rounding. However, the more generally used /ɔ/ or /o/ before /r/ is quite often pronounced /ɑ/ for the following:

forest	[fɑrɪst]
horrid	[hɑrɪd]
orange	[ɑrɪndʒ]

Before the /ŋ/, the usual /ɔ/ also becomes /ɑ/ as in *prong* as [prɑŋ] and *honk* as [hɑŋk]. The *o* before *r* is very rounded as *four* becomes [fɔə] compared with Southern or New England [foə] and General American [for]. But the /ɝ/ of General American is likely to be [ʌr] so that *worry* becomes [wʌrɪ] and *hurry* becomes [hʌrɪ].

A number of sub-standard pronunciations are attributed to the New York dialect in popular media stereotypes. These include unnecessary pronunciation of a [g] in -ng endings so that *singing* becomes [sɪŋgɪŋ] and *Long Island* becomes [lɔŋgaɪlənd]; substitution of a glottal stop for lingua-alveolar or lingua-palatal stops as in [bɑʔl] for *bottle* and [trɪʔl] for *trickle*, and the substitution of /d/ for /ð/ in *these, those,* and *them.*

New York City is not only a place people like to visit. The "Big Apple" attracts its share of residents from all three of the major dialect areas, adding further variety to the speech one is likely to hear there.

Black American-English

The Black tribes of Africa typically spoke languages different from each other, even though they might have lived in fairly close proximity. Their tribal culture was dominated politically by strong autocratic chiefs, and it featured religious rules and taboos that kept tribes linguistically separated, isolated, and relatively small. Their languages were generally not recorded with formal orthographic systems. When Caucasian and Black slave merchants dipped into this polyglot reservoir during the 18th and early 19th centuries, they assembled on the beaches of West Africa compounds of Black men, women, and older children who spoke a myriad of African languages. Regrouped into masses that were convenient to fill the holds and meet the scheduled orders of "slaver" ships, families and tribes were further separated. Their dispersion continued at the auction blocks of Richmond, Annapolis, Charleston, and other slave trade centers of the American South, as plantation owners bid to buy the strong and healthy worker, regardless of tribe or family relation.

Thus, among the slaves of a plantation there might be no two who spoke the same African language. Restrictions on their travel prohibited meeting other members of their native tribes on neighboring plantations. The overseers spoke to them only in English. Finally, their own names, the last vestiges of their African language, were replaced by their owner with first names from common Anglo-Saxon (Joe, Topsy, Ned), classic Latin (Erasmus, Hannibal, Caesar), King James biblical stories (Amos, Ezekiel, Thomas), and from heroes (George Washington, Martin Luther). Surnames were usually the adopted names of their owners. Under these conditions they turned to the only common language available—English.

Their first new world speech, a kind of English Pidgin, consisted of imitated approximations of the Southern American-English model available to them, and some remnants (tote, voodoo, gumbo) of their mother tongue. Since they were unfamiliar with orthographic systems from their African languages and were not given the opportunity to learn to read and write the new language, they did not have alphabet spelling against which to compare their aural perception of others' speech and their own pronunciation. They taught their children this oral language from the cradle, developing the plantation creole or early native American phase of Black American-English.

In 1880, Joel Chandler Harris published a record of creole, Black American-English dialect in *Uncle Remus: His Songs and His Sayings*. Upon hearing that his work was to be catalogued among humorous publications, he retorted that "-its intention is perfectly serious—to preserve the legends— and to wed them permanently to the quaint dialect." He further noted that the dialect is different "—from the intolerable misrepresentations of the minstrel stage, but it is at least phonetically genuine." By brilliant transliter-ation with our alphabet, he forces his reader to abandon the usual rapid visual scanning, and, at least sub-vocally, delight in speaking the dialect of the uneducated Black slave story teller.

> In dem days, de creeturs kyar'd on marters same as fokes. Dey went inter fahmin', en I speck ef de troof wuz ter come out, dey kep' sto', en had der camp-meetin' times en der bobbycues w'en de wedder wuz 'greeble.

Within this short passage is the characteristic substitution of /d/ for /ð/ (dem, de, dey, der, wedder), the insertion of /r/ (marters, ter, der, inter), substitution of /f/ for /θ/ (troof), omission of unstressed syllables (kyar'd, 'speck, 'greeble), omission of final cluster consonants (kep'), substitution of /w/ for /ʍ/ (w'en), and, of course, omission of /r/ (fahmin', bobbycues, sto').

Creole Black American-English is most accurately viewed as a dialect of Southern American-English, since it developed from that dialect and shares characteristics with it. The English spoken by Blacks in Africa is certainly different from that spoken by Blacks in America. As a dialect for Black Americans today, the early creole has been dissipated first by migrations out of the South to the northern and western United States, and second, by social mobility with adoption of the major regional dialect spoken by other than Black Americans.

Modern Black American-English, sometimes called "Ebonics" or "Merican," is more difficult to define and is usually attributed to low socio-economic status Black persons. Certainly, the speech of Blacks differs greatly depending upon the part of the country in which they live and upon their social status. Many Black people who grew up with Black American-English dialect have adopted one of the major regional dialects but can still speak their earlier dialect. Much that characterizes Black American-English is in vocabulary, syntax, and intonation, but some pronunciations are distinctive. Final and preconsonantal -r is omitted, as in Southern speech, so that *hammer* becomes [hæmə] and *sharp* becomes [ʃaəp] or [ʃa:p]. Many diphthongs are simplified so that *I* becomes [a:], *pie* becomes [pa:] or [pa:], *boy* becomes [bɔ:] or [bo:] and *time* becomes [ta:m]. A distinctive feature is the nearly complete substitution of other sounds for the lingua-dental sounds

/θ/ and /ð/. The /θ/ becomes /t/ initially and when following lingua-alveolar /n/, and it becomes /f/ medially and finally as in the following examples:

thumb	[tʌm]	*month*	[mʌnt]
teeth	[tif]	*arithmetic*	[rɪtmətɪk]
bathroom	[bæfrʊm]	*nothing*	[nʌfɪn]

The /ð/ becomes /d/ initially, and becomes /v/ medially and finally, as in these examples:

these	[diz]	*the*	[də]
smooth	[smuv]	*those*	[douz]
feather	[fɛvə]	*bathing*	[beɪvɪn]

Final consonant clusters are simplified by omission of one or more consonants, usually the final one. Note these examples where both members of the cluster are either voiced or voiceless:

locked	[lɑk]	*first*	[fʌs]
wasp	[wɑs]	*hand*	[hæn]
nest	[nɛs]	*rained*	[reɪn]
rubbed	[rʌb]	*messed*	[mɛs]

Final consonants are usually both articulated when one is voiceless and the other is voiced, as in [dʒʌmp] for *jump* and [bɛlt] for *belt*. Final and medial /l/ is often omitted so that *apple* becomes [æpə], *health* becomes [hɛəf], *nails* becomes [neɪəz], and *help* becomes [hɛp]. With omission of medial /l/ and reduction of voiceless consonants in a cluster, *twelfth* becomes [tʌf].

Omission of the contracted /l/ suggests to the listener a difference in syntax that may originally have been just a matter of pronunciation. When *will* is contracted and the /l/ is omitted, "Tomorrow I'll bring the thing" becomes "Tomorrow I' bring the thing." Similarly, "He'll be here in a few minutes" becomes "He' be here in a few minutes," and "I'll be working tomorrow" becomes "I' be working tomorrow." When language is transmitted to the next generation primarily by speech, these omissions of /l/ may appear to be and then become real syntactical differences. A similar phenomenon occurs with the often omitted -*ed* suffix, so that *named* becomes [neɪm] and *finished* is said as [fɪnɪʃ], suggesting the absence of past tense usage. Omission of contracted 've for *have* and 's for *has* also suggests syntactical omissions as in "I' been here for hours," and "He' gone home." A similar phenomenon in General American is responsible for people writing "might of been," derived from "might *have* been" by way of contracted [maɪt əv bɪn] in connected speech.

The use of [ɪn] for the -*ing* suffix is common to many American-English speakers but is almost universal in black American-English as in [sɪŋɪn] for *singing*. Nasalized vowels are sometimes substituted for final nasal consonants as in [mæ̃] for *man*, [rʌ̃] for *run*, and [drʌ̃] for *drum*. This is especially frequent in unstressed positions as in [meəmæ̃] for *mailman*.

DEFECTIVE SPEECH

The foregoing sections describe important ways speech differs as nonstandard productions and as dialects. Neither kind of deviation should be considered "defective" or "disordered" speech. Two useful definitions of speech defects are prevalent. Speech defects exist when the speaker wishes to change a non-standard pattern but cannot, and thus some external assistance is needed. Speech is defective also when it poses a significant handicap for the speaker, possibly influencing his social, vocational, or educational potential. The first definition refers to the speaker's own impression of his speech and his difficulty with self-improvement. The second refers to the reaction of his listeners. The speaker might analyze his own speech by comparing it with that of others, but often he is unaware even that his speech is different until he is cued by a negative listener reaction.

The following example illustrates how these definitions of defective speech might be applied. Earlier in this chapter, the difficulty of mastering the /l/ and /r/ sounds was cited. For the young child, non-standard productions of these lingual consonants are considered immature speech patterns and are to be expected. Few children master these sounds before six years of age, and before this, the /w/ substitution is not viewed with concern. If the substitution should persist into adulthood, a number of possible reactions may take place:

1. The speaker realizes, by self-analysis or from listener reaction, that his /l/ or /r/ differs from that of his peers. By careful listening and by trial-anderror attempts at articulation, he may improve his own production to a satisfactory level and have no further problem.
2. Upon realizing his /l/ or /r/ production is different, he may wish to change toward the standard, but his attempts are in vain. He cares about his speech and will need help with his speech defect.
3. Upon realizing his /l/ or /r/ production is different, he may not care to change from what he has always said. He may attempt a change himself but gives up easily with disinterest. Among his peers and in his school, or in his type of vocation, he is not penalized because of his non-standard speech. His speech is intelligible and some listeners may even think it "cute." His speech is non-standard but not defective. It serves him well.
4. Upon realizing his /l/ or /r/ production is different, he may not care to change from what he has always said. He persists in his non-standard patterns. In school classes in which oral recitation is required, his

classmates laugh at him, and later he finds he cannot get the jobs he wants because of the reactions of listeners to his speech. He retreats from communicative situations and works at menial occupations well beneath his intellectual potential. He is severely penalized by his defective speech.

5. He realizes his /l/ or /r/ production is different, but in school, where he is an outstanding athlete, he is popular and his peers take his different speech as a matter of course. He would like to change his speech but is not bothered enough to make a serious effort. In college he cannot make the varsity team, and now his fellow students sometimes laugh at his speech or imitate him. They do not seek him out or look up to him. He knows his speech defect will handicap him and he seeks professional help. Even though there was no change in the degree of difference in his speech, it has shifted from merely non-standard to defective because of the situation and his reaction to it.

In these examples, even though the speech a listener might have heard was the same, whether or not it should be considered "defective" depended upon the situation, upon the reaction of listeners, and upon the speaker's perception of his speech pattern.

Imagine, now, the problem of determining the incidence of speech defects in our population. Before the age of 9 or 10 years, since it is natural for children to be developing their articulation, many differences will be prevalent in their speech patterns, particularly among preschoolers. Then too, some listeners may judge a minor deviation in pronunciation of an adult to be a defect when the speaker does not think of it as such. It is not surprising to find studies of the incidence of speech defects giving widely varied reports. Surveys have ranged from less than 1 percent to over 20 percent of the school age population having defective speech, with summary estimates at about 5 percent. In some studies, children just developing speech have been considered defective, and in others, foreign accents and dialect differences were included in the defective group. Differences in severity, the type of defect, the speaker's reaction to his speech, and the handicap it gives him may make the task of determining incidence of speech defects in general a nearly impossible one.

REVIEW VOCABULARY

American-English—that English spoken within the United States.

Colloquial speech—the common, familiar, and informal speech of cultivated people.

Creole speech—refers to the speech of the first generation of native born speakers descended from immigrants from a foreign language background.

Defective speech—that which poses a handicap for the speaker, or that which the speaker wishes to change but cannot without assistance.

Dialect—the words, language forms, pronunciations, and speech habits peculiar to people of a geographic region who are part of larger group using the same language.

Enunciation—clarity or precision of articulation, sometimes referred to as diction.

Immature speech—those patterns different from the prevalent speech patterns of adults within a dialect group that an individual uses because of lack of experience and/or maturation.

Intelligibility—the quality of being understandable, usually limited to the recognition of speech units rather than comprehension of their meaning.

Metathesis—reversal of consonant order in connected speech.

Non-standard speech—that which is notably or remarkably different and considered poorer than general standards of speech.

Pidgin English—an adaptation of English by foreign speakers, using essential content words for conducting business and essential communication.

Pronunciation—selection among available phonemes in producing a unit of speech.

Shibboleth—a peculiarity of speech distinctive to a particular group; a password or watchword.

Standards of speech—a variety of criteria for general acceptance or approval of speech, either stated or implied, against which an individual's speech pattern is commonly judged.

Vernacular—native common usage learned from childhood by educated persons.

Voice quality—that which distinguishes one person's voice from others. The combination of fundamental frequency plus overtones, but usually includes characteristics of articulation and speech rhythm.

EXERCISES

1. Pronounce each of the listed variations for the following three words. Compare these with your own typical pronunciation and with that indicated in dictionaries.

library	*temperature*	*February*
[laɪbrɛrɪ]	[tɛmpɚətjur]	[fɛbruwɛrɪ]
[laɪbrærɪ]	[tɛmpɚətur]	[fɛbjuwɛrɪ]
[laɪbɛrɪ]	[tɛmpɚətʃɚ]	[fɛbəwɛrɪ]
[laɪbɚɛrɪ]	[tɛmpɚtʃɚ]	[fɛbwɛrɪ]
[lɑbrɚɪ]	[tɛmpɪtʃɚ]	[fɛbɚɛrɪ]
	[tɛmpətʃɚ]	[fɛbrɪ]
	[tɪmpɪtʃə]	[fɪbjɪɛrɪ]

2. Ask several friends to say each of the following sentences as they usually would speak it:

   a. "I believe my library book is extensively overdue."
   b. "Today the barometric pressure and temperature are lower than yesterday."
   c. "It begins to get just a little warmer in February and March."

   Transcribe in IPA symbols the key words *library, temperature,* and *February.* Compare to the pronunciations in exercise 1, above. Do not say the sentences to them yourself or tell them the key words. Let them read each sentence silently on a card before saying it from memory.

3. After your speakers have said all three sentences in exercise 2, ask them for the "correct" pronunciation of each of the key words. Transcribe and compare with the transcription of their usual production in connected speech.

4. From the variations in pronunciation described in this chapter, compile a single list of no more than 10 "shibboleth" words that will differentiate speakers from General American, Southern, and New England dialect areas. If possible, test the list on appropriate speakers.

5. Ask several friends or instructors to read and give you "the correct pronunciation" of the following familiar words:

with	([θ] - [ð])
herb	([hɝ] - [ɝ])
often	([ft] - [f])

data	([eɪ] - [æ] - [ɑ])
was	([ʌ] - [ɑ])

After they have said the words, ask such questions as, "Is it supposed to be [wɪθ] or [wɪð]?" "Is it supposed to be [hɝ·b] or [ɝ·b]?" Note in their responses (1) the standards criteria they employ compared with those in this chapter, (2) their level of certainty about the "correct" pronunciation, and (3) any embarrassment or emotional response related to their uncertainty about pronunciation.

6. Ask several friends or instructors to read and "say" each of these probably less familiar words:

> *struthious*
> *lucubration*
> *omphaloskepsis*
> *metathesis*
> *sesquipedalian*

Observe the strategies utilized, not only in settling upon the pronunciation but in determining the accent pattern.

SUGGESTED READING

Winitz, Harris: *Articulatory Acquisition and Behavior.* Englewood Cliffs, N.J., Prentice-Hall, Inc., 1969.

A good basic text on speech development of children from a psycholinguistic viewpoint, for the speech pathologist, especially.

Edwards, Mary Louise and Shriberg, Lawrence D., *Phonology: Applications in Communicative Disorders,* San Diego, College-Hill Press, 1983.

A substantial work for the serious student of phonology, including references on basic readings in phonological theory and child phonology. Extensive appendix.

Carr, Elizabeth B.: *Da Kine Talk: From Pidgin to Standard English in Hawaii.* Honolulu, University Press of Hawaii, 1972.

A scholarly account of the development of neo-Pidgin spoken in Hawaii today, especially its derivation from the various languages that have been spoken in the Islands, and a description of the present variations from island to island.

Dillard, J.L.: *Black English: Its History and Usage in the United States,* New York, Random House, 1972.

This basic treatise on Black American-English traces the roots of the dialect, especially pointing out "Africanisms," related to tribal languages, and the influence of Black American-English on other American-English dialects.

Chapter VIII

SENSORY PRODUCTS OF SPEECH

- **INFORMATION FOR THE AUDITORY SYSTEM**
  - **THE FREQUENCY-INTENSITY SPECTRUM**
  - **DIFFERENCES IN DURATION**
- **INFORMATION FOR THE VISUAL SYSTEM**
- **INFORMATION FOR PROPRIOCEPTION**
- **SPEECH PERCEPTION**
- **REVIEW VOCABULARY**
- **EXERCISES**
- **SUGGESTED READING**

Another important way to describe speech is to consider the results of speaking. The processes of respiration, phonation, resonation, and articulation, described in earlier chapters, result in the production of acoustic energy or sound waves that carry the code of speech to our auditory system. These sounds are the intended and the primary product of speech production. But sounds are not the only result of speaking. A number of other results occur that may be considered by-products, providing secondary level information that is available to our senses. Among these are **visible** lip movements the observer, but not the speaker, has available for the process called "speech reading," the **tactile** [tǽktɪl] impressions of touching and friction available to the speaker during his articulation, and the **kinesthetic** [kɪnɛsθέtɪk] impressions the speaker senses from muscles moving and stretching.

INFORMATION FOR THE AUDITORY SYSTEM

Acoustics [əkústɪks], the branch of physics concerned with the physical properties of sound, collaborates with phonetics to form the specialized field of study called **acoustic phonetics.** Those who pursue acoustic phonetics seek to describe the important acoustic features of speech and how they relate on

217

the one hand to speech production and on the other hand to speech perception. All speech sounds can be described in terms of three acoustic parameters: frequency, intensity, and time. We begin with the parameters of frequency and intensity.

The Frequency-Intensity Spectrum

The physiological process of phonation was described in Chapter II. A complete opening and closing of the glottis constitutes one **cycle** of phonation. The physiological cycle of phonation results in a physical cycle of compression and rarefaction of air molecules as the glottis opens and closes. When the pulses of compression and rarefaction occur regularly or periodically, a sound wave results. A special case for illustration of sound waves is the simple back-and-forth motion of a tuning fork that results in a simple sound or "pure" tone. A cycle of compression and rarefaction of air molecules of the pure tone may be represented graphically by a sinusoidal wave (sine curve), as shown in Figure VIII–1.

The physical term **frequency** refers to the number of complete cycles of openings-closings, oscillations, or vibrations of any object over a given period of time. For sound waves, frequency refers to the number of cycles of compression and rarefaction of air molecules. Figure VIII–2 compares two pure-tone sound waves, graphically illustrating both compression and rarefaction of air molecules and the sinusoidal waves that would represent this change in air pressure. The frequency of the wave at the bottom is twice that of the wave at the top. Frequency, described by the number of cycles per second, is written as **Hertz** [hɜ·ts], for the German physicist Heinrich R. Hertz (1857–1894) and abbreviated **Hz.** As frequency increases, the sound is heard as higher in pitch. A sound of 100 Hz, for example, is very low in pitch, whereas a sound of 8000 Hz (8 KiloHertz) is very high in pitch.

Intensity of sound is determined by the amount of compression of air molecules or pressure that occurs for a sound wave, related somewhat to the frequency of the sound but primarily to its **amplitude.** Amplitude refers to the extent of excursion from the center or equilibrium of a vibrating body

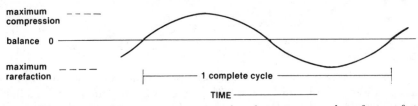

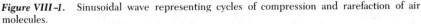

Figure VIII–1.   Sinusoidal wave representing cycles of compression and rarefaction of air molecules.

or for voice, to the extent of openings of the glottis. The greater the amplitude, the greater the intensity of the sound. Figure VIII–3 compares two pure-tone sound waves that are of the same frequency but differ in intensity. The intensity, that is the degree of condensation and rarefaction, of the wave at the top is about twice that of the wave at the bottom. Intensity, which is related to dynes [daɪnz] (unit of pressure) per square centimeter, is described in ratios written as **deciBels** [dɛ́sɪbɛ́lz] (for Alexander Graham Bell, 1847–1922) and abbreviated **dB**. As intensity increases, the sound is heard as louder. A sound of 30 dB, for example, is very soft, whereas a sound of 100 dB is very loud.

The rate of opening and closing of the glottis determines the fundamental frequency (F_0) of voice. The irregular wavelike motions of the vocal folds in their opening and closing of the glottis during phonation produce a complex sound consisting not only of the fundamental frequency but also of several **overtones**. These are a succession of higher frequencies or partials of the fundamental frequency. In a periodic sound like voice, the overtones are whole number multiples of the fundamental frequency and are called **harmonics**. The harmonics, whose amplitudes combine to coincide

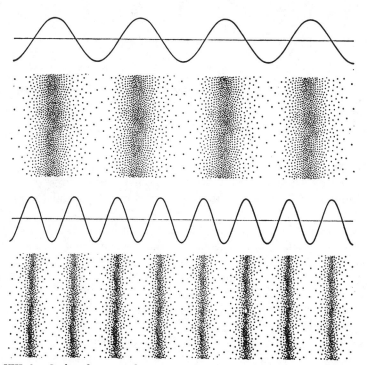

Figure VIII–2. Cycles of two sound waves illustrated by sine curves that represent pulses of compression and rarefaction of invisible air molecules (dots.) Frequency is described by the number of cycles per second. The frequency of the wave at the bottom is twice that of the wave at the top.

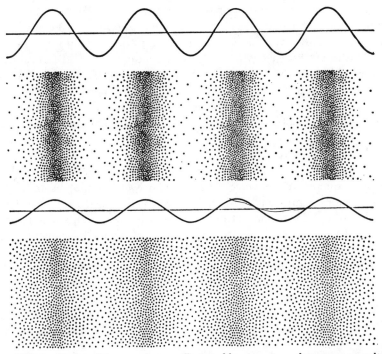

Figure VIII–3. Cycles of two sound waves illustrated by sine curves that represent pulses of compression and rarefaction of invisible air molecules (dots). Intensity depends upon the degree of compression and rarefaction in the cycles. The intensity of the wave at the top is about twice that of the wave at the bottom. The frequency of the two waves is the same.

with the amplitude of the fundamental frequency in a given period, will each be less intense or weaker than the fundamental, and each successively higher harmonic will be less intense than the previous one. A description of the acoustic **frequency spectrum** of a complex sound, therefore, requires consideration of the relative intensity or amount of energy at various frequencies.

The complex sound produced by phonation has a frequency spectrum consisting of the fundamental frequency plus harmonics of successively decreasing intensity. The rate of their decrease in intensity is about 12 dB per "octave," or doubling of frequency. Figure VIII–4(a) is a line spectrum representing the various frequencies and their relative intensities that would be produced by a glottal sound source. A sound of this type would be heard by a listener as a buzz with a particular pitch related to the fundamental frequency, having a particular **quality** of sound that is influenced by the intensity relations among the various frequencies represented in the sound.

However, the sound from the glottis is never heard in its original condition because it is immediately influenced by resonation in the vocal tract above it. The process of resonation was briefly described in Chapter II.

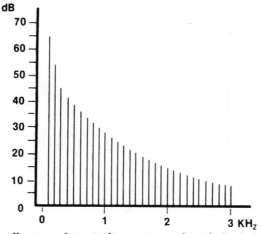

Figure VIII–4(a). Frequency-Intensity line spectrum of an idealized glottal sound with a fundamental frequency of 100 Hz (a buzzing sound).

Imagine the vocal tract in a relaxed condition, with the tongue lying flat and the mouth opened, but the nasal cavity closed off at the velopharyngeal port, much as the situation would be for the unstressed natural vowel /ə/. In this situation, the oral and pharyngeal cavities would act like a resonating tube open at one end (the mouth) and closed at times at the other (the glottis). Its resonance characteristics would be especially influenced by its length, averaging 17.5 centimeters or about 7 inches for an adult male. Pulses of compressed air can reflect through a tube of that length at a rate of about 1000 round-trip reflections or 500 maximum to minimum cycles per sec-

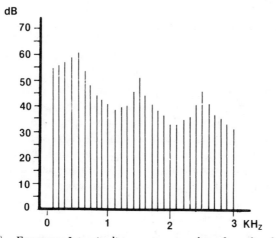

Figure VIII–4(b). Frequency-Intensity line spectrum resulting from the glottal sound *(a)*, acted upon by an idealized and relaxed vocal tract with a resonant frequency of 500 Hz (an /ə/ sound).

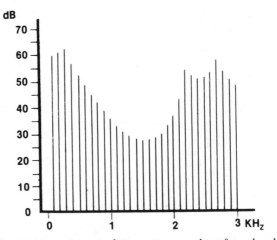

Figure VIII–4(c). Frequency-Intensity line spectrum resulting from the glottal sound (*a*), acted upon by an idealized vocal tract positioned to produce the vowel /i/.

ond, giving the tube a resonant frequency of 500 cycles per second, or 500 Hz. Thus the vocal tract, open as a resonant tube, would tend to reinforce a 500 Hz component more than all others. The new spectrum of frequencies for the resulting sound would show a peak at 500 Hz, sloping off in the higher frequencies, but with a fairly regular pattern of other overtone peaks of energy at about every 1000 Hz above the major resonant peak at 500 Hz. This creates a pattern of peaks followed by valleys at odd multiples (1,3,5,7,9) of the resonant frequency of the tube: 500 Hz, 1500 Hz, 2500 Hz, etc. Figure VIII–4(b) shows a line spectrum of the glottal sound of Figure VIII–4(a) acted upon by an idealized vocal tract with a resonant frequency of 500 Hz.

This new sound would be quite different from the glottal buzz. The listener would still hear it as having a low pitch, related to its lowest tone or fundamental frequency of 100 Hz, but its quality would sound like the vowel /ə/. The peaks of resonance in the frequency spectrum that form the new quality to make the sound become the vowel /ə/ are called speech **formants** [formænts]. They are determined by characteristics of the vocal tract and change as the vocal tract changes in length and shape. The formants are numbered from low to high frequencies and are called the first formant, F_1, the second formant, F_2, the third, F_3, and so on. Remember that the fundamental frequency of a sound is written F_0.

The frequency locations of the formants, especially F_1 and F_2, are closely influenced by the configuration of the vocal tract. It is these formants that especially contribute to perception of vowels. The factors that contribute most to the position of F_1 and F_2 are (1) length of the vocal tract, (2) location of constriction in the tract, and (3) narrowness of the constriction. The greater the length of the tract from the glottis to the lips, the lower the formant frequencies. Thus, since the average length of the vocal tract in women is about four-fifths as long as that of men, the location of formants would be higher that in men, with the same spacing of odd numbered multiples (1,3,5,7,9) of the lowest resonant frequency of the relaxed vocal tract. And an infant with a vocal tract one-half the length of an adult's would have a resonant frequency of the relaxed tract of twice that of an adult. It is not surprising, then, that lip rounding, which usually includes lip protrusion and therefore lengthening of the tract, tends to lower the frequencies of formants. Thus the vowel /ɔ/ has a lower F_1 and F_2 than /ɑ/ from which it differs primarily in lip rounding.

Although there are not always one-to-one relations between specific configurations of the tract during connected speech and the frequency positions of formants, here are two rough rules-of-thumb for these relations:

1. **F_1 is lowered by increasing constriction in the front half of the tract.** Thus the /i/, the highest of the front vowels, has a very low F_1 associated with the narrow space between the front of the tongue and the palate-alveolar ridge (see Chapter IV). Each of the other front vowels, /ɪ/, /ɛ/, and /æ/, has a successively higher F_1 corresponding to less constriction. The /u/ has the narrowest frontal constriction at the lips and thus has a lower F_1 than most other vowels, including those that have lip rounding but a wider opening such as /ʊ/ and /ɔ/.

2. **F_2 is lowered by increasing constriction in the back half of the tract.** Thus the /u/, the highest of the back vowels, has a very low F_2 associated with the narrow space between the back of the tongue and the velum (see Chapter IV). With reduced back constriction, as back for vowels /ʊ/, /o/, /ɔ/, and /ɑ/, the F_2 would tend to rise.

The alterations of the oral cavity to form vowels is reflected in considerable movement of the frequency positions of the first two formants. For example, the /u/, which has constriction in the front by the lips and in the back by the elevated tongue, would have lowered formants, fairly close together. Average F_1 would be about 250 Hz with an F_2 of about 850 Hz for /u/. The /i/, with constriction in the front and no constriction in the back, would have an average F_1 of 250 Hz but an F_2 of over 2000 Hz (often written as 2KHz, for KiloHertz). Figure VIII–4(c) shows a line spectrum for the vowel /i/. Compare this pattern with that of the idealized and relaxed vocal tract of Figure VIII–4(b).

Some average frequency positions of the first two formants of steady state vowels and resonant consonants, produced by a male speaker, are shown in Figure VIII–5. The relation between configurations of the vocal tract and formant positions is apparent, especially for the front vowels /i/, /ɪ/, /ɛ/, and /æ/. Positions of formant bands are well displayed by a filtering device called a "speech spectrograph." Figure VIII–6 shows a resulting spectrogram of /i/, /ɪ/, /ɛ/, and /æ/ in which the formant bands stand out in contrast to the softer background. Time is the horizontal parameter in this figure.

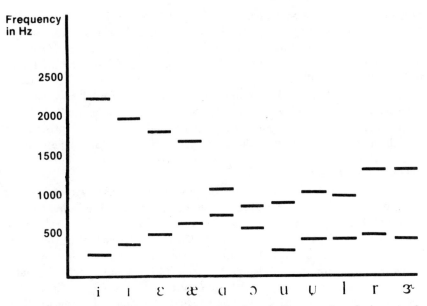

Figure VIII–5. Average frequency positions of the first two formants of steady state vowels and resonant consonants produced by a male speaker.

Fricative consonants appear on spectrograms as areas of sound energy from aperiodic or inharmonic sound production. Notice the difference in Figure VIII–7 of the frequency spread for the /s/ and /ʃ/ sounds. Fricative consonants yield frequency information both from their position on the frequency spectrum and from their spread of sound energy over the spectrum.

Nasal consonants, produced with the velopharyngeal port open, have a complex frequency-intensity spectrum. While the oral cavity is especially resonant for some frequencies, and thus amplifies them, the nasal cavity may be "antiresonant," diminishing those same frequencies, and vice versa. On spectrograms, the nasal consonants show resonant bands or formants, like vowels, but the formant bands are broader in frequency spread and more sound energy exists between the bands than for oral resonant sounds. Since opening of the velopharyngeal port for nasal sounds increases both length and size of the total resonating cavity that may act upon the glottal sound, a large concentration of lower frequency energy is created, usually at 250 to 300 Hz.

In addition to the relative intensity of certain frequency areas for each phoneme, the overall intensity of the sound varies from phoneme to phoneme. When averaged, the phonemes of American-English have a range of intensity of 28 dB, or a power ratio of approximately 1:680 from the weakest /θ/ to the strongest /ɔ/. The vowels are the most powerful and thus the

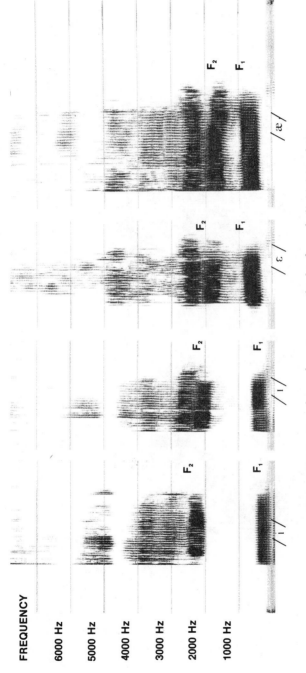

Figure VIII–6. Speech sound spectrograms of isolated vowels /i/, /ɪ/, /ɛ/, and /æ/.

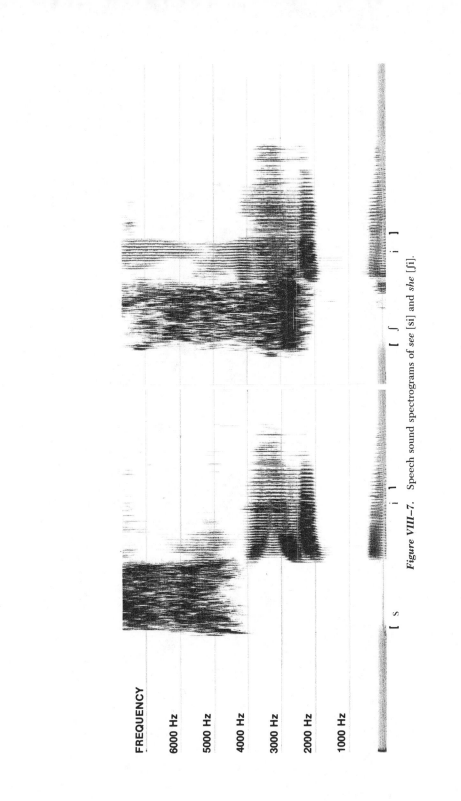

Figure VIII–7. Speech sound spectrograms of *see* [si] and *she* [ʃi].

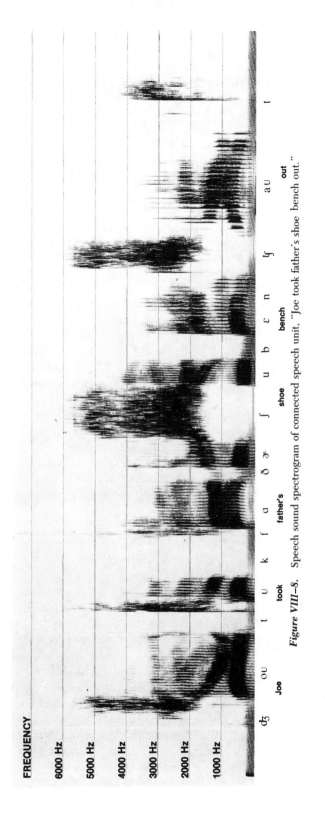

FREQUENCY

6000 Hz
5000 Hz
4000 Hz
3000 Hz
2000 Hz
1000 Hz

dʒ	oʊ	t	ʊ	k	f	ɑ	ð	ɚ	ʃ	u	b	ɛ	n	tʃ	aʊ	t

Joe   took   father's   shoe   bench   out

Figure VIII–8.   Speech sound spectrogram of connected speech unit, "Joe took father's shoe bench out."

loudest sounds. When stressed (see Chapter VI), vowels may have three to four times as much power as in unstressed syllables. Resonant consonants are next in power, followed by /ʃ/, /tʃ/, and their voiced counterparts. The stops and fricatives follow, with /f/ and /θ/ being the weakest sounds. Of course, the actual intensity of speech sounds, particularly vowels and resonant consonants, would vary from speaker to speaker, as would the range of their intensities. The intensity of voiceless consonants are less influenced by such individual speaker differences.

Just as description of the production of isolated phonemes in Chapters III and IV needed to be modified by the important effects of context and coarticulation described in Chapter V, so too must the static displays of acoustic characteristics of isolated phonemes be considered in the context of the flow of connected speech, Figure VIII–8 is a spectrogram of connected speech produced at a normal rate. Here, formant bands that appeared level in the isolated displays of Figure VIII–6 bend up and down and sometimes do not even attain their target frequency positions. The transitions between phonemes appear as prominently as do the phonemes themselves, and indeed, the transitional characteristics seem to have an important influence on speech perception. The bending of vowel formants, for example, lends an important cue to the place of production of adjoining consonants.

Speech rhythm features are also reflected in the frequency-intensity spectrum over the time period of the connected speech signal. As pointed out in Chapter VI, the physiologic force of production for accent and emphasis produces perceptible changes in intensity, frequency, and duration of the stressed word or syllable. Intonation consists primarily of variations in fundamental voice frequency over the period of a phrase. Phrasing and rate are related to the parameter of time or duration.

Differences in Duration

Along with the frequency-intensity spectrum, duration appears to be a significant contributor to speech perception. For example, given the same phonetic context, the /i/ is longer than the /ɪ/. This may be a useful difference for perception in words that are similar such as *beet* and *bit*, since the frequency-intensity difference in the two vowels is small. However, the duration of all vowels is systematically influenced by the consonants around them, particularly by the consonants that they precede. A vowel is longer in front of a fricative than in front of a stop consonant, helping the listener to determine the manner of production of that consonant. The duration of a vowel is greater before a voiced consonant than before its voiceless counterpart, so that the greater length of the [i] in *bead* compared to the [i] in *beet* is a cue to perceiving the voice-voiceless distinction of the final consonant.

Because of this influence of phonetic context, the [ɪ] in *bid* may actually be longer than the [i] in *beet*. Stress patterns also influence duration, with the vowel of a stressed syllable typically longer than the same vowel of an unstressed syllable. Of course, individual differences in rate of speaking also determine phoneme duration, especially for vowels and resonant consonants.

Fricative and stop consonants are marked by important durational differences, in addition to their frequency positions and frequency spread, and their intensity characteristics. Stops are shorter than fricatives in overall duration, with affricates falling between the two in length. The voice onset time (VOT) following an aspirated voiceless stop, such as the [pʻ] in [pʻi], is significantly greater than that of a voiced stop [b], as in [bi]. This durational difference is also an important cue to the listener in perceiving the voiced-voiceless distinction of a stop consonant preceding a vowel.

INFORMATION FOR THE VISUAL SYSTEM

In producing the sounds of speech, the jaw, lips, and tongue make movements that are generally visible to an observer. These movements, or articulatory gestures, may provide the observer with important information about the speech sounds produced. The process of using these gestures as a means of speech perception has been called "lipreading." The term "speechreading," now more common, takes into account the movements of jaw and tongue, buccal tension, upper neck movement, nose movement, and general facial expression, as well as information from the lips.

A listener-observer with normal hearing may occasionally complement his auditory perception with speechreading in difficult listening situations. In a noisy background, for example, the acoustic distinction between *free* and *three* may be so obscured that only the visual gesture of the lower lip approximating the upper front teeth can assure the listener-observer that the initial consonant was [f] and thus the word must have been *free*. We may also be assisted by **complementary perception** when speech production is unusual. When listening to a person with a speech defect, a foreign speaker, or a young child who is just developing speech, most of us avail ourselves of speechreading to receive visual cues that complement acoustic cues, some of which may be ambiguous. Speechreading is often helpful, also, when spoken language content is difficult to comprehend, as when we hear unfamiliar words in a lecture. The necessity of complementing auditory speech information with visual information is especially pronounced when we listen to nonsense syllables or to an unfamiliar language for purposes of phonetic transcription.

An observer-listener with a serious hearing impairment may habitually supplement hearing with speechreading in all situations. Or, when hearing loss is even more severe, he may depend upon speechreading as the primary source of speech reception, using hearing as an important supplement. For persons with profound deafness, without recourse to acoustic amplification by hearing aids, articulatory gestures may be the only source of speech information.

It is generally agreed that visible speech gestures carry only a portion of the information necessary for complete and accurate comprehension of the speech message, perhaps less than 50 percent. When only the visible gestures of articulation are perceptible, the remainder of the message may be supplied by (1) contextual information from the subject under discussion, (2) knowledge of linguistic rules so that a recognized word suggests what the word next to it probably was, (3) familiarity with the speaker's typical language style and choice of subject, and (4) a facility for "filling in," utilizing the first three factors, as well as a knowledge of relative frequency of occurrence of words and phrases in spoken language. It is also apparent that, when supplemented with even minimal acoustic speech information, our ability to speechread can improve markedly. Acoustic information that gives cues about manner of production, voicing, and nasality appears to be especially helpful as a supplement to speechreading.

Analogous to the phoneme of auditorally perceived speech is the visual phoneme or **viseme** [vɪzim]. Visemes are the visible speech positions that form recognizable categories of optical contrast, with variations, like allophonic variations, caused by coarticulation. There is no consensus concerning the number of visemes in English. This fact reflects the greater degree of variability in both producing and perceiving visemes as compared with acoustic phonemes. It is the conventionally accepted acoustic signal, and not the optical signal, that the typical speaker consciously produces. An acceptable acoustic signal for a phoneme may be produced by very different articulatory gestures, as was pointed out in chapters III and IV. Friction for /ʍ/, for example, can be created by tongue placement without the typical lip rounding. Therefore, we cannot expect as much similarity in how the viseme for /ʍ/ looks from speaker to speaker as in how the acoustic phoneme sounds. One of the marked visual variations among speakers is the nearly immobile upper lip, habitual with some speakers who never really round the lips but may compensate to produce an acceptable acoustic result by changing tongue position. This is an action essentially invisible to the observer.

Enunciation for speech sound production was discussed earlier in Chapter VII. Good **visual enunciation** requires speaking so that complementary visible gestures of the speech mechanism accompany the production of speech sounds. Skill in visual enunciation is not consciously practiced but those who frequently talk to deaf people who speechread develop beneficial habits of visual enunciation. These habits include lip, tongue and jaw movement, and exposure of teeth that display to the viewer important visible cues to the *place* of articulating consonants (bilabial, labio-dental, lingua-dental, lingua-alveolar) that may complement auditory information on the *manner* of articulating consonants (stop, fricative, nasal or oral resonant). The relation between place and manner of articulating consonants was reviewed in Figure III-1. Good visual enunciation can also provide information on the degree of mouth opening and lip rounding associated with vowels and with some consonants. The speaker who wishes to improve visual enunciation may have to relearn habits of producing speech sounds by observing in a mirror. It is important that the visible gestures be not grossly exaggerated so that they detract from the acoustic signal or impair normal coarticulation, speech rhythm and rate.

Ability to perceive speech visually also varies greatly among individuals. Moderately hearing-impaired observers typically read speech better than do those with normal hearing, but there is an immense range of ability among normal-hearing speechreaders. Most people improve in ability to recognize visemes after a short period of training.

Regardless of the habits of the speaker or the ability of the observer, articulatory gestures for all speech sounds are not equally visible. The bilabial /p/, /b/, and /m/, with front articulation and lip closure, are easiest to see. The labio-dental /f/ and /v/ and the vowels with lip rounding are also easily observable. Lingua-alveolar /t/, /d/, /l/, and /n/ are harder to see, and the lingua-velar /k/, /g/, and /ŋ/, made in the back of the mouth, are not visible at all during normal speech production. Among those speech sounds that are visible, however, not all are discriminable. The easily visible /p/, /b/, and /m/, for example, are virtually indistinguishable from each other so that *pie, by*, and *my* would look alike. These very similar looking visemes are referred to as being **homophenous** [homάfinəs], and words that are visually indistinguishable are called homophenous words. Acoustically **homophonous** [homα'fonəs] words such as *bare-bear, write-right*, and *so-sew* were mentioned in Chapter I. Speechreading makes available to the observer information primarily about the place of production of speech sounds. However, the presence or absence of voicing, the use of open nasal resonance, and much about the manner of production is absent from the visual speech signal. Voiced and voiceless cognates, such as /v/ and /f/, and /d/ and /t/ cannot be discriminated. The nasal /m/ also looks exactly like the oral /b/.

A promising approach to research on the parameters of visual information available for speech perception is the description of contrasting features or oppositions. This effort parallels the search for acoustic distinctive features that influence auditory speech perception. Figure VIII–9 shows a model of some visual oppositions at seven levels of increasing subtlety. The levels may correspond to progress in early speechreading development by deaf children, and could be predictive of confusions on visual perception tasks.

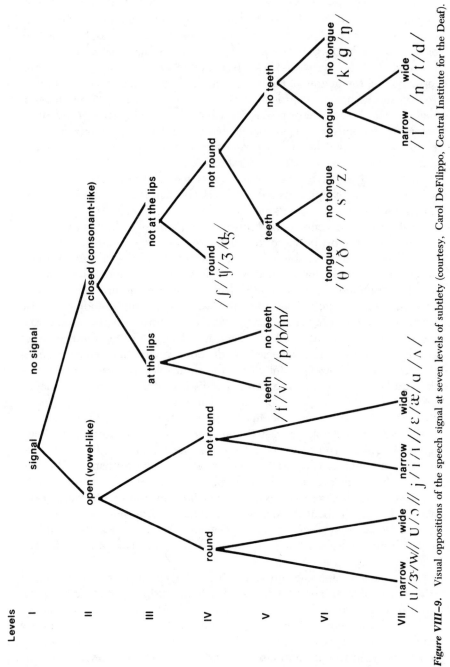

Figure VIII-9. Visual oppositions of the speech signal at seven levels of subtlety (courtesy, Carol DeFilippo, Central Institute for the Deaf).

INFORMATION FOR PROPRIOCEPTION

Speech not only produces acoustic and optical information propagated for perception by other listeners and observers, but it also results in sensory information about speech movements that is fed back only to the speaker. Such information is available for the speaker's internal perception or **proprioception** [próprios£pʃən]. Proprioception for speech serves several important purposes:

1. Proprioception provides instantaneous and continuous feedback about speech movements that helps the speaker **monitor** his speech production. Such monitoring helps him make adjustments in place or manner of production, which result in desirable acoustic output, as he is learning and developing speech. It also helps in correcting occasional speech errors or "slips of the tongue" during rapid connected speech.
2. Proprioception provides sensory information basic to the memory patterns necessary for producing speech. In the absence of hearing for speech, as would occur in a very noisy environment or with temporary hearing loss, we continue to speak by using our memory for how speech feels as it is being produced.
3. Proprioception provides a probable basis for speech perception by the listener or observer. The "motor theory" of speech perception maintains that we perceive speech in the way that we produce it, and that hearing the acoustic events of a unit of speech calls up our proprioceptive memory for how we would produce that same unit.

Proprioception includes two major kinds of sensations, tactile and kinesthetic, which apparently supply complementary information for a unified motor memory pattern.

Tactile speech information comes from touching parts of the speech mechanism; from friction and turbulence as air flows over the surfaces of the tongue, lips and palate; and from vibration associated with voicing called **vibro-tactile** information. A review of speech sound production in chapters III and IV will reveal that not all phonemes yield equal tactile information. Bilabials /p/, /b/, and /m require touching of the tactually sensitive lips, and the lingua-alveolar /t/, /d/, /n/, and /l/ involve touching the alveolar ridge with the sensitive tongue tip. Whereas these sounds provide considerable sensation from touching, the lingua-velar /k/, /g, and /ŋ/, which involve the less sensitive back of the tongue and the velum, give little information from their touching. Some consonants, such as /s/, /ʃ/, and /r/, do not require touching another part of the speech anatomy and thus provide no tactile feedback to assist in monitoring their appropriate place of production. The same is true of the vowels and of the consonants /w/ and /j/. The fricative consonants, particularly the voiceless fricatives /f/ and /θ/ which require close labio-dental or lingua-dental approximation, provide tactile sensations from the flow of turbulent breath. Less tactile sensation is available from the more open fricatives /h/, /ʍ/, /s/, and /ʃ/. Combined touching and friction occurs in the affricate /tʃ/. The voiced fricatives /v/, /ð/, /z/, and /ʒ/ provide less tactile friction sensation than do their voiceless counterparts, but they have vibro-tactile information from voicing. The vowels, which have no touching or friction, possess strong voicing vibration. The strongest vibro-tactile information comes from the nasal resonant consonants /m/, /n/, and /ŋ/.

Kinesthetic speech information comes from the movement of structures and from the stretching of muscles. The kinesthetic sensory receptors lie between muscle cells, in the surface of joints, and in the interior of tendons. They are sensitive to position, movement, and tension. Speech sounds vary in their yield of kinesthetic information as they do of tactile information. Although there is very little stimulus from movements of the velum and pharynx in closing the velopharyngeal port, movement of the lower jaw, the lips, and the tongue provides considerable kinesthetic sensation. The lip rounding /ɔ/, /u/, and /w/; the wide jaw opening /ɑ/ and /æ/ and the diphthongs /ɔɪ/, /oʊ/, and /aʊ/ offer considerable kinesthetic feedback. If the lips are drawn back for /i/ or if the tongue is retroflexed for /r/, these sounds can yield great kinesthetic sensation. The voiceless stops and affricates, particularly the /p/ and /t/, require pressure for closure, which gives some information. Among the weakest sounds, kinesthetically, are the /ʌ/, which requires no tongue elevation; the /h/, which has no position of its own; and the lingua-velar /g/ and /ŋ/, where little movement is required of either the tongue or velum.

Proprioception for speech usually occurs subconsciously but can be brought to the level of consciousness when needed for analysis of speech production. The fact that tactile and kinesthetic speech feedback information alone is inadequate for monitoring completely normal speech production is borne out by the different sounding speech of profoundly deaf persons deprived of auditory feedback. By the same token, the value of such feedback is demonstrated by those who either lost their hearing or were born with profound deafness and who nevertheless maintain functional use of speech for communication in the absence of auditory feedback. The importance of proprioception for speech is readily apparent for all of us when perception is impaired as with topical dental anesthetic influencing the tongue.

SPEECH PERCEPTION

The relations are complex among how we produce speech (physiological), what the speech signal consists of (physical), and how we perceive speech (psychological). These relations for voice, previously suggested, are summarized in Table VIII–1. As the opening and closing of the glottis grows faster, frequency increases and the pitch of the voice rises. As amplitude of the glottal opening becomes greater, sound intensity increases, and the voice is perceived as being louder. In more complex relations, the irregular wave-like motion of the vocal folds in opening and closing the glottis creates a complex sound wave that is acted upon by the supra-glottal resonating cavities, and distinctive voice quality is perceived.

In the previous chapters, speech has been described as a chain of discrete phonemes linked together by coarticulation. Linguistic theory suggests that speech may be recognized by the human auditory system converting the acoustic code of the 40 or so phonemes that constitute the limited set of American-English phonemes. Allophonic variations of phonemes, despite a multitude of idiosyncratic differences from speaker to speaker, from dialect to dialect, from context to context, and from time to time, are assumed to be sufficiently like each other and distinct enough from allophones of any other phoneme class so that the phoneme intended may be clearly perceived. This view of speech perception suggests an analogy to reading by recognizing each character in a string of alphabet letters forming words and sentences. Recognition of phonemes from within a variable acoustic signal is thought to occur by a process of determining a number of **distinctive features** characteristic of each phoneme. Early studies from confusion matrices of single syllables suggested that the distinctive features of phonemes might be such as (1) whether voicing was present or absent,(2) whether voicing was nasal or oral, (3) whether friction was present, and (4) where the place of articulation occurred. The traditional classification of consonants, as shown in Figure III–1, suggests a rudimentary set of distinctive features. Recognition of /f/ by this approach, for example, would not depend

TABLE VIII–1 RELATIONS AMONG PHYSIOLOGICAL, PHYSICAL AND PSYCHOLOGICAL DESCRIPTIONS OF VOICE

PHYSIOLOGICAL	PHYSICAL	PSYCHOLOGICAL
opening and closing of the glottis	pulses of compression and rarefaction of air molecules	voice heard
rate of opening and closing of glottis	frequency	pitch of voice
amplitude of glottis opening	intensity	loudness of voice
irregular motion of vocal folds + resonance	complex sound wave	voice quality

upon the particular acoustic (frequency, intensity, duration) characteristics peculiar to a produced [f] but would be based on determination that the sound (1) was voiceless rather than voiced, (2) was made with friction, and (3) was made at a labio-dental place of articulation. Since no other speech sound has these three characteristics, the phoneme intended must be /f/. A more elaborate theoretical set of distinctive features includes such binary opposites as vocalic-nonvocalic, nasal-oral, tense-lax, compact-diffuse, grave-acute, front-back, interruptive-continuant, and fricative-sonorant.

A number of observations cast doubt on this discrete phoneme code theory of speech perception. First is the extreme acoustic variability among the allophones of a single phoneme when analyzed in connected speech. Figure VIII–8 showed the distortions of vowel formant positions in connected speech context. The acoustic differences between the /t/ and /d/ when produced naturally as in *a liter of wine* and *a leader of men* seem almost to disappear. Many of the assumed distinctive features do not relate directly to acoustic information in the speech signal, the information that must be transmitted to the listener. Another observation is that speech can be followed by listeners at rates as high as 400 words per minute, or about 30 phonemes per second, a rate approaching the known temporal resolving power of the auditory system for non-speech stimuli. At that rate, discrete acoustic events are likely to merge into an indistinguishable buzz. Furthermore, electronic apparatus designed to recognize speech through its phonemes has not been able to succeed beyond recognition of a very few distinct sound patterns in the speech of a very few individuals. When speech-like sounds have been synthesized by electronic equipment, perception appears to be greatly influenced by the transitions between phonemes whether some of the actual phonemes are present or not.

One view of understanding speech to help account for these observations is called the "motor theory" of speech perception. Noting the close linkage between auditory feedback channels and motor control of articulation, this theory suggests that memory for speech is related to memory for how speech is produced. The speech of others is perceived with reference to the listener's knowledge of his own speech mechanism and the motor patterns that we would use to produce the same speech units. The listener, recalling the neuromuscular patterns he would use to produce the unit he hears, associates these patterns with the meaning of the speech units. Tactile and kinesthetic speech feedback is an important part of these motor patterns. It is not necessary that the listener actually move his speech mechanism through the pattern in order to perceive it. However, it is a common observation that when learning a new language or hearing an unfamiliar word, we find ourselves saying the word "under our breath" to get more familiar with it or to help recognize it. The author has observed a number of young deaf children who, having difficulty first learning to lipread, seem to need to say the word to themselves or out loud before they can recognize it. These overt manifestations of motor assistance with auditory perception may be related to the way we perceive rapid connected speech.

This theory of speech perception leaves unanswered what acoustic information must necessarily be transmitted to the listener in order for him to connect the speech unit he hears with his own neuromuscular patterns of speech production. There are clearly a number of questions still to be answered about how we perceive speech. A thorough understanding of descriptive phonetics may be one route to those answers.

REVIEW VOCABULARY

Acoustic phonetics—the field of study concerned with the acoustic features of speech.

Acoustics—the branch of physics concerned with the physical properties of sound.

Amplitude—the extent of excursions of a vibrating body, or extent of openings as in the glottis.

Complementary perception—using two or more sensory modalities to distinguish or recognize information, as in using both hearing and vision (speechreading) to perceive speech.

DeciBel, (dB)—a widely used unit for the level or strength of a sound. One-tenth of a Bel, named for Alexander Graham Bell.

Distinctive features—acoustic or visual features characteristic of a phoneme that distinguish it from other phonemes.

Formants—bands of energy in a frequency spectrum associated with vowel perception.

Frequency—the rate of the vibrations of a sound, described in Hertz or the number of cycles per second.

Frequency spectrum—the relative intensity of frequency components of a given sound.

Harmonics—overtones that are whole number multiples of a fundamental frequency.

Hertz, (Hz)—a unit of frequency used for "cycles per second." Named for Heinrich R. Hertz, a German physicist.

Homophenous—optically indistinguishable units of speech, as in *pie, buy,* and *my.*

Homophonous—acoustically indistinguishable units of speech, as in *write, right,* and *rite.*

Intensity—the magnitude of the energy of a sound, described in deciBels.

Kinesthetic—the sense of movement and position available from the stretching of muscles, tension on joints, and moving body parts.

Monitor—to maintain control by making adjustments based on sensory information fed back to the producer during an action.

Overtones—a succession of frequencies higher than the fundamental frequency.

Proprioception—sensory information perceived internally by the producer of an action, as with the tactile and kinesthetic feedback during speech production.

Quality—the intensity relations among the fundamental frequency and overtones of a sound.

Tactile—the sense of touch including that available from touching of parts of the speech mechanism, friction caused by air turbulence, and vibrations as with phonation.

Vibro-tactile—vibration that can be detected by tactile perception, as with the vibration produced by phonation.

Viseme—visible speech positions that form recognizable categories of optical contrast associated with phonemes.

Visual enunciation—producing speech so that visible information about producing consonants and vowels is apparent to a viewer.

EXERCISES

1. Line up six empty soft drink glass bottles, exactly alike and not touching each other, on a table. Leave the first bottle empty, add one inch of water to the second, two inches to the third, three to the fourth, four to the fifth, and five inches to the sixth. Tap lightly the neck of each bottle in turn with a metal spoon and note how the pitch of the resulting sound rises as the size of the resonating air cavity decreases.

2. Write at least ten pairs of words that are **homophenous** but not **homophonous.** Example, *bait-made.*

3. By saying each of the following units of speech aloud several times, and by producing each in "slow motion," analyze and describe first the various kinds of **tactile** information, and then the **kinesthetic** information each one yields:

[du]   [sæk]   [lʌntʃ]
[θʌm]   [fju]   [mɑmə]
[sɪŋ]   [æpl]   [hɛvən]

4. Analyze the proprioceptive products (both tactile and kinesthetic) of the following sounds, first describing what feedback information is available to the speaker, then placing them in rank order for the strength of overall proprioceptive information they provide.

/t/, /f/, /m/, /ʌ/, /s/, /u/

SUGGESTED READING

Bordon, Gloria, J. and Harris, Katherine S., *Speech Science Primer*. Baltimore, Williams and Wilkins, second edition, 1984.

Already becoming a classic, this 300 page text ties together concepts of speech production acoustics, and speech perception. It also includes chapters on "Research tools in speech science," and "Evolution of language and speech."

Calvert, Donald R. and Silverman, S. Richard, *Speech and Deafness*. Washington, D.C., A. G. Bell Ass'n. for the Deaf, second edition, 1983.

This text for teachers of hearing-impaired children includes a section on the perceptual features of articulation, voice and speech rhythm in chapter I, "Speech and its production," (pp. 23–39) with tables that estimate the strength of sensory feedback available from consonant and vowel production. Chapter III, "Using hearing for speech," describes acoustic information associated with speech sounds. Chapter VI, "Instructional Analysis of Consonants and Vowels," (pp. 177–234) describes the kind of tactile and kinesthetic information from each of the American-English speech sounds, and how these may be used in speech instruction.

Denes, Peter B., and Pinson, Elliot N.: *The Speech Chain: the Physics and Biology of Spoken Language*. Garden City, N.Y., Anchor Press/Doubleday, 1973.

A paperback of the Anchor Science Study Series, written by two speech scientists at the Bell Telephone Laboratories, relates speech production to speech recognition with a simplified presentation of the physics of sound and the acoustic characteristics of speech.

Lehiste, Ilse (editor): *Readings in Acoustic Phonetics*. Cambridge, Mass., The MIT Press, 1967.

This frequently reprinted collection of articles serves as a resource of basic references for a number of original ideas developed by their authors. The single volume includes some of the world's foremost authorities on acoustic phonetics, with articles reprinted from a variety of journals. Some knowledge of acoustics is needed.

Pickett, James M.: *The Sounds of Speech Communication.* Baltimore, Maryland, University Park Press, 1980.

A technically sound text on acoustic phonetics with some references to speech perception. A well illustrated introduction by a research scientist in acoustic phonetics.

INDEX